Structured Family Recovery has been a ... cess allows me to share in my recovery ... helped me understand the family disea ... of drug ... biggest lie I told myself as an addict wa... that I was only hurting myself. The SFR process has taught me that this is a lie and has been ... tal in the healing process between me and my family.

—J. F., recovering from alcohol and drug addiction

Structured Family Recovery helped me save my life. After confronting years of addiction, twelve difficult weeks in treatment, and the prospect of starting over entirely, SFR became an anchor to a loving, nonjudgmental group of friends and family. I am in a place where I feel joy unlike I've ever experienced, and my relationships with my parents, extended family, and life partner have deepened in ways I couldn't have imagined. SFR has been the perfect complement to my Twelve Step recovery journey, and it introduced and strengthened a connection with my family that most addicts I know don't have. I am so grateful for the opportunity to build my SFR identity, and I look forward to carrying the SFR program and message to the addict that still suffers.

—D. C., beloved recovering son

I found the family recovery calls to be very worthwhile. They were particularly challenging as they included my ex-wife as well as my two beloved sons, since I am not on good terms with my ex-wife. This made having an expert who moderated the calls critical to our success. As a show of support for my son, I entered the Twelve Step program. This program has been very beneficial to me as it helped me to reconnect to my faith, which had been dormant. It also forced me to fashion an action plan, which I regularly consult and work on. As a result, I believe I have improved several of my weaknesses. Both sons have said that one of the best results of the SFR meetings has been the four of us coming together—something that didn't happen before the calls. For me, the best result is having a weekly window into my sons' emotional lives— how they are really feeling. Prior to this, our family rarely shared our emotions. I feel closer to my sons as a result and look forward to our conversations. I enthusiastically recommend Debra Jay's program.

—W. M., father of a beloved recovering son

Structured Family Recovery allowed me to bridge the gap between my recovery and my family's recovery. This process is unparalleled by any type of therapy I have been part of since my journey began in 2016. It has allowed me time to process sensitive topics in my own Twelve Step meeting with the ability to bring insight gained back to my family in a safe and structured environment. SFR taught me to stay in my own lane of recovery, but if I look over, I will see family traveling down the same road, and that is a priceless gift of recovery.

—L. S., wife of a beloved recovering husband

Thank you, Debra Jay, for helping our family to find a clear path forward out of sadness and despair. Our family is working our way through your book for a second time and finding new wisdom and support on each page. We could have so easily fallen apart. And yet, with the help of the Twelve Steps and our wise and patient SFR counselor, this program has given us an opportunity to reflect, learn, and stay connected and supportive of each other.

—L. S. H., father-in-law of a beloved recovering son-in-law

The Structured Family Recovery program was a call to action for our family of four at a critical time. We had been impacted by two life-changing events: the marital separation of my husband and I, closely followed by our youngest son's thirty-day stay in rehab. Weekly SFR teleconference sessions brought our geographically distanced family together with a trained SFR counselor to help us focus on a path forward. Wary at first, each of us soon became committed to recovery, both for ourselves and for our family unit. Over time we noticed we communicated better due to the common language that a Twelve Step program offers. With our newly acquired knowledge, tools and practices, we have increased confidence as we approach the future and what it brings.

—J. W., mother of beloved recovering son

Our family was reeling. Our son was lost in addiction, with all of the attendant secrecy, lies, erratic behavior, and health issues that can accompany the disease. As parents, we alternated between denial and ineffective overreaction, guilt and excuse-making. We were all in great pain, spinning out of control until we immersed ourselves into Structured

Family Recovery. Our son is now five years sober because he, and we, committed to the program. It wasn't easy, but the journey has transformed us all in unimaginable ways. "Grateful and blessed" can't begin to express how all of us feel!

—A. R. and G. R., parents of a beloved recovering son

The Structured Family Recovery program saved our family—not just the addict but our entire family. It guided us to open and honest communication and taught us how to love and trust again while helping us realize our inner strengths and how to use them. We are forever indebted to Debra Jay and her commitment to families and her dedication to helping us find our way back to each other. What we created through SFR is a long-term, ongoing fellowship and commitment to maintaining recovery.

—D. C. and M. C., parents of a beloved recovering adult child

I remember being so afraid initially of the SFR phone dialogue, but very quickly that feeling was replaced with an eager anticipation of each meeting. It is such a well-thought-out and thorough program. The topic each week and the goal setting helped us keep focus on the importance of continually working this program. And the collaboration with all of the family members was such an integral component in the commitment and perseverance that we used to motivate ourselves each day.

A true benefit, and one that we believe would never have happened if not for SFR, was the vast array of topics discussed openly and thoughtfully by my adult children with us. We were privileged to hear deep thoughts, desires, and goals of our family. The discussions were intimate and mainly about each of us as individuals. We came away from this past year of SFR with skills and confidence to handle the crises that may come to our lives. And I happily can say that our son is in recovery and maintaining his sobriety. Structured Family Recovery is a tool to build families into stronger units and guide families on what to expect and how to respond to our person who is afflicted. It is a wonderful program that has helped us immensely.

—D. F. and S. F., parents of a beloved recovering son

The Structured Family Recovery program has offered me and my dear family the time, focus, and unfailingly positive support to have meaningful conversations. Addiction brought me to this program, but the healing of old wounds and the progress toward building even better family relationships has helped me to look forward to every SFR session.

—*K. H., mother-in-law of a beloved recovering son-in-law*

I remember the exact moment in time when I read the opening pages to Debra Jay's *It Takes a Family,* and I began to feel the slightest dawn of hope emerge in my soul. I was sitting on a bed in a hotel room in a city far away from my own and fully believing that my life was over. My spouse was in an inpatient rehab facility, and I was visiting him. I opened the pages, and I couldn't believe that someone had dedicated her entire career to helping strangers like me. I was overwhelmed at the guidebook in my hand—it was a flashlight in the dark. During our recovery journey, our SFR counselor was the first person to treat us like a family full of love rather than a broken family.

—*K. F., wife of a beloved recovering husband*

Other Books by Debra Jay

Love First: A Family's Guide to Intervention
by Jeff Jay and Debra Jay

*Aging and Addiction: Helping Older Adults Overcome
Alcohol or Medication Dependence*
by Carol Colleran and Debra Jay

*No More Letting Go: The Spirituality of Taking Action
Against Alcohol and Drug Addiction*
by Debra Jay

IT TAKES A FAMILY

SECOND EDITION

IT TAKES A
FAMILY

Creating Lasting Sobriety,
Togetherness, and Happiness

Debra Jay

Foreword by Robert L. DuPont, MD

Hazelden Publishing

Hazelden Publishing
Center City, Minnesota 55012
hazelden.org/bookstore

Library of Congress Cataloging-in-Publication Data

Names: Jay, Debra, 1954- author. | DuPont, Robert L., 1936- writer of foreword.
Title: It takes a family : creating lasting sobriety, togetherness, and happiness / Debra
Jay ; foreword by Robert L. DuPont, MD.
Description: Second edition. | Center City, Minnesota : Hazelden Publishing, 2021. |
Includes bibliographical references and index. |
Identifiers: LCCN 2020054252 (print) | LCCN 2020054253 (ebook) | ISBN
9781616499129 (paperback) | ISBN 9781616499136 (epub)
Subjects: LCSH: Alcoholics—Family relationships. | Drug addicts—Family relation-
ships. | Alcoholics—Rehabilitation. | Drug addicts—Rehabilitation.
Classification: LCC HV5132 .J387 2021 (print) | LCC HV5132 (ebook) | DDC
362.292/3—dc23
LC record available at https://lccn.loc.gov/2020054252
LC ebook record available at https://lccn.loc.gov/2020054253

Editor's notes

This publication is not intended as a substitute for the advice of health care
professionals.

All the stories in this book are based on actual experiences. The names and details have
been changed to protect the privacy of the people involved. In some cases, composites
have been created.

Structured Family Recovery® is a registered trademark owned by Debra Erickson Jay.

25 24 23 22 21   2 3 4 5

Art director: Terri Kinne
Cover designer: Sara Steifel, Think Creative Design
Interior design and typesetting: Jessica Ess
Developmental editor: Marc Olson
Editorial project manager: Jean Cook

To the women in my life who made me, saved me, and loved me.

My life is built upon the examples set by each of you.

A fine glass vase goes from treasure to trash the moment it is broken. Fortunately, something else happens to you and me. Pick up your pieces. Then, help me gather mine.

—VERA NAZARIAN, novelist

How can I know who I am until I see what I do? How can I know what I value until I see where I walk?

—KARL WEICK, psychologist and author

Give people light and they will find their way.

—ELLA JOSEPHINE BAKER, activist

Contents

Foreword

As a practicing psychiatrist and professor of psychiatry I have wrestled with addiction for more than five decades, including at the highest levels of science and government, both nationally and internationally. During that half century, my best teachers have been my own patients with substance use disorders and their families. Having long pioneered in addiction treatment, two decades ago I recognized—painfully—that relapse was the expected outcome of addiction treatment. I asked, "How good can outcomes be for addiction treatment?" I found the answer in my practice, where I often worked with addicted physicians who were involved with the state Physician Health Programs (PHPs). For these addicted individuals, lasting recovery was overwhelmingly the expected outcome of treatment.

Based on that experience with my addicted physician patients, I became the principal investigator in the first national study of the state PHPs. We found that formal, intensive treatment was valuable for these addicted physicians—half were addicted primarily to alcohol and one-third to opioids. But treatment, valuable as it was, was only their starting point. Only slowly did it dawn on me that the missing element needed to improve treatment outcomes for individuals with substance use disorders was their families. These families had a huge stake in the outcome of addiction treatment. They, like their addicted family members, were severely affected by the active addiction. They, like their addicted family members, benefited from recovery.

My new interest in the families of addicted people as uniquely valuable agents promoting recovery led me to Debra Jay's groundbreaking work. I see Structured Family Recovery (SFR) as a crucial missing link in the recovery process. SFR is not only a path to long-term recovery for the addicted person, but it is also a path to the miracle of recovery for the entire family. Although the family did not cause the addiction, the entire family can benefit from recovery.

The person in recovery from a substance use disorder is better than "well" because that person is a better person than he or she was before the first addictive drug use. Similarly, the extended family who engages with the addicted loved one in the lifelong process of recovery is "more well" than the family was before the addiction because of the positive changes family members make in their shared recovery. We get better together.

SFR recovery is a major blessing, not only for the addicted family member, but for the entire family. Using the tried-and-true methods of SFR, the family learns new ways to relate to and to respect one another, new ways to communicate more effectively and lovingly, new ways to confront and benefit from the suffering of addiction and from the many other stresses of life, and new ways to celebrate their shared emancipation from the chemical slavery of addiction.

Addiction to drugs—alcohol, marijuana, and increasingly to synthetics —is epidemic in the United States and throughout the world. Unlike the COVID-19 pandemic, this deadly epidemic did not start in late 2019 and it will not end in this year or even in the next decade. There is no prospect of a vaccine. The addiction epidemic is changing rapidly with increasing simultaneous use of multiple drugs, not just one drug at a time. Today's drug epidemic builds on the long-standing challenge of alcohol addiction. Regardless of the substances or processes involved, addiction is always personal, and its negative effects are felt most acutely in families.

In my longtime learning from addiction, the single most positive development has been the emergence of a massive global recovery movement. More than 23 million Americans are now in recovery from addiction to alcohol and other drugs. SFR extends the miracle of recovery from addicted people to their families. Recovery is a transformative, contagious, joy. SFR is a highly effective way to get the family actively involved in recovery for the benefit of the addicted person and for the benefit of the entire family.

—Robert L. DuPont, MD
First director of the National Institute on Drug Abuse (NIDA)
President, Institute for Behavior and Health, Inc.
Clinical professor of psychiatry, Georgetown University School of Medicine

Acknowledgments

This book is a product of the gift of working with families of alcoholics and addicts for three decades. They reliably show tremendous love and perseverance in the face of a disease that ruthlessly changes their addicted loved ones, sometimes beyond recognition. To each of those families, thank you. You taught me much about our higher selves and what we can achieve when we come together.

To families (the addicted loved ones included) who came together as Structured Family Recovery teams and changed the legacy of your family in the face of addiction, I have such admiration for each of you. Some of you graciously shared your stories for this second edition, passing them on to families looking for a light in the dark. Your integrity, commitment, sense of belonging, and faith to venture forth give every family that is still suffering the reassurance that a lifeline exists to a long-hoped-for future. Your words are promises of something better. Your words show families what is possible. Your words are filled with heartfelt generosity.

Thank you to the SFR family members who gave me your time, sharing thoughts and ideas and ways the book could be even better. Allowing me to see through your eyes gave me a vision I could never alone have seen. Your valuable contributions speak to the fact that doing something well really does take a family.

A special thank-you to the alcoholics and addicts who participated in extended conversations with me, candidly sharing about their addiction and recovery as well as their experiences doing Structured Family Recovery with their families. Your direct, unvarnished honesty is illuminating, allowing families to see inside your world of addiction and the road to recovery. To the parents who shared—equally candidly—their experience watching addiction take over their beloved son and the journey they have since taken together, yours is a beautiful story of what family is capable of doing when given the right vehicle. Allowing these conversations to be printed in these pages opens up a new world of understanding to everyone who loves an addict, as well as to the addicts themselves.

Thank you to all the SFR counselors who shared their experiences using this book with families, offering helpful suggestions. I especially would like to express my gratitude to two SFR counselors, both amazingly good thinkers, who gave me full access to their thoughts, ideas, and time for this new edition: Kathy Row and Sherry Gaugler-Stewart.

Jane Dystel, my agent at Dystel & Goderich Literary Management, is my guiding light who readily gives of her depth of knowledge, steadiness of purpose, and great wisdom. But more important, everything she does is ultimately informed by her unwavering integrity and heart. To say thank you is never enough.

I thank Joe Jaksha, publisher at Hazelden, for getting behind and supporting a new vision. I thank Andrea Lien, editorial director, for her marvelous sense of collaboration as she guided this project forward. A well-designed book is a pleasure to read; I thank art director Terri Kinne for her work. A book free of typos and other stumbles requires the heedful work of copyeditors. For this work, I thank Cathy Broberg, Betty Christiansen, and Victoria Tirrel. Most of all, my gratitude goes to Marc Olson, my editor, for his industriousness, exacting eye, and devoted engagement in this project. A good editor is an author's greatest gift.

I am indebted to Robert L. DuPont, MD, for agreeing to write the foreword of this book. He is a great mind in the field of addiction, and I have long admired his work. I especially thank him for being such a giving and warm person.

I am deeply grateful for the behavior design work I had the privilege of doing with B. J. Fogg, PhD, who has expanded my mind in amazing ways. His work at Stanford University on designing behavior for lasting change has added tremendous richness to this book. To use his favorite word, "Awesome!"

Lastly, I thank my dear husband, Jeff Jay, who is my inspiration and my rock. My gratitude goes far deeper than words could ever reach. Without him, I could never do what I do.

A Note to the Reader

The words *alcoholic, addict, alcoholism, drug addiction,* and *addiction* are used interchangeably. They all represent the same disease. Many people actively use multiple drugs in active addiction: alcohol, mood-altering prescription drugs, and legal or illegal addictive drugs. These words also describe anyone recovering from process (behavioral) addictions such as sex addiction, gambling addiction, or compulsive overeating. These addictions are caused by addictive changes to brain chemistry.

I do not use the terms *substance abuse* or *substance abuser* because a person can be an abuser without suffering from the disease of addiction. I do not use the new popular diagnostic term *substance use disorder* because the language is too vague and isn't used in Twelve Step programs or literature where long-term recovery happens. Treatment providers and other professionals may use these new words, but professional care is but a blip in time as compared to programs of recovery after treatment.

In this book, I refer primarily to the original Twelve Step groups. Alcoholics Anonymous (AA) was founded in the 1930s for people addicted to alcohol. Al-Anon was launched some twenty years later for the families and friends of alcoholics and drug addicts. Narcotics Anonymous (NA) was formed in 1953 for those addicted to drugs other than alcohol. Today there are a great variety of Twelve Step recovery groups for both addicts and their families. There are groups for most process addictions, too, such as sex, gambling, and food. We focus strictly on Twelve Step groups because they are optimal. There may be other groups available, and some people may look upon them favorably, but research shows that Twelve Step recovery works best. Recovery from addiction is not easy, and relapse can lead to consequences none of us would choose. So we always stick with using what is optimal.

Introduction

We Come Home Together

Structured Family Recovery is so simple, so obvious, it's a wonder it hasn't been done before. Often the truly simple is the most revolutionary.

Success doesn't come magically or accidentally. It is a result of what we do. The same can be said of failure. Usually it is a small change in one direction or the other that determines if we win or lose. Structured Family Recovery helps us make the correct choices and then steadily keeps us on course over time.

Up until now, families have been mostly left out of the recovery equation. This surely contributes to the ubiquitous nature of relapse. Structured Family Recovery starts with a family and ends with a family recovery team. We support sobriety by bringing together family and addict in a way that creates unity and mutual triumphs. Turning to social science, we learn what really creates change—challenging the things we've been taught. We apply discoveries of how the workings of the brain affect how we make real-time choices in life. We put it all together to create a family recovery program that is simple and smart.

Structured Family Recovery is a GPS system, a way of navigating through addiction and recovery using the elements we know work. It's about connectivity, not isolation. It goes beyond patient-centered care to family-centered recovery. By working together, we create a different story and unshackle ourselves from the power of addiction.

The first section of this book provides a broad scope of knowledge on addiction, recovery, and change so we can better understand what we're up against, what's required for sobriety, and how we can make change last. The second section of the book is a guide for Structured

Family Recovery, putting into action the goals of achieving lasting sobriety and rebuilding family trust and respect.

There are many ways we find help, both for the addict and the family. Treatment and family programs dot the map of this great country, giving us any manner of assistance and head starts. But these places and programs don't keep alcoholics sober or drug addicts clean; they just begin the process. What keeps the addicted from going back to drink or drugs for the long haul is outside the domain of professionals. Programs for families, marvelous as they are brief, don't prepare us for the day we're again standing in the kitchen face-to-face with our addict, who has now relapsed. I recall the panicked words of a woman who had just smelled alcohol on her recovering husband's breath: "What do I do now? I went to the family program! No one told me what I do now!"

Structured Family Recovery is not a response to crisis but a safeguard against it. We do not stand alone in the kitchen. We stand with family and an entire recovery community. We come prepared for crisis, smoothing the waters with a family living in recovery, gliding forward steadily, with perseverance, over the ripples of turbulence, looking ahead, working for something better, saying farewell to our past ways as best we can. Imperfection is in us and all around us, but we can embrace it as the place where change begins.

Coming together takes the powerless and makes them powerful. Structured Family Recovery brings this power to the family and, in cooperation with the larger recovery community, stands firm in the face of addiction, which trespassed into our homes and multiplied itself into our lives. We crowd addiction out by building a family life brimming with togetherness and recovery, even though we may start out not knowing our way back to each other.

Rather than leaving families clueless in the dark, second-guessing, hoping, and praying, we place family smack-dab in the center of recovery. This is when things begin to change. We can no longer leave lasting sobriety to chance, waiting around for the addicted person to figure out what it means to succeed. The cost to families is far too great, and sometimes we pay a price that is beyond what anyone can bear to pay.

When their families are part of the alcoholics' or addicts' journey, experiencing recovery in the most democratic of ways, newly recovering loved ones no longer feel like the identified patient, the outsider. They know that, once again, they belong to family. They know they are loved.

Follow the book as it's written. The information builds on itself to move you forward—not just with head knowledge, but in real ways to change the course of what's to come. Recovery is practical. It requires we take action. This book shows families (which always includes the recovering addict) the way into recovery with a step-by-step presentation of Structured Family Recovery. It's a place where the world begins to change, and it comes from the changes within us.

Families can engage in Structured Family Recovery on their own or work with an addiction counselor trained specifically to do this work. Whichever you choose, I have only one word for you: *commitment*. Family members must demonstrate to the addict, in deed, what this word means. Then, along the way (not always immediately noticed), recovery heals us, individually and together.

If we can trust just a bit, if not yet in each other, in the greater providence of good and walk forward with only the barest of faith, we will find what we could not see before. Too few find their way alone. Let us bring family and the beloved addict together. It is in the "we" that we find an elegance in life that is as sweet as it is powerful.

We belong to one another. Nothing can change that, not estrangement, not even death. Family is defined by belonging. When we use the word *family*, it's for each of us to know what that word means—who it is we belong to and who belongs to us. We are born into families, adopted into them, marry into them, or choose them from people we love best. But family goes beyond love; it's primordial. It defines us. We are born with a deep need for knowing there are people who will always show up when we need them, stick with us through thick and thin, and love us at our best and worst. Author and columnist Erma Bombeck described it like this: "We were a strange little band of characters trudging through life . . . inflicting pain and kissing to heal it in the same instant, loving, laughing, defending, and trying to figure out the common thread that bound us all together."

This book is about addiction and family and lasting sobriety, and, ultimately, about working together to find that place where everyone is okay and safe and happy.

What We Need to Know

This section is written to provide families with a necessary foundation for beginning a program of Structured Family Recovery (SFR).

You won't find information as usual here. Instead, you'll be challenged to reexamine what you've been taught to believe about addiction and the family. As R. Buckminster Fuller once said, "You never change things by fighting the existing reality. To change something, build a new model that makes the existing model obsolete." This section of the book lays the groundwork for moving past an old and unhelpful model of family involvement by teaching us to think differently.

The information in this section isn't an optional read. Before putting Structured Family Recovery into practice, it is very important to have a bedrock of knowledge that leads to correct thinking about addiction as well as what sustained, long-term recovery requires. We want success, so we cut no corners.

1

The Missing Elements

Fifty to 90 percent of alcoholics and addicts relapse in the first year after treatment. In the face of such grim figures, it's easy to toss around blame. *Treatment doesn't work. The addict isn't doing what she should. Doctors are the new drug pushers.* But the truth lies elsewhere for the most part and requires a new conversation.

Relapse is caused by underestimating what it takes to stay sober. Addicts, their families, and society commonly minimize what is required for successful recovery. Addicts can't simply think their way out of addiction. Recovery requires action. It's much more than leaving the drug behind, whether that drug is alcohol, cocaine, marijuana, heroin, methamphetamine, pain medications, or tranquilizers. Recovery is about changing behaviors, which leads to changes in thinking. It's about positive spirituality—honesty and willingness and letting go of resentments. It's about taking a fearless look at one's self and the wrongs of the past. It's about cleaning house and making amends. Recovery is about more than abstinence; it's about becoming the kind of person who can engage in healthy relationships.

Abstinent without recovery, the addicted person is haunted by the past, suffers in the present, and can't see a promising future. The control centers in the brain are being depleted by the constant internal battle not to pick up a drink or a drug. Relationships with family are frayed and getting no better. For these addicts, relapse is usually just a matter of time.

An old adage says it best: "When a heavy drinker stops drinking, he feels better. When an alcoholic stops drinking, he feels worse." For alcoholics and addicts to begin enjoying life again, they need to work a rigorous Twelve Step program of recovery in groups such as Alcoholics Anonymous (AA) and Narcotics Anonymous (NA). These programs work because they treat the chronic nature of addiction that affects the mind, body, and spirit. There is no cure, only a daily reprieve that requires ongoing management. If we don't understand this basic tenet of success, we don't understand recovery.

When we believe treatment centers are the heart of recovery, we base our hopes and dreams on a flawed assumption. Treatment isn't recovery, and clinical teams don't know who will stay sober and who won't. Stellar patients drink on the flight home, and seemingly hopeless cases never drink again. Treatment staff know what works, but no one knows who will follow directions and do what it takes to stay sober.

Recovery doesn't officially begin until treatment ends. It isn't dished out by doctors or teased out by therapists. It happens in a community— and not just any community. It requires working a Twelve Step recovery program with other alcoholics and addicts. Recovery requires broad changes in how addicts live their lives, the kind of changes that would be tough work for anyone. Our loved ones are attempting it with a brain so compromised by addiction that their brain scans look like Swiss cheese. With decision-making abilities impaired and emotions turbulent, it's no wonder so many don't get very far before they crumble and relapse.

The purpose of treatment is specific. It is designed to attend to the acute stage of this chronic illness. Involvement with patients is relatively short. A team of professionals tends to the most intense and severe symptoms, most notably the physical and emotional discomfort that comes with early abstinence. And many do an excellent job of it. But the scorecard we use to rate the success or failure of these facilities erroneously holds them responsible for patients' sobriety once they return home. Addiction is a chronic disease, and it must be managed by working a daily Twelve Step program. Treatment centers can only prepare patients to follow through with ongoing recovery recommendations. They can't do it for them. If addicts don't follow the directions for ongoing recovery, they are at high risk for relapse.

While not making direct promises of keeping people sober long term, with some notable exceptions, treatment centers do so implicitly. Instead, professionals need to be straightforward about what they can do, why it is important, and what they *can't* do.

This is exceedingly important because today we have so many treatment centers popping up across the country, trying out new strategies and protocols that might differentiate them from the pack but aren't necessarily effective if our goal is sobriety. This makes it difficult for families to evaluate treatment options. It's hard to be a smart consumer in a confusing arena.

The problem begins with the rubrics we're using—our scoring guide to evaluate the quality of treatment—which are flawed. *Treatment cannot be responsible for recovery outside the treatment program.* It can only be held responsible for its effectiveness in these areas:

1. Medically detoxing and stabilizing patients, thoroughly assessing their needs, and setting treatment goals

2. Working with patients to break through denial at the deepest possible level, in a respectful and dignified manner, so they accept that they have a chronic disease that requires lifelong abstinence

3. Integrating the Twelve Steps into the treatment plan (Twelve Step Facilitation has been shown to be most effective)

4. Providing patients a recovery management plan that includes relapse prevention strategies and a clear understanding of how to work a Twelve Step recovery program when returning home (encouraging the patient to go to AA or NA meetings while in treatment and connecting the patient to a recovering person in his home area help accomplish this goal)

5. Inviting the family to attend the family program and encouraging children to attend a children's program if one is available

6. Developing aftercare recommendations designed to give an appropriate level of support that will increase the likelihood that patients will engage in recovery once they leave treatment

7. Engaging the family in the entire process, as appropriate

There is also much talk about evidence-based treatment, but even though intentions are good, there are problems. *Evidence-based* doesn't necessarily mean the research is flawless, nor does it mean it is measuring the same outcome we are aiming for: lasting sobriety. Results depend on the quality of the research, the validity of the testing, replication over time by impartial researchers, and reviews by other researchers. Research bias—particularly the bias of what is actually published (mainly the positive results)—can lead to "proving" something is true when it is not true. Instead, we should be talking about "levels of evidence" and "quality of evidence."

According to Eric Topol, MD, cardiologist, geneticist, and researcher from the Cleveland Clinic, in his book *The Creative Destruction of Medicine,* "Consumers, unfortunately, are typically getting data from small, observational studies, published in obscure journals or not at all, in which there is no real control group or no randomization, and shaky end points." He goes on to say that even very large-scale observational studies have produced faulty results, misleading the public more than once. Professionals can be misled too.

Dr. Topol has coined the word *litter-ature,* denoting that too much of the research is "littered with misleading and false-positive findings." We must be smart consumers of research, he says. "I don't want to be excessively negative, but the right assumption in reviewing any new data presented to consumers is to question it . . . consider the new finding null and void unless you are thoroughly convinced that the evidence is compelling." He is speaking of medical science, but results in the field of addiction and behavioral health are even more tenuous.

Misconceptions about treatment, leading to false expectations, coupled with the frustration of relapse, have families throwing up their hands and proclaiming, "Enough! Treatment doesn't work!" Once they reach this verdict, hopelessness can settle in, and the only question left is "Now what?"

What if I told you there was a group of addicted people who almost never relapse in the years following treatment? As a matter of fact, 78 percent never have a single relapse. Less than 15 percent have one relapse but not a second. And those with more than one relapse? A whopping 7 percent. Not only that, these folks are some of the most difficult addicts to treat. When I worked in inpatient treatment, having them assigned to our caseload would elicit groans of despair because we knew our work just doubled. "They're the worst patients!"

The alcoholics and addicts in this group are getting something other addicted loved ones aren't—a team who works with them for five years after treatment to make sure they build a solid program of recovery and make the prerequisite changes that lead to lasting sobriety. Because when alcoholics and addicts are left to their own devices—in spite of the universal cry that they can do it on their own—the odds are they'll be drinking and drugging again.

Author Stephen King, in his column for *Entertainment Weekly*, writes about just this point.

> [Managing] good sobriety without much help . . . is a trick very few druggies and alcoholics can manage. I know, because I'm both. Substance abusers lie about everything and usually do an awesome job of it. I once knew a coke-head who convinced his girlfriend the smell of freebase was mold in the plastic shower curtain of their apartment's bathroom. She believed him, he said, for five years (although he was probably lying about that, it was probably only three). . . . Go to one of those church-basement meetings where they drink coffee and talk about the Twelve Steps and you can hear similar stories on any night, and that's why the founders of this group emphasized complete honesty . . . what happened, what changed, what it's like now. . . . If my own career as a drunk both active and

sober has convinced me of anything, it's convinced me of this: Addictive personalities do not prosper on their own. Without unvarnished, tough-love, truth-telling from their own kind—the voices that say, "You're lying about that, Freckles"—the addict has a tendency to fall back to his old ways.

The problem is, of course, that most alcoholics and addicts coming out of treatment don't want to work a program of recovery that requires taking action. They're convinced they have changed, with surprisingly little effort and in a remarkably short amount of time, and they often convince their poor gullible families of the same. These alcoholics and addicts think they have a better idea, which usually entails staying sober on their own with an easier, softer approach—one that eventually lands them back in the liquor store or crack house or doctor's office looking for a scrip. They do this not because they are bad but because this is the way the disease directs their thinking processes.

This lack of compliance is repeatedly used by professionals and researchers as the reason AA or other Twelve Step programs don't work. Confusing an addict's compliance with a program's effectiveness is faulty analysis. The real question is how do we increase compliance?

It isn't that Twelve Step programs don't work. It is that alcoholics and addicts, for a complex set of reasons, have difficulty adhering to *anything* in a consistent manner. Consider the struggles diabetics have trying to comply with their recovery programs—and they do not have to contend with the cognitive impairment we see in addicts. Research shows that among patients who only needed to take a medication to treat their illness, a mere 50 percent complied. Nobody would argue that medications don't work because people don't take them as directed. When it comes to addiction, the sustained commitment it takes to recover is in another stratosphere from swallowing a pill.

What if we, as families, could initiate a program with our loved ones that models those used by the recovery winners mentioned above? What if we could provide the missing element—the one that makes it much tougher to relapse? Once we appropriately identify the staff in treatment centers as the "first responders" instead of the sole providers of a stand-alone solution, our expectations of treatment change. Without a doubt, treatment has a vital job to do, but it's only the beginning. Treatment centers can keep our alcoholics and addicts only so long, and then they come home to us. This is when it takes all of us bonding together for recovery. If we're to take our place among the winners, it most definitely takes a family.

Families and close friends have a tremendous amount of influence in an addict's life, but we usually don't know it. Too often families believe they are powerless. They don't understand their power and often feel mistreated, disregarded—even disliked.

The very people an alcoholic or addict needs most are the people he often fights against. He tries to appease family, only to break the promises he makes to them. Or he ignores those closest to him, pretending he simply doesn't care. The addiction not only punishes the people the addict cares about most, but it abuses him too. The addict breaks promises to himself. He pretends none of the pain matters. And, even as he begins losing everything he holds dear, he can't stop this downward spiral. He is typically filled with shame as he strikes out in anger. He doesn't understand what is happening inside himself. That is what it's like to live under the tyranny of addiction. It doesn't have to be like this. A rigorous recovery program can reverse the insanity of this disease, making things better one day at a time.

2

Stick with the Winners

So, who are the winners I referred to earlier, the ones who mostly never relapse in the first five years of recovery? They're doctors (and other licensed professionals). And why are they selected to receive the exceptional support that safeguards them from relapse? Because no one can imagine opiate-addicted cardiologists or alcoholic neurosurgeons left to their own devices once they are discharged from treatment. If they are going to see patients, they must be sober.

Right about now, I can hear people objecting, "Of course they stay sober. They're doctors. They know better than to relapse." But remember what I told you: *they are the toughest patients in treatment*. The belief that addicted doctors take direction well or commit to doing what is required to stay sober is largely fictional. In truth, doctors are at even higher risk for relapse.

Let's put a doctor's risk for relapse into perspective by looking at something else they struggle with—hand washing. For the past thirty years, there's been an ongoing effort to persuade doctors to wash their hands between seeing patients, with little sustainable change. Hand washing is, of course, no small matter. The Centers for Disease Control and Prevention estimate that we spend $30 billion annually fighting health care–associated infections and that almost 100,000 deaths are attributable to such infections each year in the United States. The fix? Soap and water. And yet, knowing this fact has not improved physicians' hygiene practices. In response, hospitals have been forced into action. They've trained hand-washing coaches. They've installed video cameras that send images halfway around the world so workers in India can monitor our doctors. They require doctors to wear radio-frequency ID chips that register each time they walk by a sink. Good hand-washers are sometimes rewarded with cash. This provides an eye-opening perspective on how different groups struggle with compliance.

Another false belief is that doctors' success in sobriety is correlated with the fact that they have a medical license to lose. After all, retaining one's privileges to practice medicine ought to be a big motivator for staying sober. But fear alone is not enough to ensure recovery. The specter of losing something valuable can be a motivator for getting started, but long-term success requires an ongoing program of support and accountability.

Most of us are concerned about loved ones who do not have the threat of losing a medical license looming over their heads. But our addicted family members have things they value too. Things they do not want to lose. Topping the list is family, but they also value their jobs, friends, and reputation. These can serve as motivators to get started. But like doctors, our loved ones need programs that manage their recovery over time.

For most alcoholics and addicts, consequences in the distant future have little impact on what they do today. Whether it's someday losing a medical license or someday losing their family, the immediate pull of addiction has far greater power. The need to snort cocaine or shoot up heroin or drink a bottle of vodka today obliterates concerns about tomorrow. Whether or not a person is a doctor, the negative consequences that demand attention are the ones that happen right away, not in some far-off time. A drug court in Hawaii found that the future threat of a ten-year prison sentence was a poorer deterrent than being immediately sent to jail for three days upon failing a drug test. The timing of a consequence is more effective than the size of a consequence.

Doctors entering treatment tend to be sicker than most, due to a seemingly inexhaustible supply of drugs and the ability to more easily hide their problems from others. People also tend to look the other way and enable addicted doctors more than they do the average addict.

Intervening on a doctor usually occurs only after the addiction has become impossible to ignore. Consequently, addiction's progression has become quite serious before most physicians find themselves in treatment. This makes their long-term successes all the more compelling. It appears they've found the Holy Grail of recovery.

Can we find it, too? Is there something we can learn from how doctors succeed in recovery that can help our loved ones? Before we answer this question, let's examine how the model of care for doctors is unique.

First, there is a high expectation for doctors to succeed in recovery. This is paired with the support required to make success possible. Treatment programs are clearly defined as acute care providers and only a first step in the recovery process. Once doctors are discharged from treatment, they engage in a second phase of care, which is designed to support long-term recovery. Called the Physician Health Program (PHP), this program provides five years of chronic care management (depending on the state the doctor resides in). Doctors receive multiple levels of support with the flexibility to respond to changing needs over time. Even physicians who continue to struggle with sobriety longer than others are highly successful, because the program lasts long enough to give them the time to succeed.

In 2007, researchers conducted the largest study to date on addicted physicians involved in five-year monitoring programs. Studying 904 addicted physicians who participated in sixteen different PHPs, the research showed that long-term recovery rates for these doctors were notable—not because they were physicians, but because they were highly engaged in PHP care management programs. These programs are composed of what have come to be known as Eight Essential Elements.

Based on evidence and reasoning, these researchers also concluded that these same elements can be successfully used as a chronic care model for the general population of addicted people. They state, "On the basis of these findings, there is reason for renewed optimism for individuals with [addictions] and their families."

It is helpful to remember that this is the *required* care for addicted doctors. It is well documented that these Eight Essential Elements, when applied simultaneously, work.

1. *Positive Rewards and Negative Consequences.* Establishing a clear understanding of rewards for positive behavior and consequences for negative behavior is key. Addiction is linked to unacceptable behaviors, and recovery is linked to desirable behaviors. These behaviors aren't about being good or bad, but about being sick or well. We know which behaviors precede relapse. Consequences, both negative and positive, must be meaningful, timely, and sustained if we expect them to have beneficial effects.

2. *Frequent Random Drug Testing.* Doctors are randomly drug tested for five years. They call daily to learn if they need to appear for testing. Relapse is linked to consequences that are predetermined and written on a signed document, so doctors clearly understand the cost of a relapse. Since there is no room for indecision, consequences are effective in producing changes in behaviors. Consequences are not synonymous with abuse or disrespect, but rather level-headed expectations properly linked to relapse behavior.

3. *Twelve Step Programs and the Abstinence Standard.* Doctors are actively referred to Twelve Step groups, not just passively encouraged to attend. It's known that Twelve Step programs are central to long-term sobriety, so showing up isn't left to chance. Additionally, doctors are enrolled in professionally led group therapy sessions designed for recovering physicians. Doctors are expected to abstain from all mood-altering substances, not just their drug of choice.

4. *Viable Role Models and Recovery Mentors.* Doctors are paired with other recovering physicians who mentor them and provide recovery role models. These associations help doctors begin to identify positively with the recovery experience in Twelve Step programs. Mentors also build relationships with doctors' families and ask for input on progress. Newly recovering physicians receive feedback from their mentors and get report cards highlighting recovery strengths and recommendations for improvements.

5. *Modified Lifestyles.* Changes to doctors' lifestyles and professional lives position them for success in both recovery and work. For example, they may change their medical specialty or request outside monitoring of prescribing practices. Recovery-enhancing decisions are supported and encouraged.

6. *Active and Sustained Monitoring.* Designed to lay the groundwork for a lifetime of sobriety by ensuring early detection of relapse, this component includes monitoring doctors for at least five years after treatment. This extended period provides most doctors—even those who've had one or more relapses—the level of support that eventually establishes solid recovery. What distinguishes Physician Health Programs from most every other mainstream treatment model is this extended time component that addresses the chronic nature of addiction.

7. *Active Management of Relapse.* When doctors relapse, the PHP process re-intervenes and re-evaluates. Rather than simply repeating the same past treatment experiences, a more intense, specialized treatment is recommended. The researchers explain, "The blend of support and accountability, alliance and toughness distinguishes Physician Health Programs from other interventions that seek but too often fall short of creating and sustaining these important ingredients."

8. *Continuing Care Approach.* Addiction is a chronic disease that needs to be managed on an ongoing basis, just as we manage diabetes and other chronic illnesses. Lifelong recovery is achieved by managing the chronic nature of addiction appropriately. Physician Health Programs demonstrate this by sustaining therapeutic relationships with doctors for five years or more and achieving high rates of lasting sobriety.

In the treatment field, we have long understood how each of these elements is effective for treating addiction. But Physician Health Programs are the first to demonstrate that integrating all eight elements into a single, long-term program of support is the formula for producing durable, lasting sobriety. Most alcoholics and addicts don't have access to the type of care management provided to physicians through these programs. Therefore, the chronic nature of their addiction isn't well managed, and risk of relapse is high. Drawing from the wisdom and proven track record of the PHP success, Structured Family Recovery transforms the family into a recovery team with a structured program, creating a new gold standard available to us all.

How It All Started

William Duncan Silkworth, MD, was known as the little doctor who loved drunks. A Princeton graduate with a medical degree from New York University, he had a penchant for alcoholics. Even the most resistant drunks opened up to him, and some broke down and wept. He spent his entire career working with alcoholics—more than 51,000 of them.

At a time when alcoholics were thought to deliberately bring devastation on themselves, Dr. Silkworth steadfastly believed in their intrinsic goodness. He was a man with special gifts, great devotion, and a deep understanding of alcoholism. Yet, with all his talents, Dr. Silkworth reported that only 2 percent of the alcoholics he saw achieved lasting sobriety. There was little hope for the truly addicted. These were times before Alcoholics Anonymous.

One of the drunks Dr. Silkworth treated was nearing death at age thirty-nine. His name was Bill Wilson. While hospitalized, Bill had a "white light" experience during which he felt the presence of a Higher Power and had a spiritual awakening. Describing the episode to the doctor, Bill asked if he might be insane. Dr. Silkworth, having treated many alcoholics suffering from hallucinations, instinctively understood that what Bill had experienced was different. Rather than dismiss it as another drunk's crazy story, Dr. Silkworth told Bill, "I don't know what you've got, but hang on to it. You are not insane and you may have the answer to your problem."

Another doctor might have dismissed Bill's story as delusional, unwittingly dooming the future of Alcoholics Anonymous. But Dr. Silkworth encouraged Bill to take seriously the message he took from this experience: *You will stay sober only if you share your story with other alcoholics.* Bill's sudden understanding that the key was helping other alcoholics eventually led to Alcoholics Anonymous. To this day, it is the most dependable path to recovery with more than 118,000 groups in 180 countries.

Sister Molly Monahan writes of Alcoholics Anonymous in her book *Seeds of Grace*:

> I once heard a Jesuit assert that when the history of twentieth-century American spirituality is written, Alcoholics Anonymous will be judged the most significant spiritual movement of the era. I am quite sure he was not a member of A.A. I am and have been for over seventeen years. I am also a Roman Catholic nun and have been for over forty years. I am inclined to agree with that Jesuit.

The spirituality within Alcoholics Anonymous leads some to erroneously claim it is a religious organization. As Bill Wilson wrote, "There is room for all shades of belief and nonbelief." AA speaks of a Higher Power, but it is one of individual choosing. Atheists may find that power in nature, or in the Twelve Step program itself. For others, G-O-D stands for *Group of Drunks* or *Good Orderly Direction*. Still others find their Higher Power through personal religious beliefs. Whatever the choosing, one of AA's key insights is that a Higher Power—a power greater than the self—is required for loosening the grip of addiction. Personal willpower is not enough.

Over the next months, after leaving the hospital, Bill Wilson shared his story with one alcoholic after another without a single success. Exasperated, he was ready to give up. It was his wife, Lois, who persuaded him to continue. "Bill," she said, "you are sober. That is miracle enough."

Lois's pivotal role, in this particular instance, is rarely mentioned in AA history. If she hadn't insisted Bill continue his work with other alcoholics, he may have called it quits, started drinking again, and died a hopeless alcoholic. But instead, *as a family member,* Lois helped change the course of history—and probably saved her husband's life.

In 1935, six months sober, Bill Wilson traveled from New York to Akron, Ohio, in hopes of jump-starting his career. When the business deal he was counting on fell through, Bill found himself alone, despondent, and with only ten dollars in his pocket. Rather than turning to the bar in the hotel lobby, he began searching for an alcoholic to help. He called a local minister, Dr. Walter F. Tunks, looking not for religion but another drunk.

Dr. Tunks gave Bill the names of ten people. Standing at a pay phone, it wasn't until he reached the last name on the list that Bill finally got a lead. A fellow gave him a name, Henrietta Seiberling, and her home phone number.

Now imagine this for just a moment. A complete stranger, calling person after person, announcing himself as "a rum hound from New York who's found a way to keep alcoholics sober," is given a name—Seiberling—that he knows from his successful days on Wall Street. Seiberling, Bill knew, was the family name of the founder of Goodyear Tire. It must be his wife, Bill reasoned, and momentarily felt too embarrassed to call.

But a voice inside Bill's head said, "You better call the lady."

As it turned out, Henrietta was not the wife, but the daughter-in-law of Frank Augustus Seiberling, who was indeed founder of the Goodyear Tire & Rubber Company. Henrietta, who had three small children at home, told Bill, "You come right out here."

Henrietta later said that her first thought was to put this man from New York together with an alcoholic surgeon and physician in town, Dr. Robert Smith. Bob Smith was losing everything to drink, and he desperately wanted to get sober. He had long before confided in her about his alcoholism. "Henrietta, I don't understand it. Nobody understands it. Some doctor had written a book about it, but he doesn't understand it. I don't like the stuff. I don't want to drink."

Henrietta picked up the phone and called Dr. Smith's wife. "Anne," she said, "I've found a man who can help Bob. You must bring him right over."

Anne was uncomfortable admitting, on this Saturday afternoon, that Bob was passed out drunk in his bed. It was only through Henrietta's dogged insistence that Anne confessed the truth.

"Bring him over for dinner tomorrow night at five," Henrietta said. It would be Mother's Day, 1935.

Even though he had desperately wanted to quit drinking, Bob Smith did what alcoholics have always done when help is offered. He firmly declined. He wasn't moved by the promise of this man who claimed to sober up alcoholics. Bob eventually relented, but only because of his deep respect for Henrietta. He also knew she wasn't a person who took no for an answer. So, he agreed, saying to his wife, Anne, "Only fifteen minutes. Let's make it snappy."

The meeting between Bill and Bob stretched out to six hours, one alcoholic talking to another alcoholic. Although Bill didn't know it at the time, Bob would be his first success story. He and Dr. Bob, as he was affectionately called, would go on to tell their stories to other alcoholics, who would tell their stories to yet others, laying the foundation for the AA program that has brought hope to alcoholics around the globe.

It's important to note that Alcoholics Anonymous didn't begin simply with two alcoholics somehow finding each other and getting together for a talk. It began with a friend and a spouse putting two alcoholics together, even as one of them was objecting mightily. In other words, Alcoholics Anonymous began with a family intervention.

This story is important for all people who love an alcoholic or addict. We, too, have often been taught to step aside. We're told that alcoholics and addicts must feel ready to get sober before any good can come from anything. But Dr. Bob didn't feel ready to meet with Bill. The meeting with Bill happened without regard to Bob's feelings of readiness. If Anne and Henrietta had waited for Bob to take the lead, Alcoholics Anonymous may never have formed.

A few years later, after AA proved successful at keeping alcoholics sober, Dr. Silkworth was asked to contribute to the writings of the book *Alcoholics Anonymous,* more commonly known as the Big Book. In a chapter titled "The Doctor's Opinion," he wrote:

If any feel that as psychiatrists directing a hospital for alcoholics we appear somewhat sentimental, let them stand with us a while on the firing line, see the tragedies, the despairing wives, the little children; let the solving of these problems become a part of their daily work, and even of their sleeping moments, and the most cynical will not wonder that we have accepted and encouraged this movement.

Even in these earliest times, recovery was understood as a family affair. Lois Wilson and Anne Smith, the wives of Bill and Bob, played crucial roles in the formation of Alcoholics Anonymous. As Lois told writer William Borchert, "I used to think my life really began the day I met Bill. I guess I was as addicted to him as he was to alcohol. Then he got sober—and I got well."

Lois suffered through seventeen years of Bill's drinking, which included financial ruin, the loss of her family home, days when Bill wouldn't dress or bathe, and frequent hospitalizations. Eventually, she watched Bill almost die. Once Bill found sobriety and met Dr. Bob, Lois's life initially became worse, not better. "I guess I thought once he stopped drinking, everything would go back to what it was like before—happy and loving," she said. It didn't.

In 1959, Lois Wilson began Al-Anon, a Twelve Step program to help families and friends of alcoholics. By doing so, she gave the people who love an alcoholic a path to hope, happiness, and peace of mind.

A member of Al-Anon writes about family recovery:

I am sorry for families who have not taken refuge in the Al-Anon program. . . . When an alcoholic finds [AA], he often grows so fast that we must learn to grow with him or the relationship may be in danger. For this is a family disease. It needs a family answer. In order to achieve real unity, the whole family needs to practice the A.A. and Al-Anon principles, each in his individual way.

4

Introducing Structured Family Recovery

Structured Family Recovery takes family members off the sidelines and puts them in the game. It's often said that recovery isn't a spectator sport. We can no longer afford to squander one of the best resources in the lives of most addicts—*family*. In early recovery, a time when a united front is crucial, families can make the difference between success and failure.

As families, our efforts to help the addict can be hindered by misconceptions. What we believe about addiction and recovery are often myths. The newly recovering person is not only misled by faulty ideas but further hampered by a propensity for dismissing the advice of treatment providers. Once a family engages in Structured Family Recovery, the process is designed to set the entire family on the right course.

Building on what we know about what works for doctors, Structured Family Recovery is designed to bring a similar recovery team to families. We incorporate elements from the Physician Health Program as a springboard. Structured Family Recovery is a framework. It's a simple process that gets results. It works with any size family group. Team members can begin before an addicted loved one goes to treatment, while he's in treatment, or after he's completed treatment. The addicted person isn't involved at the outset but is invited to join the recovery team at the appropriate time, usually week three or four. Even when an addicted loved one doesn't join, families experience tremendous benefit.

Structured Family Recovery gives renewed purpose to a family that's been fractured by the emotional and financial upheaval caused by addiction. Sharing a common goal—sobriety that lasts—naturally draws families together again. A higher calling unites us. Pulling together, we are able to accomplish more than any one person can. In all areas of achievement, from sports to business to science, those who succeed stand up to congratulate the members of their teams: the mentors, coaches, supporters, cheerleaders, and experts. Similarly, families in recovery need teams built for success.

Structured Family Recovery is a program of action. It is therapeutic, but it isn't therapy. It supports Twelve Step recovery for alcoholics, addicts, and family members, but it isn't AA or any other Twelve Step group. Like PHPs, it supports ongoing recovery—designed so that every member of the family contributes to preventing relapse, healing the whole family, and building trust. Through structure and accountability, a new outlook emerges. Everyone participating in a recovery program changes—each individual as well as the very grain of family life. Broken relationships start to mend, and the love we have for one another begins to reveal itself.

Structured Family Recovery starts with a decision to dedicate one hour a week to a family meeting. Since meetings happen via conference calls, it doesn't matter where you live, if you are at home or traveling, in your pajamas, or in bed with a cold. People don't have to drive to designated meeting spots, find child care, or figure out how to include family members who live out of town. If the addict is in residential treatment or a sober house, he can still participate. Each meeting is as close as your telephone.

Structured Family Recovery isn't punitive or judgmental. No one is telling anyone else what they think about them or what they should do. Instead, they talk about themselves and their own strengths, limitations, and needs. By focusing on themselves rather than on everyone else, the individual members of the team regain manageability in their lives. Everyone learns where to find their power and what they are powerless over. With time, everyone can begin to forgive and eventually can trust. There are bumps in the road, to be sure, but together, as a family, they work through them.

The Williams family decided to participate in Structured Family Recovery when their mom was in treatment for the third time. All four children were grown, with families of their own. Mom and Dad were empty nesters. Mom's relapse with alcohol and oxycodone, an opiate pain medication, went largely unnoticed by the kids, who were busy with their own lives. Dad didn't want to burden the children with news of yet another relapse, so he tried to manage the problem on his own.

Eventually, Mom found it hard to get enough pills to satisfy the demands of her addiction. Law enforcement had begun cracking down on the doctors who were making it easy for her to get prescription painkillers. This is when things changed measurably. She was forced to buy what she could on the streets. Some days, when nothing else was available, she bought heroin. An upper-middle-class housewife and grandmother turned street junkie once the doctor's office—the socially acceptable supplier of her drug—was shut down.

Soon it was impossible to hide her problem. Dad still didn't mention anything, but the children were terrified by how incapacitated their mother had become. At a granddaughter's birthday party, she was barely able to speak and repeatedly nodded off at the dinner table. Finally, her daughter broke the code of silence and demanded something be done. The children implemented a structured family intervention and managed to move their mother to accept treatment.

Once Mom was admitted into a residential treatment program, her children began to discuss the seriousness of their mother's addiction and how it was ripping the family apart. They knew if she relapsed again, she would die.

Addiction had taken its toll on everyone. There was too much secret keeping, infighting, and general chaos. The adult children didn't get along most of the time and periodically stopped talking to one another. Everyone dreaded celebrating holidays. They were frustrated by their father's passive approach to their mother's addiction and blamed him for allowing it to go on. Even the grandchildren had been pulled into the family drama. They voiced their own concerns that something was wrong and began objecting to sleepovers. Something had to change.

A family decision to participate in Structured Family Recovery felt like a leap of faith. Nobody fully understood the idea of family recovery or why it was necessary. They only knew that they needed to do something more than they had done in the past, hoping it would help their mother in her struggle to stay sober. Empowered by the success of the intervention, the adult children approached their father and asked him to get involved too.

Because family relations were fractured by many years of coping with their mother's addiction, they unanimously decided they needed to work with a counselor trained in Structured Family Recovery. Most of the family resided in Chicago, but one brother lived in Indianapolis. A sister was a corporate trainer, often on the road. Since weekly meetings with the counselor were on conference calls, everyone could participate. Nobody knew what to expect, but the counselor reassured them, explaining that their mother also felt nervous and unsure about being in treatment and away from home.

The weekly meeting is the heart of Structured Family Recovery. During the call, everyone reviews their past week, determining what worked well for them and what didn't. Then members of the team discuss what they want to do in the week ahead. The counselor offers support and guidance to keep everyone moving in a positive and beneficial direction. Every member creates small, workable goals that will produce big change over time. No one worries about being perfect. The Williams family chose "Progress not perfection" as their family slogan.

The family made a pact to do whatever was required—fully engaging in the recovery process, just as they expected their mother to while in treatment. The counselor began educating them about recovery and how it worked. Everyone found a weekly Al-Anon meeting to attend, began reading recovery literature written for families, and completed simple assignments. They soon began to see the power of small changes and the effectiveness of working as a group.

Halfway through her treatment program, their mother called saying she'd packed her bags and was leaving treatment. The family momentarily panicked. As they described it, "Everyone started freaking out. We fell right back into our old ways of coping, which was helping no one." But then they realized they weren't alone anymore. They quickly called their SFR counselor and then their mother's treatment counselor. The crisis allowed the family to experience firsthand how easily they could mobilize their team. Family and professionals, working in tandem, put a plan together. They scripted the best way to talk with their mother to help her make a better decision. A conference call with the family, the treatment counselor, and their mother made it possible for everyone to participate in dignified and respectful problem solving. In less than thirty minutes, their mother agreed to stay in treatment and follow all the professional recommendations. The power of the group had become stronger than the pull of her addiction. The treatment team agreed that none of them individually could have persuaded her to stay without help from the family team.

Before Mom was discharged from her residential treatment program, the family invited her to participate in one of their SFR conference calls. They explained what they had been doing for themselves and invited her to join the family team. She readily agreed. Later, a counselor in the treatment center told the family how proud their mom was that the entire family was part of the recovery experience. She had shared what happened during a group therapy session, smiling from ear to ear.

Today, the Williams family has been engaged in weekly SFR meetings for more than fifteen months. Mom is sober a year and three months, and she is actively involved in her Twelve Step recovery program. The entire family knows the language of recovery because they attend weekly Twelve Step meetings for families of alcoholics and addicts. While not everything is perfect, the family is back together. They've begun having fun again, getting together on weekends for dinner and board games. They've even taken some short skiing trips together and are planning a family cruise. Grandchildren are at the grandparents' house for over-nighters. Everybody talks to everybody else.

The dad recently said, "I have to be honest. When we started this, I resented it. I thought, it's one more thing I have to do every week. But now I see my wife sober, and I'm so proud of her. And I hear what comes out of my kids' mouths during our meetings, and I'm amazed. I think to myself, did I raise these wonderful children?"

Structured Family Recovery transforms recovery into a journey the family takes together. Ultimately, it gives families back the most important thing of all—each other.

A Shared Gift

On a lovely summer afternoon several years ago, my phone rang. The woman on the other end spoke with a most genteel Southern accent and informed me she was from Mississippi. She was calling for a friend who had concerns about her daughter. After we talked about the problem, she paused and said: "My daddy's been in recovery over twenty-five years. He was a successful man around town, but at home his alcoholism was bad. Now, with all this sobriety behind him, our relationship is as sweet and clear as moonlight through the pines."

After another pause, she added, "What a lot of people don't know about me is that every morning when I wake up, the first thing I do is thank God for the disease of alcoholism.

"You see, if my daddy hadn't been an alcoholic, we would never have belonged to a family in recovery." Recovery, she said, made them better and happier than they ever could have been without it.

Family involvement isn't just about motivating the addict to accept treatment. That's just the beginning. We need a systemic solution that heals the entire family, not just one person. Family recovery requires refocusing on our own actions for the purpose of recognizing and rooting out the ways addiction has changed our behaviors, especially the ways we relate to one another. Family recovery is defined by an unwavering belief in the integrity of the family.

When the disease of addiction is active, it's common for alcoholics to lie about everything. What is not often recognized is how dishonest the rest of the family becomes. We lie to protect the addict and to spare ourselves from embarrassment or loss. We make promises and then don't keep them. "I'm not going to put up with this for another minute," we pledge. But we do, often for years—even decades. We do whatever it takes to survive. In the grip of her addiction, our loved one is doing the same thing.

Alcoholics and addicts don't ask to get sick. They take a drink, maybe a drug, and somewhere down the line, the drink or drug takes them. They can't see it happening, and neither can we, until things get much, much worse. We loved each other before things got bad; then we mix up the illness with the person and aren't so sure anymore. It's hard to feel love when we're consumed with anger, fear, and resentment. We think this is something our loved one is doing to us, and we can't understand why he doesn't stop.

Addicts can be just as puzzled. Still wanting to be the good guy, most create endless rules around drinking and using, and they are astonished at their inability to maintain them. But their brains are in a downward spiral, marked by a growing loss of control and varying forms of negativity. With everyone in the family unhappy with them, they can become filled with anger, fear, and resentment. Once they get sober, addicts often still smart from the stinging words they suffered from fed-up family members. Meanwhile, the family, who also suffered due to their loved one's addiction, can't believe the addict is angry with them. Nobody seems to understand that they've all been reacting to the effects of a disease that disrupts the brain and the spirit.

Addiction turns us into adversaries; Structured Family Recovery brings us back together. Moving toward the solution in unison, we create a sublime kind of accountability. We become accountable in partnership. Accountability isn't just about the addict; it's about the entire family. That's when a new sense of harmony begins to emerge.

By the time addicts are discharged from treatment, their brains have been drug-free for weeks or months. They've worked through some acute emotional, psychological, and spiritual problems. Their bodies usually feel much healthier, and they look better. It's easy to believe they're fixed. We might even say, "It's up to you now."

As soon as we're lulled into that trap, we must remember the doctors we talked about earlier. No one trusts the neurosurgeon to achieve lasting sobriety alone. So, neither should we expect it of the schoolteacher, lawyer, waitress, homemaker, student, executive, or retiree. No matter how great they look when they walk out the door of the treatment center, no matter what they say, no matter what we believe, they are not cured. Addiction is a chronic disease, and the road to long-term recovery starts now.

Recovery means something specific. There is a goal. Most alcoholics, addicts, and their families, when asked, say the goal is sobriety. Once the addict is clean and sober, they reason that all will be well. But the absence of alcohol or other drugs doesn't mend lives or families. This comes as a shock to many. Although sobriety is essential, recovery is much more than sobriety. It concerns itself with the way alcoholics and families live their lives *together.*

When families get involved in recovery, they find a new and vital integrity. People learn to say what they mean and do what they say. Each person strives to admit when they are wrong, forgive others for their shortcomings, and honor the progress everyone is making as a group. Truth is not used as a weapon, and love is not used as an excuse for inaction. With everyone in recovery (emotional sobriety for family members, which leads to healthier self-regulation), the family—which now includes the addict on this shared journey—begins to feel safe.

Recovery is accomplished just one day at a time, but it radically alters our future. Most families who have successfully put Structured Family Recovery into practice say they are better than they ever were. A twenty-seven-year-old said of Structured Family Recovery, "In the past ten years, my mother relapsed multiple times. As a family, we all stood outside the circle, passing judgment and pointing fingers. Now we're all inside the circle, holding hands, doing recovery together."

With recovery, we begin to see each other's goodness more clearly. We celebrate together. Life still throws its curve balls, but we are better at handling them and less likely to fall into blame. The good news is that we don't have to find our way blindly. We know what works.

As they say in recovery circles, "It works if you work it." Structured Family Recovery helps families work it. By doing so, we experience a spiritual shift. It's no longer "me against you and you against me." We are family, and we stand together.

5

A Misunderstood Disease

It's a commonly held belief that defining addiction as a disease is a relatively new development, but this understanding was established well before the founding of AA—dating all the way back to Greek and Roman philosophers. In the early sixth century BCE, it was noted that mental disorders can come from compulsive drinking. Nearly two thousand years ago, Roman writers Pliny and Seneca described symptoms that closely resemble current observations of alcoholism: character defects, loss of memory, the shakes, antisocial behavior, swollen liver, insomnia, and untimely death. Seneca wrote that wine destroys the mind with tragic consequences, using Marc Antony as an example of a great figure taken down by alcohol.

The word *alcoholism* was coined in 1849 by a Swedish physician. It eventually became the commonly accepted term for addiction to alcohol, eventually replacing the term *inebriety,* which was popular well into the early twentieth century. It continues to be used in Twelve Step programs and throughout society today.

An article published by *Scientific American* in 1877, titled "Inebriety as a Disease," differentiates between drunkenness as a vice and drunkenness as a disease: "The man who drinks for pleasure, it holds, may look for benefits in the counsel of others or in his own strength of will; but he who drinks because he cannot help it, being led by an irresistible impulse, is a sick man, and needs a physician not a temperance pledge."

An 1885 issue of the same journal addressed the topic again, concluding that "to refrain from alcoholic indulgence is obviously not always within the voluntary power of the . . . inebriate."

By the mid-nineteenth century, the idea of addiction as a distinct disease, rather than a form of insanity, achieved international recognition. Edward Turner, a physician specializing in the treatment of inebriety, described it as hereditary, a disease that could be passed down to offspring. Treatment, he said, required complete abstinence.

During this period, many who studied and treated addiction undertook the task of educating medical professionals, lawmakers, clergy, and the general public in hopes of changing the ways alcoholics and addicts were treated. The preface for a paper written in 1885 by Isaiah de Zouche, MD, reads, "Much misapprehension exists as to the nature of Inebriety, which has led to mistaken treatment of the inebriate by his friends, and to his wrongful punishment by the law."

These same advocates would surely be shocked if they could see how many of these old beliefs still exist in the twenty-first century. Even with the success of AA after the publication of the Big Book in 1939 and the eventual confirmation in 1954 by the American Medical Association of Dr. Silkworth's groundbreaking case for alcoholism as a disease in his "Doctor's Opinion" that opens the book, we continue battling misguided notions that addiction is caused by a deficit of character or loss of willpower.

Media outlets commonly use the word *lifestyle* as a euphemism for addiction, as if it were a preferred choice. Even with recent research showing that addiction has a neurological basis and is a genetic-based disease, many physicians still believe alcoholism is at least partially chosen by its victims. In many societies, including the United States, alcoholics and addicts are more likely to be punished than to be treated. As a result, families often still approach addiction as a moral failing rather than a chronic illness. Addiction remains the most misunderstood disease.

One of the great puzzlers for many is the question of how putting intoxicants into one's body could possibly be considered a disease. After all, most people who use mood-altering substances don't become addicted.

There are many examples of conditions triggered by environmental substances entering the body, most commonly allergic diseases. Hay fever is triggered when allergens such as pollen are inhaled by people with sensitized immune systems. Others can breathe the same pollen with no adverse reaction. Likewise, food allergies are caused when the body mistakenly identifies a protein as an enemy and begins fighting against it. While most people have no problem eating dairy, soy, shellfish, fruits, vegetables, and nuts, those who are allergic to these foods experience symptoms ranging from mild (itchy mouth, hives, hoarse voice) to severe (anaphylactic shock, loss of consciousness, death). There is no cure for allergies.

Some newborn babies test positive for a mutated gene that results in an inability to break down amino acids in proteins. The disease is called phenylketonuria. For these children, the simple act of consuming proteins can cause intellectual disabilities as well as seizures, behavioral problems, and other mental disorders. The solution for living with this disorder is to maintain a low-protein diet and to avoid foods with artificial sweeteners that are made with phenylalanine. The warning "phenylketonurics: contains phenylalanine" is printed on certain food labels—such as diet sodas—to alert people with this disorder.

Addiction to mood-altering substances also requires consuming something from the environment. Some people metabolize intoxicants differently, setting off what Dr. Silkworth called "an allergy of the body and an obsession of the mind that condemns one to die." Since he wrote those words, sophisticated genetic research has shown that addiction isn't a learned behavior but an inherited disease, like so many others caused by our differences in genetic coding. To activate it, we add alcohol or other drugs from our environment. As Mehmet Oz, MD, said, "Your genetics load the gun. Your lifestyle pulls the trigger." In a drinking and drugging society, many triggers are unwittingly pulled.

The Genetics of Addiction

The concept of alcoholism as an inherited disease is time honored, but it ultimately required scientific study to determine whether children *learn* to be alcoholics or *inherit* the disease through their genes. Research over the past seventy-five years has consistently found a genetic link to addiction. It's estimated that 50 to 65 percent of the risk is inherited. The remaining threat is supplied by the environment.

Due to the complexity of genetic factors, there is no reliable biological testing for a genetic propensity toward addiction. Addiction isn't caused by one single gene, but by multiple gene variants that can change from family to family and individual to individual. According to geneticists, alcoholism is one of the most complex genetically based diseases to study.

Children who have a genetic predisposition to addiction and who are born into heavily drinking families are more likely to model drinking behaviors in their homes as they get older, thereby activating the disease. However, when these same children grow into adulthood and choose to abstain from alcohol and other drugs, the disease never manifests itself. Many people decide not to drink precisely because alcohol is so problematic in their families. Others go headlong into abusing substances, risking addiction. Even children who detest a parent's alcoholism will often begin drinking and drugging in their teenage years, believing they know better than Mom or Dad and won't become addicted.

There are, of course, many gray areas when it comes to addiction. The onset of this illness doesn't occur in the same way for each person. The amounts and duration of a drug needed for triggering the disease vary widely. Some people report being addicted from their first try at drinking or drugging. Others experience a slower progression, drinking fairly normally for several years before crossing the line into addiction. Some drugs have a shorter addiction cycle than others, such as heroin, meth, and crack cocaine.

Other people have periodic problems with addiction. For example, a young woman may show signs of alcoholism but quit using all substances while raising her children. Years later, perhaps when her last child is graduating from high school, she decides to have a glass of wine, and the disease is activated once again. In many such cases, people report that the addiction is worse than it was when they left off, as if it had been progressing all the while. The ability to stop is no longer within their control, and negative consequences quickly mount.

An example of the power of genetics is clear in the case of a forty-year-old wife and mother. Having witnessed the destructive nature of alcoholism in her grandfather's life and the toll it took on his eight children, she was vehemently anti-alcohol and never took a drink. In her late thirties, she was in a skiing accident and sustained a severe back injury. During her treatment, she was given powerful pain medications and quickly became addicted. Over time, she began visiting several doctors for multiple prescriptions, eventually taking more than twenty pills a day. She spent much of her days in bed. Her husband and children believed it was due to her back pain, not an addiction to painkillers. Eventually she lost interest in family activities, stopped making meals and cleaning the house, became irritated when her children invited friends over, and grew increasingly unreasonable and argumentative. When her husband became suspicious of the pills after finding bottles hidden in drawers and closets, she accused him of not caring about her suffering. A woman who had never once taken a sip of an alcoholic beverage became a full-blown addict in response to a pain medication prescribed for a legitimate purpose. Consuming the powerful medication activated her genetic coding.

Our beliefs as a society are informed primarily by the idea that everyone should drink (or use other "recreational" drugs) responsibly. Drinking and, to a lesser degree, the use of these other drugs is encouraged in many circles. Marijuana is legal in some states, and doctors easily prescribe a host of addictive, mood-altering medications. Alcohol isn't even considered a drug by many, and those people who don't drink are sometimes viewed with a degree of suspicion. In some social settings, people try to goad nondrinkers into drinking. *Come on, have a drink and join in on the fun!*

Everyone who uses intoxicants is expected to follow certain social norms, but these rules are generally vague and malleable, so it's not always clear when someone has initially crossed the line. In a drinking culture, it requires considerable progression of the disease before alcoholics and addicts are seen as rule breakers. Once identified as such, they're expected to shape up or risk the contempt of their families and contemporaries. They may try to follow the rules, but the disease continues onward, making it increasingly difficult. Even those closest to them simply don't understand.

Addiction as a disease may be part of our vernacular, but it's our emotional reactions that betray our true beliefs. People who are addicted continue to be blamed for their disease. They are frequently portrayed as *self*-destructive. Addiction is seen as something they are doing to themselves. In truth, many alcoholics and other drug addicts fight fiercely against the pull of addiction. They win some battles—even abstaining for various periods of time. When they fall off the wagon, families interpret their return to drinking or drugging as a choice or a failure, not as a symptom of a disease. The very thing that is destroying their lives has an irresistible pull that few can resist. In fact, the addict's brain is the major contributor to that loss of control.

Understanding that our loved ones do not choose to become addicted makes it easier for us to let go of our anger and replace it with compassion. In the words of Nelson Mandela, "Our human compassion binds us the one to another—not in pity or patronizingly, but as human beings who have learnt how to turn our common suffering into hope for the future."

A Changed Brain

As addiction progresses, it's easy for families to see the decline of their loved one's state of mind. Personality is explosive and less stable. They become increasingly withdrawn and malcontent. Without the drink or drug, they become irritable and agitated.

Addiction-created negativity extends beyond active drinking and drugging. In all their undoing, addicts often stand in judgment of everybody and everything. *The treatment team knows nothing. My family is plotting against me. I'm being brainwashed.*

Regardless of the ongoing destruction caused by addiction, many alcoholics and addicts stubbornly oppose any help, most notably from Alcoholics Anonymous or other Twelve Step programs. The resistance and denial that characterize the way alcoholics and addicts think can drive families crazy. What causes this? Most likely, it's what addicts see as the life-threatening prospect of having to give up their drugs.

In the past, we could only study brains of alcoholics and addicts by autopsy on cadavers, many of whom were alcoholic men who died living on the streets. It was difficult to know if brain abnormalities were caused by addiction, some other disease, or malnutrition. Today, modern science has advanced in neurotechnology, allowing us to look into brains of living, breathing people. We can see in real time how substances change the structure and functioning of the brain. Researchers assign tasks to addicts and then take images of their brains to understand how they operate in the realm of thought and higher-order activities. With today's technology, addicted brains can be compared to nonaddicted, healthy brains.

The most popular technology for brain imaging is the fMRI, or functional magnetic resonance imaging. It differs from the MRI, which takes snapshots, because it's able to create movies of brains in real time. Scientists can now observe brains while they are *functioning* (thus the *f* in fMRI). Researchers aren't just interested in what makes a brain light up, but in higher-level questions: How does an addicted brain make decisions, complete tasks, switch strategies, or process information?

The *reward systems* and *anti-reward systems* are two brain systems that give us the capacity to feel both good and bad. When brains are properly balanced, our moods aren't too high or too low. Alcoholics and addicts change the balance of these systems as they impulsively use mood-altering substances to boost their reward centers.

In the beginning, addicts are filled with great anticipation of their next high, because it feels so good to use the drug. Just thinking about it creates excitability. Emotional rewards spike far beyond what is normal, driving addicts to repeatedly stimulate the brain's reward center. Nothing else can compete—food, family, friends all drop in value. The addict's brain is preoccupied with one overriding thought: *When can I get high again?*

But then something interesting happens. Repeated substance abuse begins to deplete the reward system. No amount of alcohol or other drugs achieves the same high, because the reward circuitry is desensitized. At this point, the anti-reward system—which brings on adverse emotions—becomes dominant. Now, without alcohol or other drugs in their systems, addicts feel miserable. The brain is only producing emotional lows. More drugs are required to escape the darkness of the anti-reward brain. This is when the compulsion to drink takes over. The addict needs the drug just to feel normal.

By this time, addicts are now living in an ongoing negative emotional state caused by a decrease in the reward functioning of the brain and an increase in anti-reward functioning. This negativity is a hallmark of addiction. Alcoholics and addicts become chronically malcontent. When family members attempt to help them get treatment, addicts don't feel gratitude. They're suspicious of the motives of others. During periods of abstinence, they become irritable, restless, and obsessed with getting their hands on alcohol or other drugs. Anxiety and depression become the new norm.

The unrelenting stress addicts experience at this stage of addiction can be intolerable. There is no relief until alcohol or other drugs hit the brain. Even then, an addict no longer gets a great high but instead achieves something closer to emotional stability. The alcohol or other drug is primarily helping the addict find a way back to normalcy and equilibrium in the world. Drinking or drugging is now experienced as a *need* rather than a *want*. A need is a necessity that must be fulfilled, such as breathing and eating. So even though an addict may feel guilty, may be sorry, or may promise to never do it again, he cannot regain control. The drink or the drug isn't his problem; it's his solution. To learn more, search the work of George Koob, PhD.

Harry Haroutunian, MD, former physician director at the Betty Ford Center, describes his personal experience with this phenomenon in his book *Being Sober.*

> I remember the day Nancy Reagan suggested that everyone "just say no" to drugs. And I tried. I tried to say no and failed miserably. I felt different and apart from the norm. It made me think of myself as a broken person who could not live in a society ruled by dignity and courage. No matter how hard I tried, I could never just say no; I felt shame.

When I learned that the area of the brain affected by
this fatal disease is the same area from which emanates
my heartbeat, my next breath, and all my vital functions,
I finally understood I could no more say no to that next
drink than I could say no to that next breath.

Decision making and the higher functioning of the brain are compromised by addiction too. This is something Alcoholics Anonymous
has long understood, but science ignored until fairly recently. With
brain-imaging capabilities, researchers now observe how the prefrontal
cortex—the thinking brain—is disrupted, making it difficult for addicts
to change their behavior, even in the face of punishment. Family members are dumbfounded by loved ones who continue to drink and use
drugs even under the threat of losing children and jobs, going to jail, or
being evicted. Understanding that an addicted brain functions in much
the same way as an injured brain provides some insights.

The prefrontal cortex is the CEO of the brain. It's largely responsible
for our success or failure in life. When we think of ourselves—who we
are—it is this part of the brain that gives us our sense of identity. It reg-
ulates behaviors, makes choices between right and wrong, takes in and
processes information, and controls social interaction. The prefrontal
cortex makes decisions on how we should behave—what actions to take
and what actions to avoid. It is primarily responsible for our intelligence
and personality, and it allows us to plan ahead and create strategies. It
helps us focus so we can set goals, pay attention to the world around us,
and learn. Active memory—the ability to keep in mind recent events or
bring to mind information from long ago—originates here. It is through
the prefrontal cortex that we feel empathy for one another.

When this part of the brain is damaged or disrupted, the whole brain
can be thrown off. Personalities can change, turning a mild-mannered
person into someone who is aggressive or reckless. An extrovert may
withdraw from social interactions and avoid even close family and
friends. As addiction progresses, it's not unusual to witness the addicted person becoming increasingly self-absorbed and filled with self-
pity. Diminished ability to differentiate between right and wrong affects

morals and ethics. Disruption of the prefrontal cortex often shows up in chronic lateness and procrastination as well as emotional distress, loss of self-control, and socially inappropriate behaviors. Planning, reasoning, and problem solving are also diminished. Ultimately, addicts lose the ability to consider the long-term consequences of their drug use. Without regard for harm or punishment, they increasingly make decisions based on immediate gratification.

Families who witness these changes often interpret them as a refusal to accept personal responsibility. The two most common questions posed by families are "Can't she see what she's doing to herself?" and "When is he going to learn?" They don't understand that addiction erodes an addict's ability to act responsibly. The ability to switch strategies when things are going badly is disappearing. It is becoming increasingly difficult for an addict to make good decisions. Addicts keep doing the same things over and over, expecting different results. This is the definition of *insanity* commonly held in Alcoholics Anonymous circles.

The emotional brain, known as the *limbic system*, is also changed by addiction. This ancient part of the brain is responsible for motivation, learning, emotion, and memory. It is highly interconnected with the brain's pleasure center and controls mood and attitude. Our ability to bond with others is centered here. The limbic system filters how we see external events through our internal events, or what is called *emotional coloring*. In other words, how we see the world is largely determined by how we feel. The seat of our spirituality, our passions, desires, and joy for living emanate largely from this area of the brain. The limbic system sets the emotional tone for everything about life: ideas, memories, emotions, and dreams.

When addiction causes disturbances in the limbic system, alcoholics and addicts become highly sensitive—especially to criticism—and increasingly malcontent. They experience mood swings and irritability. A disrupted limbic system floods the brain with negative emotions like depression and aggression, which, in turn, feed self-centeredness and paranoia. Addicts become increasingly isolated emotionally and, sometimes, physically. Enthusiasm for living wanes, because, as social animals, we need a healthy limbic system to ensure our survival in the world.

Our society values intellect more than emotional health. But neurologists tell us that we are not thinking machines that *feel*; we are *feeling* machines that *think*. Our thoughts and emotions don't operate separately but are interactive, one always influencing the other. When our emotional brain is not working well, neither is our thinking brain. It cannot properly engage in problem solving, decision making, or planning.

To understand the addicted brain further, it is important to examine another function of the brain: the capacity for self-control. Until late in their addiction, alcoholics and other drug addicts commonly believe they can stop drinking or using on their own—and they prove themselves right time and time again. The problem, however, is staying stopped. Alcoholics, addicts, and their families view these periods of self-control as proof that quitting is within their power if they want it badly enough. The return to drinking and drugging is attributed to weakness of character or a stubborn refusal to do the right thing. But it is neither. Self-control is a limited cognitive resource. We only have so much available; when it's used up, we lose control.

The implication of this insight—that as a resource, self-control is finite —supports two important concepts that we'll develop more in the next chapter: (1) Motivation doesn't produce long-term changes in behavior, and (2) alcoholics need the right level of support to succeed over time.

As a finite resource, self-control only works for a limited time. When circumstances require sustained, long-term self-control, there will eventually be a breakdown. Therefore, with our addicted loved ones, when we overvalue motivation and undervalue support, we get relapse.

Researchers Mark Muraven and Roy Baumeister, at Case Western Reserve University, explain it this way:

> Exerting self-control may consume self-control strength, reducing the amount of strength available for subsequent self-control efforts. Coping with stress, regulating negative affect, and resisting temptations require self-control,

and after such self-control efforts, subsequent attempts at self-control are more likely to fail. Continuous self-control efforts, such as vigilance, also degrade over time. . . . It is concluded that the executive component of the self—in particular, inhibition—relies on a limited, consumable resource.

Forty years of research have shown that only 15 percent of dieters succeed in keeping weight off for three years or more. Among those who are successful, a high percentage participate in ongoing group support. Presumably, these people don't deplete reserves of self-control—or what some would call willpower—because they also rely on help from others.

One of the practical applications of this research is its value in helping addicts and their families understand why self-control isn't a reliable solution for overcoming addiction. The researchers at Case Western Reserve University noted that "addiction counselors may find it useful to realize that addictive and relapse patterns are hardest to overcome when the person is subjected to depleted resources—including depletion by factors that seemingly have little or nothing to do with the addiction itself."

We know that addicts experience escalating negative consequences in many areas of their lives before they receive treatment. They have problems with their jobs, relationships, finances, health. They sometimes exhibit co-occurring disorders such as depression, anxiety, and post-traumatic stress disorder (PTSD), or sexual, spending, and gambling addictions. In an attempt to overcome them, they apply varying degrees of self-control to these problems.

But since the brain's capacity to control and change behavior is limited, this strenuous overuse of self-control depletes the reserves, making it difficult to exert control in areas of life unrelated to addiction. In other words, there is a growing sense of unmanageability in life generally. Families often experience this as promises made and promises broken. The addict believes his promises when making them but no longer can muster enough resolve to follow through consistently. As the disease progresses, it requires greater amounts of self-control, using a brain that is "running on empty."

We create the perfect recipe for relapse when we expect addicts to exert self-control over drinking and drugging, with the added burden of an impaired thinking brain and emotional brain, and no proper support. Many try, and fail, multiple times. Repeated relapse creates hopelessness because the addict believes he is incapable of staying sober, and the family often gives up.

Many people continue to define addiction as *drinking or using too much,* and the solution is simple: *drink or use less.* But addiction is a complex disease, and recovery is highly challenging. Brain imaging has helped us understand how an addicted brain is changed. But addiction also causes a spiritual sickness that prevents the addict from reaching out for help, making it all the more difficult to get well.

Alcoholics and other drug addicts might be able to quit for periods of time, but they don't know how to live every single day sober. Without a program of recovery, the addict experiences abstinence as a grim existence. The brain is impaired and exhausted. It's no wonder so many fail. Twelve Step recovery programs that include working the Steps and attending meetings, coupled with establishing mutual trust and support with loved ones, exercise the mind and spirit in a particular way. For millions of alcoholics and addicts, this has resulted in contented, lasting sobriety. The brain heals, and addicts remember how to love life again. As a recovering alcoholic wrote in the Big Book of Alcoholics Anonymous:

> When I had been in A.A. only a short while, an old-timer told me something that has affected my life ever since. "A.A. does not teach us how to handle our drinking," he said. "It teaches us how to handle sobriety." . . . God willing, we members of A.A. may never again have to deal with drinking, but we have to deal with sobriety every day.

6

Motivation Isn't the Answer

Before AA founders Bill Wilson and Dr. Bob Smith ever met, both men were highly motivated to stop drinking and had tried many times. Despite their efforts, alcoholism was incrementally destroying every aspect of their lives. Bill Wilson lost a successful career, fell into financial ruin, and almost died by age thirty-nine. Dr. Bob once said, "Well, I can't conceive of any living human who really wanted to do something as badly as I think I do, who could be such a total failure." Motivation to quit helped both men leave alcohol alone for various periods of time, but lasting sobriety eluded them. Even after experiencing the benefits of being alcohol free, they always returned to the drink. Family members were dumbstruck, unable to fathom why.

Where recovery from addiction is concerned, long-term success isn't correlated with motivation. Its value is in the short term—to get us going—but long-term change requires something more. We're taught to believe in the power of motivation, but the evidence of its limitations is all around us. Sit in an airport and watch people walk by. Americans are increasingly overweight and out of shape. How many people, do you suppose, are highly motivated to lose weight and begin a regular exercise program? We know the weight loss and diet control market is now worth about $72 billion, with an additional $30 billion spent on health and fitness clubs. For all this investment of dollars and good intentions, how many succeed in meeting their goals in a way that lasts? The Centers for

Disease Control and Prevention (CDC) reports that over 70 percent of adults in the United States are overweight.

By reviewing articles and reports on dieting—something many of us are personally familiar with—it's easy to see that motivation isn't the solution for long-term success. A small minority of dieters keep off the weight they lost. Most lose weight in the short term, then gain it all back. These results lead people to believe that diets don't work. Experts now emphasize lifestyle change as the answer, but this hasn't resulted in the slimming of a nation, nor a reduction of weight-related health problems.

Danish researchers reviewed 900 scientific articles on dieting to determine its value. The first thing they learned was that 883 of the articles they were evaluating were based on unreliable research. Of all the dieting studies published over the past thirty years, only 2 percent were considered worthy of review—which is a cautionary tale in itself. In the remaining seventeen studies, only 15 percent of the dieters maintained their weight loss over a three-year period. The most successful dieters, it turns out, were also participating in group therapy. Evidently, the power of the group works for more people than just the alcoholics and addicts of AA and other Twelve Step groups.

What researchers found is that diets actually can work. It is people who fail. And when they do, they tend to blame their failures on inadequate motivation or insufficient willpower. They are blaming themselves for failing at something that most dieters find exceedingly difficult to maintain over time. Even though following the diet would lead to weight loss, most dieters lack a level of support that would increase their probability of sticking with it and succeeding in losing weight and keeping it off.

We're Often Wrong about How We Change

Jeni Cross, PhD, a professor of sociology at Colorado State University and national public speaker, says that our greatest obstacle to change isn't that change is hard but that our beliefs about how we create change are wrong. Dr. Cross points to three common myths.

The first myth claims that education will change behavior. It presumes that people who aren't motivated to make change simply don't know any better. By educating them, according to the myth, we motivate them to take action. While education is very important for many reasons, it is a poor predictor of changes in behavior. When it comes to addiction, many have long assumed that educating addicts on the ways that addiction damages their bodies, brains, and family lives is enough to motivate them to stay sober. But if education alone changed people, we would have stamped out addiction long ago.

The second myth claims that we need to change attitudes before we can change behavior. Sociologists tell us we have it backward. Over forty years of research proves repeatedly that a change in behavior will change attitudes. Families often say, "She'll never go to AA. She hates AA." The belief is that until she changes her attitude, she won't change her behavior. But we cannot depend on attitudes to change behavior or predict it. A change in attitude—*Okay, I guess AA is a good program for alcoholics*—doesn't mean she will attend meetings. And disliking AA doesn't mean she won't attend. It's seems counterintuitive, but it's played out in real life all the time.

A mother called about her alcoholic son who had just landed in treatment for the fourth time: "He won't go to AA. He's tried it, and he doesn't like it." That didn't leave many options, other than a miracle or death, so we suggested he work with a recovery mentor who could reintroduce him to AA in a more promising way. After he worked with the mentor for a few days, the son's attitude changed completely. He loved AA. He was introduced to great people and enjoyed their company, both learning from them and having fun again. He listened to how others overcame addiction and felt understood for the first time. He began to believe he could succeed by following the AA program. His recovery mentor didn't try to change his attitude. By helping him change his behavior, everything else fell into place.

One of the secrets to changing behavior, according to social scientists, is setting up *behavioral expectations.* The recovery mentor, in this case, set a behavioral expectation: "We are going to AA meetings together." The alcoholic wasn't given an option. He could have said no to mentoring, but it would have meant going against the wishes of his family, who were ready to involve his boss in setting consequences. This made it easier for him to comply. The behavioral expectations led to a change in his behavior, which in turn transformed his attitude.

The third myth claims that we know what motivates us to make change in our own lives. Much to our collective astonishment, social scientists have repeatedly shown that this is not true. For instance, while most people claim they are not affected by what other people do or say, social scientists tell us this is the greatest of all influencers. Social norms, which indicate the established and approved way of doing things, are powerful forces for change. Whether we know it or not, we have a strong tendency to do what we see other people do. For this reason, surrounding oneself with successfully recovering people is one of the most powerful influencers for lasting sobriety.

Research has shown that when we are exposed to positive social behaviors—such as "nearly all people recycle" or "most people reuse their towels in hotel rooms"—we change our own behaviors in favorable ways. Consistently stressing high expectations through social norms produces desired results. Reporting negative social behaviors, however, changes people's conduct in an unfavorable way. For instance, when it was announced that people were pilfering petrified wood from national forests, the number of people taking petrified wood increased. Research repeatedly shows that emphasizing a social norm, either positive or negative, increases behaviors that conform to that norm.

There is a growing trend in the treatment world to reframe relapse as a normal part of the process. Addiction is defined by some as a "chronic relapsing brain disease." Is this what we want to tell addicts? Setting a negative social norm for relapse, according to what social scientists know, would make relapse more likely. It is more accurate to describe addiction as a chronic illness that requires proper ongoing management and, without it, the result is a high probability of relapse.

The impetus behind this trend is the sense that reducing feelings of shame associated with relapse will make addicts more likely to return to treatment once they've started drinking and drugging again. We really don't know if having a lower level of shame is a primary motivator for returning to treatment. It would be easier to argue the opposite. It is reasonable to assume that shame (which is quite different from the toxic experience of being shamed by others) is a normal response to failing to maintain one's sobriety and not meeting the expectations of those who mean the most to you.

Shame has fallen out of favor in therapeutic circles, but it seems that some behaviors appropriately elicit shame, while others trigger shame's first cousin, guilt. For example, if I steal money from my beloved grandmother's purse, feeling shame is an appropriate emotional response. Such a behavior should give rise to questions such as "Is this who *I* am? Is this who *I* want to be?" Whereas, if I borrow my sister's sweater behind her back when she asked me not to wear it, my experience of guilt would trigger a different kind of self-examination. "Should I have done *that*?" When the transgression is attributed to the general value we place on ourselves, we feel shame. When it's attributed to a short-lived behavior, we feel guilt.

Webster's Revised Unabridged Dictionary helps highlight the differences between the moral emotions of shame and guilt. *Guilt,* it states, "is a feeling of regret or remorse for having committed some improper act." But *shame* is a different emotion, described as a "painful sensation excited by having done something that injures reputation." The *Century Dictionary* further clarifies the emotion of shame as a feeling caused by an awareness of "having done something unworthy of one's own previous idea of one's excellence."

Interestingly, cultural differences determine how people respond to shame and guilt. When one values *feeling good,* as is common in many North American contexts, the idea of being evaluated by others is presumed to be bad or something to be avoided. In this context, shame is viewed more negatively than guilt. But in cultures that value interdependent concepts of self, such as in European, Asian, East Indian, African, and many Native cultures, other people's thoughts and feelings are as important as one's own feelings and thoughts. Compared with ours, these cultures generally view shame in more positive terms, seeing it as an instructive emotion that triggers a need for self-improvement and checking and correcting one's behavior.

Not everyone survives a relapse, and many who do, do so at great cost to themselves and their families. This most certainly triggers negative moral emotions. With Structured Family Recovery, people closest to the addict can respond to these emotions with care and loving concern, modeling the road back to recovery and setting up behavioral expectations.

It is important to consider, based on what sociologists know about social norms, that normalizing relapse might have the opposite effect of what we're after, actually triggering relapse. By creating an expectation that relapse is a normal part of the recovery process, we might be signaling that it is the normal and approved way. Negative social norms are powerful influencers of behavior.

As a long-recovering alcoholic told me, "It's a good thing this wasn't the thinking when I was getting help. My addict brain would have grabbed on to that idea immediately. The first time I wanted to go out with my old drinking friends, I would have reminded myself that relapse is a normal part of being an alcoholic."

These trends give us greater cause to become more involved in creating positive social norms within our families. When an entire family is participating in the recovery experience, we raise the bar and create our own normal. Relapse is most often a symptom of the lack of adequate support over time. As we've seen, doctors participating in Physician Health Programs experience extraordinarily low relapse rates. Their social norm is successful recovery, and the results tell the story.

So let's review what social scientists ultimately teach us about getting alcoholics and addicts to stay sober. *Never depend on motivation to carry the addict into long-term recovery.* Motivation plays an important short-term role. Motivation is good for a sprint; recovery is a long-distance race. Motivation, solely relied upon, eventually fails. Therefore, we want to keep it simple so we aren't required to amp up motivation. Twelve Step programs and Structured Family Recovery are built on the idea of simplicity.

Education, while important, does not lead to lasting change. If it did, we would have changed the world by now. If we believe someone isn't changing a behavior simply because they don't have enough information, we will experience more failure. Education must lead to clearly laid-out action steps. These are the specific behaviors required to reach a desired outcome.

We've also learned that we waste a lot of time trying to change attitudes when it is behavioral expectations that get results. If we want to change an attitude, we must first change the corresponding behavior. When we, as family members using Structured Family Recovery, model recovery behaviors, we set up behavioral expectations in the form of social norms. But the opposite can also be true. When we model a lack of commitment and involvement in recovery, we create a social norm that supports the opposite of what we want the addict to achieve, and we create a behavioral expectation that works against recovery. We need to repeatedly ask ourselves, "What social norms are we demonstrating today?"

The paradox is that if we are resistant to recovery, which, as we've learned, is true of most addicts, it takes getting involved in recovery to change these attitudes. Lasting recovery is the result of what we do, not what we think. Our actions will change our thinking. These words are found in the Big Book of Alcoholics Anonymous:

> There is a principle which is a bar against all information, which is proof against all arguments and which cannot fail to keep a man in everlasting ignorance—that principle is contempt prior to investigation.
>
> —Herbert Spencer

Contempt prior to investigation keeps us in our heads, dependent solely on our own thinking and opinions, which, when generated by the addicted brain, are likely to resist new experiences and ideas. This applies to families too. To change our thinking, we change our behaviors. It results in creating a new world for ourselves.

It isn't difficult to identify the limits of motivation in the journey from drinking to sobriety in each alcoholic's history. Motivation alone, as we will see in the following story, is not effective when it's up against the closed mind and distorted thinking of the addict. Involvement of a family team gives motivation muscle. But even then, it can't be relied on as the foundation for lasting sobriety. True change happens by incorporating shared goals of a recovery community into our daily lives.

Greg is a thirty-six-year-old husband and father. He's been drinking heavily since high school and started smoking pot in college. For the past four or five years, he's been doing cocaine, first with his buddies and now in the mornings to get a start on the day. As a backup drug to his cocaine, Greg obtained a prescription for Adderall, a stimulant. He made plans to go to a psychiatrist for a second prescription for the drug as his need to build his supply increased.

Greg began to experience negative consequences. He was spending too much money on cocaine, squandering funds from the family's monthly budget. His wife became furious about the shortfalls and interrogated him about where the money was going. He borrowed from his parents to secretly cover drug costs and didn't pay them back. Using Adderall and cocaine, he felt like a powerhouse on the job, but his boss brought him into her office one day to ask him if he was all right. She said he didn't seem quite like himself. Greg could tell she thought something was up.

Greg's wife found a tiny bag with a residue of white powder in his jeans pocket. She called him at work demanding to know what was going on. She threatened to call his parents. Greg told her a friend had left it in his car and he put it in his pocket, planning to throw it in the trash. She accused him of lying. The pressure was building, and Greg was getting nervous. He made a pledge to himself that he would quit the cocaine and cut down on the booze. He'd allow himself an Adderall in the morning and two or three beers to get to sleep at night—nothing more. He was highly motivated to get things under control and get everyone off his back. Greg's resolve lasted a week and a half before he called his coke dealer.

A few months later, he was spending more money than usual for cocaine. When his wife was paying bills and balancing the checkbook, she discovered they didn't have enough money to write the mortgage check. It was the last straw. After a blowout fight with Greg, she called his brother. "We have to meet right away," she said.

Greg's brother called a clinical interventionist, and together they formed an intervention team of family and friends. Intervention, they learned, creates a moment of clarity, and in that moment, most alcoholics and addicts agree to treatment. But the resulting motivation to accept help is short-lived. For that reason, they prepared to take Greg to treatment immediately after the intervention, when his motivation was at its highest.

Once admitted into treatment, Greg was actually relieved. He was tired of the secrets and lies. He burned with shame when he thought of the loan from his parents and the financial troubles he had caused his family. He thought about cocaine all the time—how to buy it and how to hide it—and it was exhausting. Getting caught filling double prescriptions for Adderall at two different pharmacies was something he couldn't even think about.

But ten days into treatment, Greg began feeling agitated. He wanted out. Everything was irritating him. His counselor told him he was experiencing cravings, but Greg insisted he was never going to drink or drug again. He complained to his wife that his roommate was a heroin addict on probation for theft. "I'm not as bad as the rest of these people," he said. "I'm ready to come home. I've learned everything they have to teach me. I know better than to use another drug."

His wife might have been convinced by his arguments, but by then, the entire family was engaged in Structured Family Recovery. They were prepared for Greg's motivation to fail and had learned that education and "knowing better" weren't cures. The family team quickly consulted with the professionals. They scheduled a family conference call with Greg and his counselor. The conversation had been carefully planned in consultation with their interventionist; each person knew what to say. They were loving and supportive of Greg but firm in standing behind the recommendations of the treatment team. Though the family was prepared to introduce negative consequences, they never needed to use them. The negotiations went well, and Greg agreed to stay. By the next day, he was feeling positive and, once again, engaged in treatment.

When Greg returned home after completing treatment, he was highly motivated to stay sober. He said his desire to drink and drug was gone. He began going to AA meetings. But the family knew that motivation in early recovery can eventually dwindle down to nothing—just like it did while Greg was in treatment—so his optimistic mood didn't give them false hopes. They knew by then that the urge to drink or drug could hit at any time. For that reason, they invited Greg to join their SFR team. Everyone on the team was already engaged in family recovery (emotional recovery) and the Twelve Steps of Al-Anon. The team members met weekly by conference call. As a family team, they created and embraced powerful positive social norms. As a result, Greg agreed to random drug testing and remained involved in AA. He enjoyed being part of a family in recovery.

His family's involvement created in Greg a strong desire to be successful in his own recovery. Participation in Structured Family Recovery set up behavioral expectations for the entire family, which led to a common empathy and a growing intelligence about recovery. Working as a team, the family returned to their values, determined not to let addiction win. These values and behaviors created a positive social norm for the entire family, not just Greg.

Following the wisdom of AA—"One day at a time"—Greg took his recovery in extremely small bites. He made a commitment to set aside one hour a day for an AA meeting. At each meeting, he'd introduce himself to one person, saying, "Hi, my name is Greg. I'm new in AA." He'd ask for that person's phone number, knowing it was one more person he could call for support. Greg took five minutes every morning and every night to read his recovery meditation book.

Initially, Greg was mostly going through the motions. He followed directions and did what he was supposed to do, but his heart wasn't completely into it. But with time, he experienced a growing sense of belonging. In the long tradition of Twelve Step programs, he began to laugh. As a result, he started looking forward to the camaraderie he experienced in meetings.

He often arrived at a meeting feeling weighed down by frustrations and discontent, but by the time he left, his load was lightened and his mood elevated. He began to follow the AA slogan "Easy does it." He learned he didn't need to solve all of his problems at once. The most important thing he could do was not make things worse by picking up a drink or a drug.

By going to a meeting every day, Greg was practicing new social norms. He was modeling a group of sober people, learning to relax and have fun. He gradually gained confidence in his ability to stay sober one more day. Reading the literature at night quieted his mind before sleep. These simple steps took much less time than his drinking and drugging had taken.

Greg made many new friends at the meetings. Some had long-term sobriety, measured in years or decades; some had only weeks or months. He chose one meeting for his home group and agreed to help organize the snacks. He started coming earlier and staying later. He'd become acquainted with an older and wiser member of AA and finally worked up the courage to ask him to be his sponsor. They began working the Steps together.

For Greg, staying sober was now part of sticking with the group. These weren't choirboys, and Greg appreciated their sharp humor and willingness to help. They were an unusual group, people who otherwise had little in common, coming from all walks of life, but he valued their experience. It was like finding his way from a sinking ship into a lifeboat with other castaways—a place where everyone worked together for a common survival.

Rather than looking forward to evenings as a time to drink, he looked forward to his AA meetings and the easy camaraderie he enjoyed with his new friends. When he arrived home to his wife, he was a man who could be part of a family.

7

A Closer Look at Relapse

When an alcoholic or addict relapses, everything is up for grabs. Even one drink or hit of a drug creates a change of mind and spirit. Of course, one is never enough when you're addicted. It's as if a demon is unleashed, launching an insatiable lust for more alcohol, more cocaine, more pills. It becomes a singular focus. Work, home, friends, children, and spouse are again shut out by the obsessive need to use the drug and hide the truth. As one relapsed crack addict described it: "My mind was constantly saying, 'I need it, I need it, I need it, I need it.'"

A friend of mine, Grayson, a former heroin addict with twenty years of abstinence-based Twelve Step recovery, tells a story that perfectly illustrates what happens when a drug is reintroduced into an addict's system. It began when he was hospitalized for surgery. After the operation and back in his room, the nurse hooked him up to an IV with a morphine drip to manage his pain, which was quite severe. Grayson describes what happened next. "The very second the morphine hit my blood, the reaction was instant and vicious. I wanted to get my wife, pregnant with our first child, out of the room and get the nurse back in. All I could think was, I need more of this now."

The demon awakened by Grayson's morphine experience, however, was up against his solid recovery program. "I keep myself right in the middle of AA," he said. "That way I always have thirty eyeballs on me." Both before and after surgery, he called his sponsor to openly discuss the fact that he would be given an opiate for pain. He talked about it at meetings. He and his wife had discussed it. Grayson knew he wouldn't be able to depend on himself once the drug coursed through his bloodstream. He needed other recovering people and family to create a safety net. By being forthcoming and applying rigorous honesty, Grayson placed himself in the hands of people he could trust. The disease of addiction couldn't stand up to the power of that kind of recovery. Grayson never acted on his desire to get more morphine. His wife stayed by his side, and he immediately got honest with her about what he was thinking. "It's just the difference between life and death," he said.

Relapse isn't random, like a cancer reoccurring. A medical team can do everything possible to eradicate cancer, only to have it come back with a vengeance. When a relapse in addiction occurs, however, it isn't a mystery. It's usually a sign that a recovery program is lacking something. Most people who relapse can point to exactly what was missing and describe quite incisively how they slipped back into drinking or drugging. The signs and symptoms of relapse are well established.

With Structured Family Recovery, we decide on an action plan in advance of a relapse. The alcoholic or addict is central to making decisions about how the team can best help if she were to fall back into her addiction. By communicating and planning together, relapse doesn't have to mean failure or a full return to active addiction. Regardless of how bad the addict might feel about herself, when the family team comes together with love, guided by the predetermined relapse plan, most alcoholics and addicts respond positively and accept an appropriate level of care. Family members also need extra Al-Anon meetings for added support while coping with the stress of a relapse.

Kerry was sober twenty-six years. He owned a fly-fishing shop in a small town in the Northwest and was a mainstay in the AA community. Everyone knew Kerry; he was funny, outgoing, and an open book about his recovery. He loved AA and the legion of sober friends he had made there over the years. When the economy crashed, his once-thriving shop began to suffer. There were times when he looked at his checking account and wondered if he'd have to shutter the business he'd spent much of his adult life building.

As the economic downturn lingered, Kerry managed to keep his fly-fishing store open, but he had to cut down on employees and do more of the hands-on work himself. Although days were long and stress was high, he always had his AA meetings and his recovering friends. "But then," he said, "I started slacking off. It seemed harmless. I'd been sober a very long time and hadn't experienced a craving for a drink in twenty-five years."

Eventually, he stopped going to meetings altogether. Looking back, Kerry says he could see the shift that took place in his thinking. Once recovery wasn't central to his life anymore, it slowly lost its importance until he had all but abandoned it. "I did what you are warned about over and over again in AA," he said. "I became indifferent. Other things increasingly got in the way of my meetings, and I stopped going." Kerry explained that once he became disconnected from the recovery behaviors that kept him sober, he was already in trouble. "I wasn't drinking, but it was a full-blown relapse nonetheless. The drink was simply a matter of time, but I couldn't see it happening to me."

Kerry began visiting a casino and entertaining himself with small-time gambling. He thought he could sit at the bar if he just ordered a diet soda. "One night, I went to play video poker and this guy I'd met a few times bought me a beer. The bartender set it down in front of me. I looked at it, and even though I knew it was wrong, I picked it up and took a sip," he said.

"When I tasted that beer, all the flags went up in my head telling me this was absolutely the worst thing I could ever do, but, inexplicably, I downed the entire glass." He said, "What I'd always heard is true: 'AA ruins your drinking.'" Sober all those years, Kerry had a well-developed conscience, and it led him to feel miserable about himself. Still, he couldn't stop.

"That first beer awakened my disease, even after all my sobriety. I totally lost control over alcohol," he said. "Throughout that week, I'd return to the casino to drink, worrying someone might see me. Then I'd think, 'I don't care! I hope you see me!' It was that crazy alcoholic mindset: 'I'll show you, I'll hurt me!'"

It was pride that kept Kerry from telling his friends in AA. "I almost didn't make it back into the program because of pride," he said. "But the terrible shame and guilt, and the relentless pain it caused me, trumped my pride."

An old AA saying kept replaying in Kerry's head: "You can't save your face and your butt at the same time." It finally pushed him to pick up the phone. "I called my longtime friend Sam, who told me exactly what I needed to hear: 'Get yourself to a meeting. You have to admit to it.'"

"Once I did that," said Kerry, "my shame and guilt were cut in half. I began to feel hope again. I knew I could make it." People in AA didn't shame Kerry for his relapse; they embraced him. An old friend with thirty-two years of sobriety said to him, "Come on, let's go to lunch so you can save my life." The friend took Kerry's admission of relapse as a gift, saying it was a powerful reminder that "There but for the grace of God, go I."

"Pain," said Kerry, "is an addict's best friend." He then recited his favorite quotation from Proust: "To goodness and wisdom we make only promises. Pain we obey."

Attending to the chronic nature of the disease is a prerequisite to avoiding relapse. Whether early in recovery or after years of sobriety, when a person stops working a thorough Twelve Step program as part of a recovery plan that includes building a support system of family and friends, the risk of eventually drinking again is almost certain. Knowing better doesn't keep people sober. Alcoholics and addicts can go on a dry drunk—abstaining from mood-altering substances but still behaving like an addict—for varying lengths of time. But eventually the pain of living with emotional unmanageability leads to relapse.

People who abuse alcohol or other drugs, but who are not suffering from the disease of addiction, can stop on their own. But among true alcoholics and addicts, quitting on their own is risky business. It's estimated that 96 to 98 percent eventually relapse or switch addictions. The alcoholic switches to pot; the cocaine addict gets a prescription for Adderall; the opiate addict starts drinking. The new drug eventually becomes a problem or sets off cravings for the former drug, or both. The brain, once addicted, reacts to all mood-altering substances. This change in the brain doesn't go away with time or by switching drugs.

I was walking with a recovering friend through Greenwich Village, a neighborhood in New York City, where she had lived while attending college. She was telling me about the severity of her cocaine addiction in those days and that this was the place where she had bought her drugs. Suddenly she stopped and turned toward me, "You won't believe this," she said. "I can taste cocaine in the back of my throat." After eighteen years of sobriety, her addiction was triggered by strolling through the streets of her past cocaine use, and she could taste the drug as if she'd just used it. This illustrates how powerful the imprint of drug addiction is on the brain.

The addict may know what actions are required for lasting sobriety, but if there isn't a rigorous recovery plan and consistent family support that ensures he'll follow through, an addict will be vulnerable to all kinds of triggers. Relapse can happen in many different ways. Here are some of the most common rationalizations that can lay the groundwork for relapse, as well as how Structured Family Recovery can prevent these problems from growing.

I've been through treatment. I can do the rest on my own. This is a combination of false pride and underestimating the power of the disease and what it takes to stay sober. The addict, fresh out of treatment, often has an inflated opinion of himself, called *grandiosity*. He puffs up his self-importance to disguise feelings of inferiority and may resist going to AA or other Twelve Step groups because of stigma. An SFR team can reassure him by setting an example. "We are with you all the way. We understand the insidious nature of this disease. We are teaming together for success." When the addict finds himself in the middle of a recovery family, he no longer feels like the odd man out. When the entire family is working at recovery, attending family Twelve Step groups, discussing what they've learned and how they're struggling, recovery becomes the social norm. The addict feels the warmth of belonging, something he may not have felt in a very long time, disarming his sense of inferiority.

I attend meetings but don't have a sponsor. The addict may be show-ing some effort and a modicum of commitment, but it won't be enough. Perhaps the addict has learned how to get along in life by giving less than full effort. She translates these past experiences to her recovery program. The addict thinks, "I'm doing enough; this works for me." Again, this is the mark of underestimating what it takes to stay sober. By engaging in Structured Family Recovery, the family sets up behavioral expectations for everyone. By modeling a program of recovery and maintaining unity and accountability with weekly family meetings, the alcoholic follows suit, not to please her family members and comply with their wishes, but because she knows they willingly do it for themselves out of love.

I have a sponsor, but our relationship is superficial. When the ad-dict remains emotionally removed from his sponsor, he is usually reluc-tant to reveal the true nature of his problem, especially the resentments he has against others. He presents an idealized image of himself rather than getting to the truth. This is his protective shield of pride, driven by fear. When family members embrace their alcoholic through the lens of their own recovery, accepting the fact that no one can change the past and knowing it is what we do today that defines our tomorrow, the need to assign blame goes away. With acceptance from his family, demon-strated through the action steps of Structured Family Recovery, the al-coholic may develop enough self-acceptance to stop fearing the truth. Bill Wilson, in *Twelve Steps and Twelve Traditions*, wrote, "We began to get the feeling that we could be forgiven, no matter what we had thought or done."

I get to meetings late and leave early. The addict is isolating even while attending meetings. By coming to a meeting late and leaving early, she avoids personal interaction with others. She's fulfilling a cursory re-sponsibility to attend meetings, but without engaging others and build-ing supportive relationships or making friendships. Addiction is an isolating disease; recovery requires connecting with others on the same path. With no emotional connection to people in AA, the addict feels like a perpetual outsider. She'll soon fall away from her meetings, tell-ing herself she has nothing in common with those people. When a fam-ily engages in Structured Family Recovery, the expectation is exactly the reverse. From the start, the addict is no longer isolated. *We are in this to-gether.* As the family members define a new norm through their actions, the addict begins to see recovery through a more positive lens. As the family members connect with Al-Anon and the growth of their own recovery, the enthusiasm is contagious.

I don't bother with service work. It's easy for the newcomer to see service work as unimportant or to think he has nothing to offer. Making the coffee, putting out the snacks, arranging the literature—it all seems small and insignificant. But it is insignificant only on the surface, in the thinking about it. In the doing, it has the deep, resonating significance of giving back. AA is not only about getting help; it is about giving help. This, you'll recall, was Bill Wilson's life-changing insight. Ultimately, it's through helping other alcoholics that people stay sober.

People tend to think those new to AA aren't ready to help others, but they can set up chairs, greet people at the door, or make sure the lights are turned off as they leave. Even more important, any time the addict tells his story or shares in a meeting, he may be giving others exactly what they need to hear to help them stay sober. These seemingly small actions are critical first steps in learning to give. Each creates a sense of belonging to the group. Families do the same in Al-Anon. In Structured Family Recovery, as we share about our service commitments, we create a spiritual expectation of giving back.

I've been sober a long time. I really don't need meetings anymore. This is the reemergence of the inflated ego, and it gets alcoholics and addicts in trouble. The fewer positive and constructive recovery experiences addicts have in the early days of recovery, the less emotional and social capital addicts build up against relapse. Some relapse happens when life seems to be good. The addict assumes she no longer needs to do the work that recovery requires, instead of understanding that her life is good because of her efforts in recovery. For families who are not participating in recovery, this rationalization can sound sensible. Some might say, "I don't see why you need to go to AA anymore. You're doing great." But families in Structured Family Recovery know better. Moreover, when an entire family is involved in Twelve Step recovery, an addict sees recovery as a normal way of life.

I don't make time for spiritual practice. Alcoholics Anonymous is a spiritual program, but newcomers frequently misunderstand this to mean religious or see it as having no real significance. When they do this, they miss a great deal. Keith Humphreys, a professor of psychiatry and social sciences at Stanford University, explains that in AA, "Someone will say something profound that everyone can connect to beyond themselves, and it can be very moving. That is a spiritual process." He goes on to say that "the basic frame is about minimizing selfishness, minimizing grandiosity, giving to others, accepting character flaws, and apologizing when you're wrong."

Spiritual practices also include reading recovery literature (such as meditation books), taking time to reflect, and connecting to other people in the program. These practices help prevent the disease from once again gaining strength. Spiritual practices are action steps that create positive attitudes and fortitude. Positive spirituality spreads to the emotional brain, which sends positive messages to the thinking brain. This process is as important for the family as it is for the addict. Anger, resentment, and blame, which keep families tied to the pattern of addiction, are put into a new perspective when family members experience a power greater than themselves at work. Structured Family Recovery helps each member of the team set up spiritual practices that are simple, consistent, and effective.

I have thoughts of drinking that I don't talk about with others. This is a combination of pride and perfectionism. Even in AA, the addict wants to look as if he has no problem. In recovery, honesty is a sign of growth, even when it is embarrassing. Lack of honesty is a lack of humility and a retreat back into the isolated self. Recovery flourishes in the light of sharing and support; addiction grows in the darkness of self-deception and secrets. For this reason, rigorous honesty is one of the main tenets of the program. When alcoholics and addicts aren't honest, they eventually relapse. In Structured Family Recovery, the family begins to let go of blame and the individual members begin to focus on themselves and what they need to do to foster recovery. The entire family team learns to model humility and honesty about themselves. As they focus on themselves, the family members discover a newfound acceptance of one another. In this atmosphere, the addict learns that it is safe to be honest with himself and others.

Monica is a forty-year-old executive for a multinational corporation who travels the globe for business. Hers is a glamorous life from the outside, but for years, alcoholism was destroying her from the inside. Finally unable to hide her drinking problem, she agreed to attend a world-renowned treatment center. Once home, she joined AA and then relapsed in early recovery. What follows is her narrative of a journey into relapse and back into recovery.

> Once I entered recovery, my life began to turn around quickly. My health came back, my liver healed, relationships were restored, and I made several new friendships. I was no longer the target of office gossip, and even my golf game was improving. Shame was starting to lift, and I was experiencing a freedom I had long forgotten. It was due to my recovery, and I was working what I believed to be a strong program: I attended daily AA meetings, committed to service work, read, prayed, and worked the Steps with my sponsor.
>
> After my health improved and my confidence returned, life was on an upswing. I quickly forgot the pain, fear, and shame that alcohol ultimately produced, despite hearing about it nightly at my meetings. I forgot how grateful I was to have been given another chance in this world. I began to get bored with my routine and started missing the glamour associated with alcohol. I began fantasizing about the conviviality of drinking with others in swanky bars. I desperately wanted the feeling of 'ahhh' again, as alcohol washed away my cares.
>
> It was the type of dangerous thinking that I should have been discussing in meetings and with my sponsor. Instead, I let my ego run away with concerns such as *What will they think of me?* Even while dreaming about drinking,

I wanted to look like the AA poster child. It wasn't clear to me at the time, but I hadn't grasped the concepts of acceptance, surrender, and honesty. My obsession with alcohol was still very present.

Before long, it became a daily fight to stay sober. Despite the forewarnings from people in AA who said, 'It just takes the first drink,' or 'The disease progresses even when you're not drinking,' or 'Relapse is planned,' my disease was telling me that I was smarter than those people—and besides, no one ever needed to know. I began to believe drinking would be different this time. Without taking that first sip of alcohol, I had already relapsed.

My secret thoughts finally drove me to drink. There was no 'ahhh' feeling with that first drink, nor with the ones that followed. Instead, each drink brought stronger feelings of guilt, shame, and self-loathing. There was no conviviality or companionship or swanky bars. I drank alone in fear of being found out, having to hide from anyone who knew I was in AA, which included my husband and my entire family.

Not only had I been unable to re-create my fantasy about drinking, there were so many precious things I lost: clarity, self-respect, confidence, serenity, and, most of all, freedom. While no one suspected yet, I was consumed by planning my next drinking escapade—where I could go, how I could hide it, how much I could have before it was noticeable, how much I could drink and still drive, what to say and how to say it, what excuses to make, how to minimize the aftereffects, how to push what I'd done out of my mind. It was an all-consuming, horrible feeling.

The next day always brought some version of a hangover and a sick feeling of doom. I needed to get back on track, which of course required a few stabilizing drinks. Even though the slip went unnoticed to the outside world, the cycle had started. The cravings and obsession were back in full force. It was all I could do to maintain any semblance of control. I was determined to portray myself as successful to everyone around me, fearful that unless I conducted myself perfectly, they would catch on. It was exhausting. I felt like a complete fraud.

I had achieved freedom with recovery, but with that first drink, I relinquished it. Again, I felt captive to alcohol and the paralyzing fear that went along with it. In the end, it was fear that led me to prayer, which led me to only one answer—the one I was desperately trying to avoid—honesty. My relapse started with self-deception, which manifested itself to outward deception, which then turned into shame, guilt, and fear. I was now drinking to drown out the terrible negativity and emotional pain.

There was only one way to break the cycle: I had to get honest with myself, others, and the God of my understanding. It is humbling and terrifying to make an admission of relapse. But I really wanted to get better, and I knew there was only one way out. There was something in me that had changed in those early months in AA, and I simply could not continue to act one way and live another. Of course, I was afraid of judgment, looks of disgust, and dismissal, but that fear originated with the way I was judging myself. In my ego-driven head, I was afraid people would think less of me. It was far from the truth. What I found instead was support, care, concern, and, yes, some colorfully worded candor. I found love, acceptance, and the strength to move forward. Today, by working an honest program of recovery, I have more than two years' clean and sober.

Recovery in AA, NA, and other Twelve Step programs replaces a drinking and drugging life with something of enduring value. In working the Twelve Steps, addicts embrace a higher set of principles that support a higher standard of behavior. Working a program gives addicts and their family members a framework for realizing major changes in character and personality. Maintaining these changes requires staying active in recovery. For those who don't, even after years of sobriety, tales of relapse abound. The story line almost always begins with the same admissions: "I stopped going to meetings" and "I wasn't being honest."

Families can relapse too. Behaviors and attitudes well practiced while addiction raged don't work in recovery. Resentments and anger often burn long after alcoholics get into recovery. In many cases, families believe it's the addict's job to make everything right again. But it's not possible for a recovering person to do what family members need to do for themselves.

Recovering alcoholics who receive criticism from their spouses, as compared to alcoholics who have their support, have a higher relapse rate, according to research from the State University of New York. The study found that families who work together in recovery, however, have greater success.

8

Tiny Tasks

In the words of Irish author Derek Landy, "Every solution to every problem is simple. It's the distance between the two where the mystery lies." As we've discussed, finding better ways to motivate alcoholics and addicts to stay sober is an ongoing and misguided pursuit. We educate, we attempt to change attitudes, and we ask alcoholics to tell us how they can best motivate themselves. None of these alone has proven to have the power to sustain lasting change. It isn't as though effective strategies for sustaining change don't exist; it's that we're not using them in a consistent way.

Behavior-change expert B. J. Fogg, PhD, is professor of social sciences and director of the Behavior Design Lab at Stanford University. In his *New York Times* best seller *Tiny Habits: The Small Changes That Change Everything,* Dr. Fogg describes a model he created that helps us think clearly about behavior change. Designing for behavior change is systematic, he says. It's not guesswork. There are just a few things that drive behavior.

Before listing these methods that effectively drive change, he describes five mistakes we often make while attempting to create sustained changes in behavior:

1. Present information, hoping it will change attitudes,
   and new attitudes will change behavior.

2. Give people a big goal and then focus on amping up motivation and sustaining willpower.

3. Move people through psychological stages until they are ready to change.

4. Assume all behaviors are a result of choice.

5. Make persuasion techniques, such as scarcity and reciprocity, the starting point for a solution.

What's startling is how often these five approaches are relied upon for creating lasting sobriety. They may result in short-term change by advancing alcoholics and addicts forward from one stage of care to the next: from intervention to treatment to aftercare planning to Twelve Step groups. Each move forward represents a short-term goal. When families want to motivate a loved one to accept treatment, they use a short-term motivator called intervention. It's what's needed to get the job done, and then treatment takes over for the next phase. But when we rely on such motivators for sustaining long-term behavior changes in recovery, we're setting ourselves up for disappointment and probable relapse.

As families, we have been expecting a kind of success from people suffering from the disease of addiction that not even dieters have achieved. Our myths about what works can lock our hopes onto false solutions, which invariably lead to disappointment, resignation, and even estrangement. People in general are resistant to change, alcoholics and addicts only more so. Our loved ones are suffering from a disease that discourages its victims from reaching out for help. We cannot expect them to reliably self-motivate for recovery. This is an important fact to keep in the forefront of our minds.

As we've learned, decades of research have found that traditional motivational approaches alone usually only produce temporary change. Dr. Fogg concurs, "Relying primarily on motivation to change your behavior long-term is a losing strategy, and similarly for will power." He is speaking for all people. But addiction creates the added burden of dismantling the will and defeating motivation. Given this, knowing that these two forces—motivation and willpower—aren't central to lasting change is good news for addicts and the people who love them.

The addict also experiences competing motivations. Dr. Fogg writes in *Tiny Habits,* "Sometimes the complexity of our motivations amount to a psychological tug-of-war. I want to rest. I want to work. . . . These conflicts can seesaw depending on what's happening around us." For the newly recovering alcoholic or addict, these conflicting motivations might be *I want to keep my family by staying sober* and *I want to go out and have fun with my old drinking buddies.* Since the brain resists things it perceives as hard to do, which of these competing motivations will win—especially without a good recovery program? Going out with friends is perceived by the brain as easy, and muscling through another lonely sober night is hard. Structured Family Recovery (SFR) works to change this calculation. When the entire family is engaged in Structured Family Recovery, recovery doesn't seem so hard, and family relationships are pleasurable—minimizing the power of competing motivations.

Change doesn't happen by placing our focus on the outcome; it happens by focusing on the behaviors that produce the outcome. Most of us get this exactly backward. This harkens back to our misreading of treatment's role in the recovery process, leading us to the false belief that the required behavior changes all took place during treatment—a *fait accompli*—and now we can just sit back and witness the results. It is the expected outcome of treatment—staying sober—that we typically fixate on, rather than directing our energies toward the post-treatment behaviors that lead to ongoing sobriety. As we've seen, it is more accurate to say that when treatment ends, recovery begins. This is when the make-or-break work of managing a chronic disease gets underway. It calls for an acquisition of new behaviors and skills. If simply announcing, "I will never drink again!" is an addict's recovery plan, he's heading for relapse. Why? Because he is skipping over the behaviors required for sobriety, such as going to AA meetings, getting a sponsor, and working the Steps. Instead of paying attention to what the journey demands, he's aiming directly for the imagined outcome. It's a sign of overconfidence.

Alcoholics and addicts who utter such proclamations usually can't explain how they will make "never drinking or using again" possible, other than through sheer willpower. If you ask them, you're likely to learn there is no reasonable plan. What you want to hear is "I am following my aftercare plan and going to my AA or NA meetings!"

Alcoholics Anonymous and other Twelve Step programs are based on the premise that behavior drives attitude change; their slogan could be "Action before motivation." Still, we commonly hear people theorize, after an alcoholic has relapsed, "I guess she wasn't ready." This presumes readiness as the key ingredient for success. In other words, the right attitude will lead to the right behavior. It also sends a message that feelings of readiness are unwavering or that they can somehow be measured. Nothing could be further from the truth. Every day, approximately 350 alcoholics and addicts in the United States die before they feel ready to get sober.

Where does all of this leave us? If motivation, willpower, education, changing attitudes, and psychological stages of change aren't reliable means for creating sustained change, what do we have left? The answer lies with social scientists, the experts on creating change.

Dr. Fogg and his Stanford team break the process of change into three steps:

1. Define what you want and the behaviors required to get there.

2. Make it easy, because simplicity changes behavior.

3. Trigger the behavior, because no behavior happens without a call to action.

When all three steps happen at the same time, the desired behaviors materialize.

Let's take a look at each of these three steps and how we can use them to create reliable programs of recovery that lead to lasting sobriety. Both Structured Family Recovery and Twelve Step programs were built upon this three-step model of change. Combined, they present a serious challenge to relapse behaviors.

1. Define what you want and the behaviors required to get there.

Alcoholics, addicts, and families don't need to guess at what behaviors keep people sober. Twelve Step programs have it well figured out. For close to a century, alcoholics and addicts in AA and other Twelve Step groups have demonstrated precisely how to stay sober—and how not to stay sober—by taking a few simple actions:

- Go to meetings.
- Choose a home group.
- Get a sponsor.
- Work the Steps.
- Read the literature (especially the basic texts, *Alcoholics Anonymous,* known as the Big Book, or *Narcotics Anonymous*).
- Volunteer for a service position (make the coffee, greet people, put out the snacks, or help clean up).

Attending meetings is the glue that holds it all together. Taking these simple steps one day at a time changes the lives of alcoholics, addicts, and their families in immeasurable ways.

The spiritual principles that underlie these actions are equally simple. They are represented in the acronym HOW, which stands for honesty, open-mindedness, and willingness. This is what members refer to as the "HOW of the program." This may seem like a tall order for an addict, but these spiritual principles can be broken into a series of tiny tasks—behaviors that are very small, making them much easier to do. An addict can start by being honest with his sponsor. He can practice open-mindedness as he learns about the principles of the program. He can become willing to do the small things every day that lead to big changes over time. The Big Book of Alcoholics Anonymous provides the following clarification:

> Many of us exclaimed, "What an order! I can't go through with it." Do not be discouraged. No one among us has been able to maintain anything like perfect adherence to

these principles. We are not saints. The point is, that we are willing to grow along spiritual lines. The principles we have set down are guides to progress. We claim spiritual progress rather than spiritual perfection.

2. Make it easy, because simplicity changes behavior.

Social scientists at Stanford and members of Twelve Step programs understand that keeping it simple is a route to lasting change. It doesn't take much motivation to do something simple. Simplicity removes blocks and difficulties that get in the way of a desired behavior. This doesn't mean the task of recovery is easy, of course. In practice, it's said that recovery is simple but not easy. *Easy* suggests it requires few efforts to get results. AA members correct this notion with a few words from the Big Book of AA: "Half measures availed us nothing." We're up against a disease that regularly drives people to risk everything, even their lives, for the next high. Approaching recovery with simplicity means alcoholics aren't required to tackle the whole problem all at once. Instead, they're asked to take small, manageable steps forward.

On his deathbed, Dr. Bob famously told his AA cofounder, "Remember, Bill, let's not louse this thing up. Let's keep it simple." Indeed, "Keep it simple" is a favorite slogan among people in recovery, both addicts and their families. We are only expected to do what we can do today, which is captured by another popular slogan, "One day at a time." Alcoholics and other addicts quickly learn that they stay sober with small goals: twenty-four hours at a time. Al-Anon's meditation book *Courage to Change* says:

> Al-Anon reminds me to "Keep it simple." Instead of approaching the task as a whole, I can simplify it by taking it only one step at a time. . . . That takes the pressure off having to know all the answers and solve every problem that may arise before I've even begun. . . . By focusing on one thing at a time the impossible can become likely, if I keep it simple.

Speaking at AA's first international convention in Cleveland, Ohio, during the last days of his life, Dr. Bob said:

> There are two or three things that flashed into my mind on which it would be fitting to lay a little emphasis. One is the simplicity of our program. Let's not louse it up with Freudian complexes and things that are interesting to the scientific mind, but that have very little to do with our actual AA work. Our Twelve Steps, when simmered down to the last, resolve themselves into the words "love" and "service." We understand what love is, and we understand what service is. So, let's bear those two things in mind.

3. Trigger the behavior, because no behavior happens without a call to action.

Certainly, we've long understood triggers that lead to relapse, but "triggers for recovery" isn't a common concept in Twelve Step circles. If we want to make a behavior a lasting part of our lives, Dr. Fogg and his Stanford team say we must pair it with a trigger—another behavior we already perform every day.

Let's look at an example that's easy to understand. About a year ago, I set out to do twelve push-ups a day. I was struggling with a goal that was unrealistic, and soon, I quit entirely. Twelve push-ups were very difficult for me to achieve. In the back of my mind, I had a lingering regret over my lack of fortitude and blamed myself for being uncommitted. I decided to try again, this time following Dr. Fogg's model of behavior change. First, I created a tiny task. I would only do two push-ups at a time. Then I paired my push-ups with something I already did several times a day—wash my hands. Since I wash my hands about ten times a day, I was immediately doing twenty push-ups without needing to motivate myself. As time went on, two push-ups were so easy that I increased it to three and so on. After a couple of months, I was doing about eighty push-ups a day. I've successfully maintained this new behavior day after day, week after week, month after month without losing my resolve because I didn't need any resolve.

It's possible that many alcoholics and addicts have relapsed precisely because they didn't have access to this simple strategy of matching recovery behaviors with triggers in daily life. Addicts who've completed treatment have been given a lot of information. They are told what to do for their recovery, but they don't always do it. Who among us isn't guilty of the same? The heart patient who doesn't take her daily walk, the diabetic who forgets to check his blood sugar, the student who doesn't keep up on daily reading assignments. It's important to understand that one of the reasons for inconsistencies or failures is that all of these things mentioned above are goals, not behaviors. We need to break goals down to very small yet meaningful behaviors to increase compliance. What simple behaviors do I need to put together to reach my goal of going to a Twelve Step meeting every day? How do I trigger these behaviors? We must begin by differentiating between goals and behaviors.

There are a number of goals associated with lasting sobriety. Let's look at meeting attendance and consider some possible triggers for behaviors. To discover the right trigger, an alcoholic can ask herself, "At what times did I drink?" If it was after work, leaving work is the trigger to drive directly to a meeting. If drinking started after dinner, then finishing dinner triggers going to an evening meeting. A morning drinker gets out of bed and heads directly to an early bird meeting. For a midday drinker, it's a lunchtime meeting.

By combining these triggers with the desired recovery behavior of getting in the car and driving to a meeting, alcoholics no longer have to make decisions about what meetings and what times. "I always started drinking by lunch, so I go to the Lunch Bunch meeting," says a stay-at-home mom, who brings a bag lunch and looks forward to the camaraderie. "I don't have to wonder when I'll fit a meeting into my schedule. At the same time I normally reached for the wine bottle, I'm in my car and on my way to my group."

Motivation and the Role of the SFR Team

We need to revisit motivation. Remember, the Stanford team's first step to behavior change requires defining what one wants and the behaviors required to get there. Alcoholics and addicts typically do not want to change their behavior, at least not for long. Social scientists' clarity about motivation informs us of its specific usefulness: some motivation is necessary for initiating change. Not everyone has the same drive to change, and some have none. This is when families and professionals can play a crucial role, creating just enough willingness to light a spark. Motivation is a powerful stimulus that points alcoholics and addicts in the right direction and gives them a little push to get them going.

Motivation generally comes in the form of a family intervention, where family members express their needs and concerns, or when upheaval and suffering in the addict's life are so sufficient that treatment and recovery look like a good option. However, as soon as pain recedes, so will these types of motivation. That's why families are able to play such a major role in an addict's desire to change. They can either create motivation by expressing their needs and concerns, thereby modeling honesty and willingness, or extinguish motivation by trying to fix the addict's problems (eliminating pain).

Treatment centers do considerable work to create motivation. They do it primarily by dismantling the denial system—which actively sends messages telling the addict that change isn't necessary. Treatment professionals are continually stoking motivation to keep patients moving in the right direction. They strive to keep patients from leaving treatment early and work to persuade them to adhere to their aftercare plans. A family working as a team in Structured Family Recovery is in the best position to support the efforts of the treatment team.

An addict leaving treatment may initially be eager for AA or NA and all things recovery, and dive right into the meetings, but if he doesn't make connections with other recovering people, including finding a sponsor, he can feel like a fish out of water. Not knowing anyone, he sits in the back quietly and leaves meetings as soon as possible, too uncomfortable to speak to people. He was close to his peers in treatment, but his Twelve Step meetings don't feel the same. Everything is new and unfamiliar. He no longer has a team of professionals to direct his behaviors. So he drops away from his meetings without giving them a chance, reassuring his family that he has no plans to drink again, but he simply can't find the time to go—and they're not doing much for him anyway.

We often hear that alcoholics and addicts must want to stay sober for themselves. The unspoken message is, "If you don't want it for yourself, it won't work." This assumes that having a reason to change is the motivating factor for a person's success. But, since social science research repeatedly shows that we don't do well at identifying the single factor that truly motivates us to change, this is unlikely. These same scientists have proven repeatedly that social norms are the most powerful drivers of behavior. Being motivated by the people you love is normal and desirable. Why worry about what fuels the call to action? Our only concern should be that we and our addict keep working our recovery programs.

Anne went to treatment after a family intervention. She initially refused to accept help, so her family established bottom lines as a method to motivate her to say yes. It was her husband's bottom line that persuaded Anne to change her mind.

> You know I love you and want our marriage to work. But first I have to say, I haven't been a trustworthy husband or father. I've done nothing to help you these last years, letting this disease overtake you and our home life, ultimately affecting our children. I was blaming you for something you could never have done on your own: just quit. But now I know better, and I apologize with all my heart. Today, we must join forces to eradicate addiction from our home and our lives. If you can't join our recovery team, it is important that you leave our home until you can choose treatment and recovery. You and I must protect the children from this insidious disease. Only with recovery can we rebuild our lives together.

The entire time Anne was in treatment, her motivation for staying sober was to save her family. Counselors and peers said she needed to stay sober for herself or she would relapse. When she joined AA, she heard the same. But she couldn't quite muster the impetus to be motivated just for herself. It was keeping her children and her husband that mattered. Some might say her attitude wasn't optimal, but as we know, changing attitudes doesn't change behaviors. Her early motivations were perfect for jump-starting change. We don't really care what fuels motivation as long as it sparks new behavior. Driven by her desire to save her family, Anne did everything that was asked of her: she went to meetings, got a sponsor, worked the Steps. With a daily program of recovery, Anne was eventually able to say, "I'm doing this for my family, but I'm also doing it for me."

Once an addicted person has completed treatment, an SFR family recovery team keeps the ball rolling by modeling new behaviors that support recovery. Creating a strong social norm within a family inhibits relapse behaviors. Regardless of all the talk of individuality, it is in our nature as human beings to want to conform and belong. We are social animals. When addiction separates and isolates us, we experience pain. When we reunite through recovery, it is easier to be happy, joyous, and free.

The sixth chapter of the Big Book, titled "Into Action," describes the result of working the Twelve Steps. These are the Promises that recovering alcoholics and addicts around the world have learned to be true. And so have their families.

> We are going to know a new freedom and a new happiness. We will not regret the past nor wish to shut the door on it. We will comprehend the word serenity, and we will know peace. No matter how far down the scale we have gone, we will see how our experience can benefit others. That feeling of uselessness and self-pity will disappear. We will lose interest in selfish things and gain interest in our fellows. Self-seeking will slip away. Our whole attitude and outlook upon life will change. Fear of people and of economic insecurity will leave us. We will intuitively know how to handle situations which used to baffle us.

Source: The Promises text is reprinted with permission of Alcoholics Anonymous World Services, Inc. ("A.A.W.S."); see Notes for full citation.

Speaking on these very promises, Father Joseph Martin, a Roman Catholic priest, recovering alcoholic, and renowned educator, said, "You are learning lessons of life from those who lived it and lost it and regained it. It's a beautiful way. . . . We are the thrice blessed of the world."

9

A New Look
at Enabling Addiction

The word *enabling* has found its way into our everyday vocabulary, popular media, and armchair psychology. It's often thrown out blithely to draw attention to dysfunctional behaviors in every corner of life. It is commonly acknowledged that families of alcoholics and addicts are culpable as enablers, much to the detriment of their addicted loved ones. If you are being called an enabler, it's not likely a compliment. Given this, why is it so hard for families to stop enabling their drug addict? Is there more to the story than we think?

Enabling is commonly defined as taking responsibility for another person's harmful conduct in ways that prevent that person from experiencing negative consequences—especially consequences that might motivate her to accept help. What this definition doesn't reveal is why. Why do families, once they learn how enabling exacerbates addiction, continue to do it? We tell people to stop, but we don't explore why they don't. Most don't even know themselves.

Oftentimes, our beliefs become well-worn paths that are too easily traveled again and again without considering if they are still relevant or accurate. Beliefs about enabling are so universally unquestioned that exclaiming, "Mother, you're such an enabler!" requires no further explanation. But this comfort with words and beliefs can easily put our critical thinking skills to sleep.

A shallow understanding of enabling serves to pit family member against family member. A sister is furious with her parents for enabling her brother. Husband and wife are on the brink of divorce over disagreements about enabling their son. Family members argue, stop talking, blame, and fume over the notion of enabling. Everyone can get bogged down in the problem with no visible way out. The resulting chaos makes it easier for addiction to thrive, because families have little chance of making meaningful change until they unite. Of course, unity is impossible when we define each other as the problem.

If we slow down and take a closer look at what is happening within a family, we will see that saving the alcoholic from negative consequences is not the end of the story, but rather a means to another end. When we enable an addict, we're really doing it to save ourselves. If our loved one dies or gets arrested or fired from a job or any of the other bad things that tend to cascade downward in the addict's life, we suffer in a multitude of ways. Like it or not, our lives are linked. When we're told to simply detach, the risk feels too great.

A young mother of small children needs her husband's paycheck to keep a roof over their heads and food on the table. An aging couple can't bear to watch their son die before they do. Parents' hearts are shattered by the thought of the sweet little girl they raised turning to prostitution to feed a drug habit. A dad doesn't know how to cope without a mom tending to the children. People closest to alcoholics and addicts intrinsically understand they hit bottom along with the alcoholic, so it is in their interest to make every effort to keep that from happening. We conventionally called it enabling, but calling it survival might be closer to the truth.

Saving the addict is about saving our families. Addiction crashes into lives, altering families in a manner that threatens all we hold dear. When we rescue the addict, it feels as if we're saving the family, but we aren't. We're protecting the addiction. Our well-intentioned rescues result in the progression of the disease, mounting problems, and ongoing damage to the entire family system. Yet we believe, in our heart of hearts, that we are doing the right thing. In the words of the American writer

Robert Brault, "An old belief is like an old shoe. We so value its comfort that we fail to notice the hole in it."

We all hold dear our own version of our family's story, and no two stories are exactly alike. Each member of a family has a perspective and a history unique to that person. Stories have parallel plot lines, defining who we were before addiction took hold, who we are now, and who we could be if things were different. The actions we take to maintain and defend our families against addiction are usually forms of enabling. How we enable is usually determined by our version of the family story.

A father and son, both attorneys, shared the same suite of offices in a small southern town. Since the first day the son expressed an interest in law, the father had dreamed of passing his thriving law practice down to him. Working with his son for the first five or six years after he graduated from law school was a joy. Then this bright, engaging young man began to change. His moods were erratic. He missed important appointments and court dates. He showed up to work late, always with a reasonable excuse. Dad began working overtime, checking up on his son's clients and cases. He instructed his assistant to monitor his son's calendar closely, making sure he showed up for appointments. When a fellow attorney asked him if his son was having problems, he vehemently denied it. When his daughter told him it was drugs, he blew up. "Nonsense, he's just going through a rough patch. He'll pull himself through." Dad was determined to preserve the dream he held so dear.

Enabling is hope for achieving something better or avoiding something worse. We need to solve the problem now. We need peace now. We don't want to believe that our actions in the moment are going to contribute to more unmanageability later. Each enabler takes on a specific role in the family story. The closer a person's fate is tied to the alcoholic, the more furious the enabling. A cousin who isn't close to an alcoholic or involved in her daily life, for instance, is probably not engaged in enabling behaviors because the alcoholism isn't central to his survival. But it's different for a spouse, a parent, or a child who lives with the alcoholic and experiences the ravages of her drinking or drugging directly.

The wife of a senior executive of a large company puts up with his glass after glass of scotch every evening. To avoid triggering his wrath, she tries to stay out of his way until he stumbles off to bed. She's lonely with all the children grown, but she believes that leaving him would feel worse than staying. He is central to her family story. Her home, car, clothing, travel, and social status are tied to him. She likes having the children and grandchildren in the big house for holidays and at the lakeside cottage for summer weekends. Divorce would mean giving that all up at this late stage in her life. She fears if she rocks the boat, he'll find a younger woman, and she'll be turned out to live alone in an apartment. Being sixty-something and divorced is not in her story.

People want solutions for addiction that preserve family rather than break it apart. If solutions seem to force them into positions they're madly trying to avoid, they're not likely to move forward. If a wife who doesn't want a divorce is told she needs to leave her husband if he keeps drinking, it's likely she will dismiss professional help or sabotage the process. Divorcing her husband is asking her to give up the story she spent forty years creating. She doesn't really care that she is enabling if doing so results in preserving her home life.

However, if a solution offers her a way to strengthen her family and help her husband, she'll probably listen. Creating a recovery team with her grown children, their spouses, and other close family members can change the dynamic. It feels good to work together as a team. Group decisions can be made about intervention, treatment, practicing Structured Family Recovery, and the best ways to support one another. These actions preserve what is best about us and rebuild what addiction has torn asunder.

Even when family members say they want to end their relationship with the addict, there is usually a wide gulf between the saying and the doing. Family members often announce decisions that feel good to say but not to put into action. When they back away from these decisions, it appears they are returning to old enabling ways, frustrating other family members and professionals. But it's more likely that it wasn't the end result they truly wanted. Most people want to come together, not fall apart.

And we know, in our heart of hearts, that when we're family, we're never really free of one another.

Certainly, there are cases when a relationship with an addicted person needs to end. Sometimes so much bad has happened it's impossible to look toward the future with that person. Even so, the web of relationships for the addict can include other family members and mutual friendships. The story doesn't generally allow for a clean severing of ties. A mother must send her child off for shared custody. A woman's brother is still invited to holiday and birthday celebrations by their parents. An ex-husband tries to juggle friendships he shares with his former wife.

Separation also doesn't guarantee an end to unmanageability. With family members, a physical change rarely leads to emotional emancipation. Simply getting away from a person doesn't automatically change everything for the better. Anger and resentment can persist and grow with new problems that we hadn't anticipated. It isn't that we don't have a relationship anymore; we now have a different relationship. We're still tied together, often through emotions, memories, regrets, family, friends, children, and geography. We struggle to create a new story that makes sense of how this relationship now plays out in our lives and the lives of others.

Even while we are fighting against the worst, our brains want to believe in the best. But when we feel the need to enable, it signals we're in trouble. It takes a great deal of faith to let go of enabling, because we fear what might happen. For this reason, we need a good solution to grab on to, and then it isn't as difficult. And when we do this as a family team, we find a power we didn't know we had.

The Power of Enabling Recovery

Enabling is a family's attempt to solve the problems that addiction has created. Left to their own devices, however, and following their survival instincts, families often unwittingly contribute to prolonging the addiction. It doesn't have to be this way. When provided with good direction, and when they learn to work together for both the addict's and their own health, families are transfigured into a remarkable source of energy and strength for enabling recovery.

It doesn't matter if family relationships are rocky at the start. Addiction always damages relationships to one degree or another. The process of working together rebuilds family ties of trust and belonging. Structured Family Recovery creates a framework that helps families succeed at recovery and avoid the pitfalls that lead to relapse. We make it together not by fixing each other, but by mending ourselves simultaneously. Instead of enabling addiction, we enable recovery.

One dictionary definition of *enabling* is "rendering capable or able for some task." This functional definition empowers us to do something about the problem we face. Simply put, it means we can support each other in developing the qualities or skills necessary for the work ahead. We can begin "rendering ourselves capable and able for" recovery at any point on the road to sobriety. Family participation is a game changer before, during, and after treatment. It's never too late to begin. Whenever we connect with each other in a meaningful way, we strengthen our family.

Alcoholics and addicts don't respond well to empty words. Actions attract their attention. When the entire family is on the same page—not telling the addict what to do, but actually doing it themselves—it is clear that something has changed. When families model recovery—not one or two people, but everyone—it has a tremendous force that goes way beyond words. It is so radical a shift that the addict can be momentarily stunned. As a recovering alcoholic said to me, "I thought, could this really be my family? I was so moved by what they were doing that, of course, I pursued my own recovery."

Working together is the key to enabling recovery, but we don't have to do it perfectly. Each member of a family must have a degree of willingness to put aside past grievances for the greater good. Our daily practice of recovery behaviors will help us begin to let go of anger, resentments, and other unhelpful emotions in a more dependable way. We cannot enable recovery when we are full of venom. In a television interview, author Toni Morrison said of anger, "It's helpless . . . it's absence of control—and I need all of my skills, all of my control, all of my power . . . and anger doesn't provide me any of that. I have no use for it whatsoever."

When we get stuck in our anger, just as the alcoholic was stuck in his addiction, no one is going anywhere.

Enabling recovery returns us to our integrity, because we can't enable recovery if we aren't participating in the solution, just as we can't enable addiction without participating in the problem. Rather than staying stuck in the quagmire, we move toward a sense of purpose with productive behavior and clear goals. We'll never get worthwhile results with anything less.

Sometimes families engage in Structured Family Recovery on their own, before their addicted loved one finds her way into recovery. In this way, the entire family begins creating a positive social norm that paves a path for recovery for the alcoholic or addict. The addicted loved one must be in treatment or active Twelve Step recovery before joining the family recovery team. Structured Family Recovery is not a substitute for treatment. The alcoholic or addict must be free of all mood-altering substances first. It's a prerequisite that they are engaged in a recovery program for addiction. For this reason, enabling recovery often begins with a well-planned, structured family intervention.

Following are two different scenarios of families reacting to a crisis caused by a loved one's addiction. These examples illustrate the difference between enabling the disease and enabling recovery.

1. A thirty-two-year-old alcoholic loses his job and begins burning through his savings.

He spends most days on the couch drinking and watching television, telling his family he's out looking for work. Running out of money, he can no longer pay his mortgage and is soon receiving notices. He calls his mother for help. Filled with panic, she pulls out her checkbook. The alcoholic's sense of emergency spreads throughout the family, whose immediate reaction is to fix the problem. Once the mortgage is paid, the mother is relieved, and the alcoholic makes some half-hearted attempts to find work. But mostly he drinks, setting up the groundwork for the next crisis and the need for more enabling.

In this example, the mother reacts to her son's crisis by paying his mortgage bill, unwittingly supporting his addiction. However, alleviating his panic over losing his house, she misses a perfect opportunity to launch him into recovery. Writing a check was an easier, quicker solution. It didn't require thinking, communicating, or planning. It gave her relief in the moment—crisis averted. But for this mother and son, things got progressively worse. Negative consequences continued to pile up, costing more money and producing ongoing stress.

2. A mother receives a call from her alcoholic daughter asking for help.

The daughter's house is going into foreclosure. Mom listens carefully and then tells her daughter she will call back after talking with her father. Mom and Dad decide to retain the services of a clinical interventionist. They bring together a family team and execute a well-planned intervention. Their daughter is admitted into a treatment facility. Crisis created a sense of emergency in this family, too, but they chose actions that enabled recovery.

In this scenario, the mother doesn't react to the crisis with panic. She buys herself some time by telling her daughter she needs to talk with her father. Together, the parents decide to seek professional advice and, working with other family members and friends, leverage the crisis by implementing a family intervention. For this family, the up-front work required more effort and some stressful moments. It was not as easy as writing a check. But in a relatively short period of time, their life became easier. Gathered as a family, they began enabling successful recovery. Once the daughter was in treatment, the family team began Structured Family Recovery with plans to invite the daughter as soon as her counselor felt she was stable in treatment.

During the planning and implementing of a family intervention, families have a well-defined and powerful role to play in initiating treatment. It's after the alcoholic is discharged from treatment that families once again may not know what to do or what to expect. Their beloved addict, who was wildly out of control just a few weeks earlier, is now making major life changes, essentially on his own. Is he really going to AA meetings? Is he resisting the urge to drink and drug? Is he hanging out with old friends who do drugs and frequent the bars?

The family isn't sure what's right or what's wrong. The alcoholic tells them what his counselor recommended, but they don't know if it's true. Is it okay to drink nonalcoholic beer? Is going out bar hopping okay as long as he sticks to drinking cola? Should family get-togethers still revolve around lots of drinking? Is a little pot okay if he doesn't drink? Is it true he only needs one or two AA meetings a week?

With so many concerns, the family's fear of relapse looms large. They have no system in place that allows for meaningful family communication and mutual support. The family is left on the sidelines, with limited information and no role to play. This is the all-too-familiar situation Structured Family Recovery was created to avoid. Without a systematic plan designed for enabling recovery, too many factors work against recovery. When everyone in the family has a way to participate in recovery, the family dynamic changes—and the addict begins following directions too.

As we noted earlier, finding ways for people to sustain their commitment is key. It cannot be stressed enough that the biggest problem in recovery from addiction—as is true across the spectrum of health care—is a lack of compliance. The World Health Organization reports that effective interventions that lead to patient compliance are more valuable than the creation of new treatments. Noncompliance is a primary cause of relapse. Structured Family Recovery is designed to create compliance. As a team, we all do what we need to do to make recovery work.

Let's look at two more families and compare how they respond to their newly recovering addict's return home after treatment.

1. Sam is home after treatment for alcoholism and marijuana addiction.

His wife, Janelle, is elated by the changes in him. For his part, Sam is on what is commonly referred to as a "pink cloud." Treatment was great. He feels like a new man, and he knows he'll never drink or drug again. Sam goes to some Alcoholics Anonymous meetings but is not really connecting with anyone and begins to think the meetings aren't for him. Unaware of his private struggles, Janelle proudly tells her in-laws that he's going to meetings and doing great. She's sure everything will be better now that Sam is sober.

Sam joins a gym to get into shape and works harder at his job to catch up for lost time. Soon, he's only hitting a recovery meeting now and again. Janelle begins suspecting that he's going less often than he claims. She asks him about it, and he snaps back, "It's my program. Quit looking over my shoulder." She and Sam have no system that allows for recovery communication, and she's never seen his aftercare plan developed by his treatment team. One evening, when Sam returns home from work, she swears she smells a whiff of marijuana.

2. Mariana was admitted into treatment after a family intervention.

The clinical interventionist recommended to her husband, Lucas, and extended family that they participate in Structured Family Recovery. In their intervention letters, they wrote, "Addiction is a family disease, so we are all committed to Structured Family Recovery. You are not alone on this journey. We're in this together."

While Mariana was still in treatment, her family scheduled their first SFR meeting and continued meeting weekly by conference call. Before Mariana was discharged from treatment, her family invited her to join the team. Now the individual team members are all working their own recovery program—the family is in Al-Anon, and Mariana is in AA. Random drug testing has eliminated the need for guesswork. Everyone talks openly about their progress, and if someone is struggling, they have the support of the entire family. Everyone knows and speaks the language of recovery.

The differences between these two families' experiences of early recovery couldn't be starker.

After an initial thrill of excitement and hope, Sam's wife, Janelle, feels isolated and alone. She can't bring herself to tell her in-laws that Sam is smoking pot again. Without a family recovery team or her own Twelve Step program, she doesn't know where to turn or whom to talk to. Sam's anger frightens her, so she keeps her mouth shut. She hopes for the best, but she's filled with dread. All the no-talk rules are back in place, offering no safe place for communication, openness, or problem solving.

Mariana, on the other hand, moved from treatment into a family recovery team that had already made commitments to change. Everyone was living a transparent life, talking about their recovery programs and what they were learning. It was a smooth transition from treatment, and Mariana now feels that she fits right in with the rest of her family. She knows they are working together and rebuilding trust. She and Lucas plan recovery date nights. He attends Al-Anon while she attends her AA meeting across the hall. Afterward, they have a nice dinner and take time to enjoy each other's company.

The quality of our future is determined by the actions we take today. It is not where we begin that counts, but where we end up. Living in recovery, we can begin to forgive. As Leo Buscaglia so beautifully wrote, "Too often we underestimate the power of a touch, a smile, a kind word, a listening ear, an honest compliment, or the smallest act of caring, all of which have the potential to turn a life around."

10

Families Pay a High Price

Chronic stress changes our brains. It also causes disease. There is a great deal of truth in the statement "I'm worried sick."

While short-lived stress doesn't hurt us, stress reaches a point when it can become toxic. Since emotions impact every cell in the body, when stress persists over time, we are set on a course for declining health and even premature aging. As this doesn't happen instantly (in the way a heart attack or a broken bone does), chronic stress doesn't always set off our alert systems. We don't worry about how much we worry; instead, we learn to live with it.

Families of alcoholics sometimes suffer from *psychosomatic illnesses* caused by emotions (psyche) changing the body (soma). Often described as psychological factors that affect medical conditions, these diseases aren't imaginary. They are very real. The ongoing stress that can be caused by another person's addiction and its consequences is able to change the health of our bodily systems. This kind of stress can lead to conditions like hypertension, stroke, and irregular heartbeat. Stress also damages our immune system, which decreases our ability to defend ourselves from bacteria, viruses, and, at the extreme, cancerous cells.

According to Robert M. Sapolsky, PhD, professor of neuroscience at Stanford University, in his book *Why Zebras Don't Get Ulcers*, "Stress can wreak havoc with your metabolism, raise your blood pressure, burst your white blood cells, make you flatulent, ruin your sex life, and if that's not enough, possibly damage your brain." He goes on to say that if we experience each day as an emergency, we will pay the price.

When we feel we are in danger—which is what stress is telling us—our body undergoes rapid changes. It releases two hormones, called cortisol and adrenaline. Adrenaline creates an instant state of readiness by increasing our pulse rate and blood pressure, creating a sudden burst of energy. Adrenaline can also temporarily increase our strength, make us more agile, and allow us to take in information more quickly. Cortisol is released after adrenaline to calm us down. We begin breathing normally, our heartbeat slows, and our muscles relax. This hormone-fueled defense reaction is designed to keep us alive by protecting us from dangers that are brief, such as escaping from a fire or evading a suspicious person or even running from a bear. Fortunately, most of us don't encounter bears on a routine basis. In modern life, most stressors are less obvious, and they can persist for months or years.

When we are under constant stress, we produce too much adrenaline and cortisol. If these emergency hormones circulate in our bodies long enough, they hurt us. Overdoses of adrenaline scar blood vessels, which can cause heart attacks and strokes. Cortisol can damage cells in an area of the brain called the hippocampus, affecting our capacity to learn and remember. When we experience prolonged episodes of stress, our bodies get exhausted, preventing us from functioning well in everyday life. In adulthood, the areas of our brain that normally decline most rapidly as we age are vulnerable to the destructive forces of stress hormones.

According to John J. Medina, MD, developmental molecular biologist and brain development expert, the worst kind of stress we can experience is a sense of hopelessness—the feeling we have no control over a problem. The more out of control we feel, the greater the stress. This is how most families of alcoholics and addicts experience stress.

In his best-selling book *Brain Rules,* Dr. Medina writes:

> Stress hormones can do some truly nasty things to your brain. . . . Stress hormones seem to have a particular liking for cells in the hippocampus, and that's a problem, because

> the hippocampus is deeply involved in many aspects of
> learning. . . . Stress hormones can disconnect neural net-
> works, the webbing of brain cells that act like a safety de-
> posit vault for storing your most precious memories. They
> can stop the hippocampus from giving birth to brand-new
> baby neurons. . . . Clearly, stress hurts learning. Most im-
> portant, however, stress hurts people.

Every structure in our brain is influenced by what is happening
in our surroundings. If our family environment isn't healthy, it's likely
our brain isn't either. According to Elizabeth Gould, PhD, of Princeton
University, chronic stress causes the brain to starve. Her groundbreaking
research in neurobiology shows how stressed brains stop creating new
cells. Our existing cells retreat inward, and the brain becomes disfig-
ured. Stress is changing our neural anatomy. Dr. Gould explains, "When
a brain is worried, it's just thinking about survival. It isn't interested in
investing in new cells for the future."

What stress does to the brains of family members is similar to what
drugs do to the brains of alcoholics and addicts, damaging the thinking
and the emotional brain systems. Researchers at Yale have found that
the prefrontal cortex—the thinking brain—is most affected by stress. As
nerve tissue in this area of the brain begins to diminish, we lose gray
matter, which affects our emotions, self-control, and ability to adapt to
life's challenges.

The mood center of the brain also shrinks, resulting in increases
in depression and anxiety. These reductions in brain function make it
more difficult for families to deal with stressful events. This is particularly detrimental since addiction is a progressive disease; over time,
we can expect more problems. When we have less capacity to handle
stress, problems appear unsolvable. Families resort to temporary solutions, which do not eliminate the impact of addiction or the resulting
stress. Similar to the alcoholic's and addict's relationship to alcohol and
other drugs, families now experience enabling as a need, not a choice—
as a matter of survival.

Stress can also lead to insomnia. Alcoholics don't sleep well because the toxic effect of alcohol disrupts sleep patterns. Family members also experience a lack of sleep caused by worry, anxiety, and depression. Stress can make it difficult for many to fall asleep and stay asleep, and it affects the quality of sleep. According to the National Sleep Foundation, stress causes hyperarousal, which upsets the balance between sleep and wakefulness. Poor sleep creates more stress, compounding the problem.

Chronic insomnia disrupts the brain's ability to pay attention, analyze information, and concentrate. It also seems to slow the brain's ability to do its maintenance work. Scientists are now learning that losing sleep also leads to a reduction in the brain's ability to clear out a buildup of waste, specifically a type of protein associated with Alzheimer disease and other forms of dementia. This may age the brain, damaging it in ways that could make it more vulnerable to the early onset of brain diseases such as dementia and Parkinson disease. It also turns out that chronic loss of sleep isn't easy to make up; brains don't fully recover. More research is needed, but studies thus far offer evidence that sleep is more important than we thought. Sleep aided by medication isn't the same as natural sleep. Reducing stress and using nonmedication sleep techniques boost brain health.

Another stress-related phenomenon that affects people in addicted families is called *learned helplessness*. It was discovered in 1965 by two scientists, Martin Seligman and Steven Maier, who exposed animals to prolonged and unpredictable stressors over which they had no control. When the animals were then given a way to avoid the stressors, they didn't do it. For example, when rats were given a series of shocks they could not avoid, they quickly developed learned helplessness. When they were put into cages with safety zones and lights warning of upcoming shocks, the rats continued taking the shocks rather than escaping. The control rats, who hadn't been previously shocked, easily avoided the shocks. When the light flashed, they quickly fled to the safety zone.

Rats who developed learned helplessness demonstrated motivational problems. They had difficulty handling ordinary tasks and rarely engaged in activities that were life improving. They no longer paid much attention to the world around them. When they would attempt to cope, they showed confusion, not knowing if their efforts were working. They didn't interact with the world in the same way that normal rats did.

Another scientist, Donald Hiroto, has conducted experiments showing how little it takes to create learned helplessness in humans. First, he exposed a group of subjects to piercing noises they couldn't escape. The second group of subjects had access to a mechanism that turned off the noise. Later, when both groups were presented with a simple task that would end the noise, the first group did considerably worse, demonstrating learned helplessness. They also showed diminished abilities in performing other tasks, such as solving word puzzles and functioning in social coping situations. The deficits led to feelings of hopelessness, lowered self-confidence, poor problem solving, and a limited attention span.

Learned helplessness is common in alcoholic families. A close relationship with an alcoholic or addict causes prolonged, unpredictable stress and a sense of having no control. Families never know what the alcoholic or addict might do next, and nothing they do stops it from happening. This creates laboratory-perfect conditions for learned helplessness.

It's easy to recognize family members who are impaired by learned helplessness. When offered help, they usually refuse to take it. Much like the animals being shocked, they don't see a way out. They famously use the phrase "yes, but . . ." to dismiss solutions. They can't believe anything could possibly work. Efforts to help an addicted loved one will be hampered by a family member who suffers from learned helplessness.

Michael, a forty-five-year-old husband and father, is addicted to alcohol and sedatives. His older sister, Betsy, decides something must be done after he's lost yet another job. Their parents are retired and can't keep bailing him out financially. She approaches Kathleen, her brother's wife, who agrees to help her intervene. But as Betsy moves forward, consulting with a clinical interventionist and building a family team, Kathleen begins subtly sabotaging the process. She's too busy with the children to attend a meeting. She isn't sure, anymore, that intervention is the best idea. She talks to Michael's parents without Betsy knowing, telling them about promising job interviews. "Treatment is going to interfere with Michael getting a job," she says. Betsy finally confronts Kathleen out of frustration, asking, "Don't you even care about your kids?" But Kathleen can't see solutions. Instead, she talks in circles about why Michael will never accept treatment. Lacking the ability to evaluate her situation properly, Kathleen can't organize her resources in ways that might protect her children or help her husband. In anger, Betsy lashes out: "You are keeping my brother sick! You are crazier than he is!"

Not understanding how Kathleen's learned helplessness is related to the crisis of addiction, the entire family defines Kathleen as "a little nutty." Intervention plans fall apart, Michael gets another job, and the addiction goes unaddressed. Betsy never forgives Kathleen, and family relationships sour. The entire debacle has made it much easier for Michael's addiction to progress unchallenged.

This same situation is approached very differently when the family quickly understands that Kathleen is experiencing learned helplessness. Rather than thinking she is "sick," they realize she is responding to the ongoing crisis in an expected manner that is beyond her control. Kathleen can't see how she's been changed by her husband's addiction.

Betsy and her parents temporarily postpone the intervention and call a meeting with other relatives who are close to Michael and Kathleen—a favorite uncle and aunt, a cousin, and a younger brother. They create a recovery team and initiate Structured Family Recovery. By doing so, they demonstrate something very important to Kathleen: You are not alone. As a family, we are standing together. We are here for you, Michael, and the children, not for a few days or weeks, but for the long haul. The family creates a growing sense of safety for Kathleen, presenting her with an entire team of trusted people to lean on.

By participating in Structured Family Recovery—before, during, and after treatment—Kathleen isn't the only one who benefited. Stress throughout the entire family began to dissipate. Michael achieved more than lasting sobriety. He found a closeness with his family he hadn't felt in a very long time.

When it comes to the disease of addiction, the costs are too great to ignore, and they are not limited to the person doing the drinking or drugging. Some people give addiction a pass, saying, "He's not hurting anyone but himself, so if that's what he wants to do, let him." This simply isn't true. Addiction hurts everyone close to the alcoholic in very real ways. Addiction is everybody's business, and so is recovery.

We Begin and End with Family

A woman recently said to me, "My sister and I disagree on many things, but I know if life hands me a lemon, she's the one who'll be there holding my hand." After all, the highest goal of any family is to sustain its members. It's telling how often we hear someone say, in the face of loss or tragedy, "As long as I have my family, I can overcome anything."

There is so much talk about *dysfunctional families,* but I think this catchphrase does us a disservice. What exactly does it mean to be dysfunctional, and who decides? Where do we draw the line between functional and dysfunctional? Does this word unfairly imply something is inherently wrong with the many families who are responding to crisis?

I find it interesting that families facing the crisis of addiction are commonly called dysfunctional, yet the same word isn't prevalent when describing families who are responding to Alzheimer disease, another brain disease. Both groups often cope with years of crisis and similar correlating emotions and consequences: denial, depression, anxiety, guilt, anger, uncertainty, grief, isolation, embarrassment, secret keeping, multiple losses over time, difficulty explaining the illness to others, concerns about safety, not knowing where to turn for help, and financial stress.

To call a family dysfunctional is stigmatizing. It is far more accurate and supportive to describe a family coping with addiction as *a family in crisis.* By doing so, we remove the implication that something is wrong with the people who make up the family. Instead, we signal that they are in a state of emergency and in need of help. Most of us, when called dysfunctional, will adopt a defensive position. But when other people acknowledge our suffering and see the truth of our crisis, there is a sense of being cared about and understood. Others are more willing to reach out to a family in crisis than to a family labeled as dysfunctional. One elicits compassion, the other condescension.

Families living with addiction know too well how this disease breaks down relationships. Many books recount the devastation. But rarely do we talk about the many noble ways families demonstrate resiliency. Working with families of alcoholics and addicts for more than twenty years, I've stood in awe of families time after time. Determined to help someone they love get into treatment, fortitude and goodness of spirit is the norm, not the exception. They sacrifice so much and work so hard to ignite a spark of willingness in their addict. After receiving solid, reliable direction, they follow instructions willingly, show amazing vulnerability, and drop their resentments and anger in favor of love. They walk through fear and trepidation to do what needs to be done. They put aside differences and hurts in favor of what is important for the well-being of the addict and the family.

So often when I meet with a family preparing to do an intervention, the first thing they do is show me photos of their beloved addicted son, brother, mother, daughter, father, or sister. They want me to see the real person—the person they cherish—so that I'll know there is more to him than addiction. It's the humanity of the person they want to share—the kind heart, sense of humor, generosity. "He's a good son and a good friend," they might say, and then tell me all the wonderful things about him. And I want to hear these things, because then I know what this family is fighting for. It is the magnificence of the loved one, not the addiction, that inspires everything we do. Standing up to addiction requires the fuel of love.

The alcoholic may seem undeserving in a thousand ways, and the family may be seething with anger, but under it all lies the smoldering power of love. That's what drives families. Love. Not wimpy sentimentalism, but courageous, never-giving-up love. I've worked with families who struggled to think of nice things to say about their alcoholic or addict, but they, too, were there to intervene against the disease because of love. Some might say this is illogical, but in spite of the many difficulties they may have had with the addict, they share a rich and complex history that isn't always easy to capture in words. If we fail to factor in the power of belonging to one another, we'll rarely understand the true depth of family relationships.

Several years ago, I began working with a mother concerned about an adult daughter. The professional who referred her to me warned that she was impossible to work with and exhibited signs of emotional insta-bility, so I was expecting the worst. During our first meeting, however, it became clear to me that she was simply a mother who wasn't going to let anyone tell her she couldn't do anything more to help her daugh-ter. She was dogged and intense, but her resoluteness was understand-able, and she made sense. Her only child was a bright, beautiful young woman terribly addicted to alcohol and other drugs. She had watched over the years as addiction robbed her daughter of all her accomplish-ments and left her dependent on any man who would have her. Now, she believed, her daughter was at risk of dying. She was going to do what-ever it took to turn things around and make sure her daughter had a chance at life, and she didn't care what anyone else thought. Together we devised a well-thought-out plan, designed not only for her daugh-ter's needs, but possibly more important, built to her strengths. It was by invoking a higher calling that we reached her daughter's heart, creating enough spiritual clarity to give her the capability of saying yes to receiv-ing the help she needed.

When families are not given a meaningful role to play after their loved ones enter treatment and recovery, and don't have a clear direc-tion in the recovery process, they often start falling apart. Teams cre-ated for the single purpose of intervention splinter, and the momentum dies. Feeling out of the loop, family members can retreat into relying on old survival skills. Where once they used these skills for dealing with ad-diction's crises, now they attempt to apply them to addiction's recovery. Using the old ways in this new world of recovery won't work. Just as ad-dicts cannot bring the old ways of an addiction lifestyle into recovery, families cannot keep using their old coping methods if they hope to sup-port recovery for the addict and the family.

Our strengths—the bedrock of who we are—are often buried under the many disturbed emotions that come with our response to addiction. We can't always feel love because anger, recrimination, and hurt seem more urgent and truer at times. But these are simply clouds—family symptoms of the disease of addiction that prevent healing for the addict and her loved ones. It's not unusual for families to hang on to disturbed emotions in the same way alcoholics hang on to drugs. Oftentimes, an alcoholic is in recovery, yet her family refuses to move forward. Without a way to embrace their own recovery, her family members are still tending to their anger.

Have we been trained to always look for the negative in our families? We can just as easily, and with better results, view each other with understanding and compassion. Just as medicine is changing to be more health-oriented rather than disease-oriented, we need to be more strength-oriented when talking and thinking about our families. This requires a clear-eyed inventory of ourselves that will allow us to make decisions to let go of what isn't congruent with our values.

Structured Family Recovery is about strengths—the ones we have and the ones we need. Over time, the crisis of addiction creates unhealthy patterns in families. Engaging in recovery as a team changes these patterns in much the same way a solid recovery program changes the alcoholic or addict. We can learn to loosen our grip on disturbed emotions just as the addict loosens his grip on drugs and the emotional and spiritual damage they've caused.

Utilizing the wisdom of the Twelve Steps, Structured Family Recovery promises a spiritual change that can reveal who we really are as a family. As the haze of fear and mistrust lifts, our true selves are revealed. We see our loved ones for who they truly are again. We witness this powerful spiritual shift that comes with recovery, not just in behaviors, but in the very countenance of addicts and their loved ones—the look in their eyes, the sound of their voices, the glow of their skin. Healing truly changes a family.

11

Don't Forget the Children

By age three, a child's brain is twice as active as an adult's. During the teenage years, the brain is going through the last phase of rapid development. If toxic stress interrupts any of these prime periods of brain growth, a child's development is compromised.

While toxic stress is occurring, whichever brain system is developing at that time will be affected. The hippocampus, important for learning and memory, is most vulnerable to stress before the age of twelve. The prefrontal cortex, responsible for cognition, personality, decision making, and social behavior, is most susceptible between ages twelve and eighteen. By introducing recovery into addicted homes at the earliest possible time, we can reduce stress and create emotional environments that allow children's brains to develop in normal and healthy ways.

Since young brains still have a high degree of neuroplasticity, they can begin to reorganize if given the opportunity. There is no better reason for an entire family to pursue recovery together. An alcoholic going through treatment by herself isn't enough. We all need to participate in the recovery process if we hope to heal as a family. We may fool or trick ourselves into believing otherwise, but brains of children won't be deceived.

Sis Wenger, president emeritus of the National Association for Children of Alcoholics and advocate for children who suffer from adversity due to addiction in the family, says, "In the face of clear evidence that children with alcohol- or drug-addicted parents are harmed emotionally and sometimes physically, we are stunned that so many children are allowed to suffer in silence without any meaningful intervention or support from adults they encounter in their everyday life."

In any given addicted family, there are many people who could break the silence and potentially change the trajectory of a child's life. Sadly, most people do nothing—not because they are uncaring, but because they can't see a workable solution. But solutions exist. When families work together, including grandmothers and grandfathers, aunts, uncles, godparents, friends—whoever is close enough to care—we have power that can be harnessed for the good of the child. When we join together as a family recovery team, we accomplish amazing things, even things we cannot see, that have profound and lifelong effects on our children.

When an addicted woman is pregnant, swift action is required. *Intervention* has become a household word. Done properly, with good guidance, family interventions are very successful. If you are concerned about a pregnant mother, locate a clinical interventionist to help you get her into treatment immediately.

Getting the addicted parent into treatment is just a beginning. Too many go to treatment, stay sober for weeks or months, and then relapse, plunging the entire family back into turmoil. Structured Family Recovery is important for keeping recovery on track and building a family recovery team that protects the children. The youngest in our families need trusted loved ones who are capable of helping them, especially when their parents cannot.

Consistency offers children a predictable world. They need to know what to expect in their daily lives. Beyond sobriety, children need harmony and love. They need regular schedules, so they know what time to go to bed, what time to wake up, and when they're going to eat. They need to know the rules and the consequences of breaking the rules. They need play and laughter. They need to trust. With consistency, they don't need to worry so much. Their brains can open up to all the good things the world has to offer them.

In Structured Family Recovery, we build great families. We want the kids to grow up saying, "I am the luckiest person ever! I grew up in the greatest family!" Recovery, after all, is about finally finding happiness. Children thrive when home life is happy. It creates wonderful futures and marvelous memories. We grow together rather than apart. As children get older, marry, and have families of their own, they come back to us with love. They want to spend time together. Siblings like each other and are good friends. We change the future of our family by what we do today.

Sister Molly Monahan says it best in her book *Seeds of Grace* when she speaks of families in recovery:

> Imagine the lives of those babies if their alcoholic parent or parents were still drinking. The erratic behavior, the emotional turmoil, the fights, the terror, the shame they would experience. Instead, even given the genetic factor in the disease of alcoholism, there is a good chance that the awful chain linking one alcoholic generation to another will be broken.

Recovery often happens later in life, when children have been living with the addiction for years—or even their whole lives. Some children might be in kindergarten or third grade or middle school or older before a parent gets help. Just because a child's mom or dad or brother or granddad is sober, that doesn't mean all of the child's troubles are solved. The child needs a place to begin healing, time to reframe the experiences of a parent or other family member's addiction, and the chance to learn about the gifts of recovery. Children impacted by a parent's addiction need to understand, both in their heads and their hearts, that they didn't cause the addiction. They need to know it isn't something Mom or Dad purposely did to them but is a sickness that hurt everybody and is no one's fault. They also need to understand that there are things people do to get well from this disease all the time.

If at all possible, your recovery team should find a facility that has a children's program. If one isn't available, get help from a therapist who specializes in working with children of alcoholics. This can provide a strong foundation for children as they participate in Structured Family Recovery at whatever level their age allows. They will discover their own roles in the mutual healing that takes place. Too often, families don't make this choice because they are still mired in secrets and shame. Both are terribly toxic for these little souls. Our secrets and shame are often the reasons we are afraid to get help for our children. But children's programs, family therapy, and Structured Family Recovery can liberate a child from the grip of this disease and, as a result, the entire family can experience a new freedom.

When young children go through programs designed just for them, learning about addiction and recovery in a manner they can readily absorb, they demonstrate acceptance and love in amazing ways. Children can inspire the whole family. They stand up and say, "This is my dad," pushing out their little chests with pride. "He has a disease. It's not my fault, and it's not his fault. But he's getting better, and he loves me."

Today's children get help at much younger ages than at any other time in history, experiencing the joys of recovery as they grow and develop. Where children once entered adulthood carrying all of the pain brought on by growing up in an addicted home, parents now have resources to help their children grow up with skills and tools that prepare them for dealing with the daily challenges of life. The Hazelden Betty Ford Foundation has pioneered a marvelous program for children. Besides its own program, which focuses on children ages seven through twelve, it offers listings of other programs available around the country. Call them and ask.

Jerry Moe, director of the Hazelden Betty Ford Children's Program, says:

> It takes much courage and strength for parents or grandparents to bring kids to the children's program. With the silence and secrecy so pervasive in addicted families, many children make up a story to make sense of all the stress and chaos. These stories are usually way off base and add to the guilt and shame children carry. Without

help, these stories can become life scripts which severely limit one's potential and actualization. Providing accurate age-appropriate information about this insidious disease helps children to realize that it's not their fault, they are not to blame, and they are not alone. This liberates kids in enormous ways.

Then equipping youth with a "feelings vocabulary," a safe place with structure and consistency, and counselors who listen with their hearts encourages kids to get real by pouring out their feelings, worries, and concerns. Slowly, their true self emerges. Empowering them with coping skills, self-care strategies, and ways to stay safe gives them hope. Children build a strong spiritual connection to the group and one another as they truly believe they belong. The beginning of a new future blooms as the possibility of changing the family legacy takes root.

12

Our Beloved Alcoholic or Addict Pays Dearly

As you venture forward into the next section of the book, remember that addiction is a chronic disease with no cure. Alcoholics and addicts have to get drunk or high, but they aren't having fun while they do it. They may say they like to drink or drug, but it's more like having a burning itch that must be scratched. It's a great relief while you're scratching, but the itch never goes away. A friend of mine, a former heroin addict with decades of abstinence-based recovery in AA, described what he thought families most needed to know about a loved one who is addicted: "They really, really need to understand it's a disease. Regardless of how their alcoholic or addict behaves, at the very root, they wake up every morning terrified. They live in a constant state of dread. They hate their lives. They see it as nothing more than overcoming one obstacle after another."

In a video essay entitled "Pleasure Unwoven," Dr. Kevin McCauley points out that when people say they are "craving" chocolate, they mean they really want chocolate a lot. "Craving for an addict," he explains, "is an intense emotional obsessive experience. The addict wants to think about other things, but his brain is constantly bringing him back to the drug. The addict is up in the middle of the night, can't sleep, his pulse is at 120, and he's thinking over and over again, 'Just one more time.' That's craving, and make no mistake, that is genuine suffering."

Addiction tricks the brain into believing that the alcohol or drug, above everything else, is the most important thing for survival. The drug and survival become indistinguishable. As Dr. McCauley makes clear, addicts' behaviors can be very bad, but bad acts do not equal bad actors. The degradation of behavior and morals is symptomatic of the disease's disruption of the brain.

The anonymous author of *Mr. SponsorPants: An AA Sponsor Blog*, explains the difference between a problem drinker and an alcoholic.

> The problem drinker gets pulled over and arrested for driving under the influence. Sitting in the holding tank, they shake their head and think to themselves, "Man, not my brightest move. Maybe I should cool it a little. At the very least, I should have called a taxi or something."
>
> The alcoholic gets pulled over and arrested for driving under the influence. Sitting in the holding tank, they shake their head and think to themselves, "[Damn] cops. Next time I should take surface streets."
>
> Alcoholics are wired for defiance, and an inability to take responsibility for our actions—when under the influence of alcoholism, it is almost impossible for us to see—and believe—a cause and effect between what we do and what happens to us.

Also writing anonymously in the Big Book of Alcoholics Anonymous, a physician shared about his life as an alcoholic and addict (in the chapter "Acceptance Was the Answer"). His words provide more insight into how trying to manage the disease of addiction on your own leads to a downward spiral, even when the person suffering from it is a well-educated medical professional.

> I drank my way through schools and always got honors. And as I went through pharmacy school, graduate school, medical school, internship, residency, and specialty training and, finally, went into practice, my drinking kept increasing.... The longer the drinking continued, the shorter

the time alcohol would keep me asleep; I would have to drink myself back to sleep again and again throughout the night. . . . It became progressively harder to get up in the morning, until one day I asked myself what I would do for a patient who felt this rotten. The answer came right back: I'd give him something to pep him up. So, I immediately started taking and shooting pep pills. . . . I'd take tranquilizers to level off. . . . [In the garage], I would put the needle in my vein and then try to figure out exactly how much medication to inject to overcome the pep pills . . . in order to get just enough to be able to pull out the needle, jerk the tourniquet, throw it in the car, slam the car door shut, run down the hall, and fall in bed before I fell asleep." The addicted physician goes on to explain, "Before A.A., I judged myself by my intentions, while the world was judging me by my actions."

In the next chapter, we will hear from another addict, now in recovery. He describes what it's like to live with addiction and how his true self, still existing beneath the addiction, experienced the resulting negativity that infused all areas of his life—especially his relationships. With a clearer understanding of living with addiction, we will be better prepared to venture into the next section of the book and begin responding to the urgent need to make a strong commitment to move out of the problem and into the solution together.

13

A Conversation
with a Recovering Addict

James is in recovery from heroin, meth, and Xanax addiction. He's been clean and sober since May 1, 2016. We sat down and had a conversation with the purpose of learning how an addict experiences addiction, early recovery, and relationships. Many of the insights James provides are similar for those who are addicted to alcohol or other types of drugs.

> **Debra:** When we speak about alcoholics and addicts being in denial, people often struggle with this idea. They say, "You can't tell me that alcoholics don't know they're drinking or that addicts don't know they are shooting heroin or smoking crack." But denial is tricky and not always so obvious. For instance, alcoholics and addicts develop different narratives about themselves. These are stories designed to counter the reality of addiction. Was this your experience?

> **James:** Yes, it was an ever-changing image that I conjured up about myself. The further down I went, the more I'd cling to other versions of me. It might be the high school version when my drug use made me cool or charming or endearing or whatever. A time before my addiction hit a catastrophic end, and everybody could see what was happening and nobody wanted me around anymore. But in my mind, I was still the same

person I'd always been. The delusion got stronger and stronger as I became further and further removed from reality and everyone in my life. Being isolated for so long with addiction, whatever you conjured up in your mind is your perception. It's way off the mark from reality, as anybody close to an addict can tell, but in the addict's mind it all makes total sense. There's also so much imagery in our society to grab on to—like the successful rock star still doing drugs. It makes everything seem normal in your life of addiction. You never want to admit, I'm basically just a junkie cockroach and nothing more than that. I can't hold a job, I'm really capable of nothing, and I am a burden on my family and society at large.

Debra: Isolation is a common symptom of addiction, whether it's physical, emotional, or both. Did you create other stories in your head to combat the really awful realities of your addiction? Thinking you were going to achieve great things or that you knew better than everyone?

James: I believed I was going to change the world. I would sit reading books and articles and watching videos on quantum mechanics and particle physics. I would get these grandiose ideas. With the kinds of drugs I struggled with, I would some-times stay up for weeks on end, and obviously things would get very, very strange and chaotic. But when you are living this, it makes total sense to you. Families see their loved ones do the most insane things, but in the addict's mind, at that moment, it makes perfect sense.

Debra: When you talk about being isolated as an addict, can you describe what that was like for you?

James: Addiction is extremely isolating. At first it was exactly what I wanted. I just wanted to be left alone with a whole pile of drugs and no responsibilities. That's what I really wanted, and when I got it, I saw just how horrifying it was. It was not like walking through hell; it was like taking up residence in hell for a very long time. I felt there was no escape. I'd wake up every day and know it was going to be a little worse than the day before, which was a bad day in and of itself. That's a horrifying prognosis. Really, it's a fate worse than death. As far as the insane notions that we come up with in our minds, we're so isolated that there's no one to put our thoughts in check. So, they start to get crazier and crazier, but they make more and more sense to the addicted brain. I swear, for a long period of time after getting sober, I held resentments toward people for things they never even did to me. I know for a fact they didn't, because they weren't even there. But it was so real to me that I would have visceral responses to the memories. I was actually holding on to memories with my sane, sober mind that never happened. I was really hurt by these things I thought people did to me, as if they really happened.

Debra: The workings of a damaged brain can be quite interesting. The brain starts to confabulate—making things up. These confabulations are so real, the emotional brain continues to produce feelings of hurt even when you are confronted by the fact that it didn't happen.

James: Yes, I had actual physiological responses. It was so emotional that my heart rate would spike, and I'd feel all these things going on as if they really happened.

Debra: This brings me to something I think is difficult for families to understand. Addicted loved ones feel the hurt of everything that was said and done against them during their addiction. Once addicts get into recovery, hurts and resentments don't automatically vanish. While families still feel their pain and nurse many bad memories, they often don't see this as a two-way street. Newly recovering alcoholics and addicts struggle with the unkind words hurled at them during those difficult times too.

James: Yes, that's right. I mean, obviously people get hurt. Families are feeling hurt because the perception is that the addict is doing this to them. Today, I work with addicts living in a sober house, and I go through these same feelings. Emotionally, it's as if they are slighting me. It feels malicious. But it's not. It's absolutely not. I know better than that. So, obviously, I should be able to deal with the resulting emotions better than I do. Just think of how difficult it is for family members who really don't know anything about the internal workings of addiction and that it really isn't about them. Families are dealing with a person who is delusional because of the way the brain operates. I can see why my family felt the way they did. My parents were extremely frustrated with me and my addiction. Everything I said, after a time, was dismissed immediately. Nobody listened to me at all. In my addiction, I had no voice and, of course, it was justified because what I said didn't make any sense. What I was talking about wasn't good for me or anybody else. But with recovery, there's a point when the addict and family need to grow beyond this lack of trust. It has to change. When the addict starts doing the right thing, they've earned their voice back. With sound decision making and consistently doing the things recovery requires for staying sane and rational on a daily basis, addicts need to have a voice again. You can't go through life feeling like you're the scum of the earth and expect to be successful at any level.

Debra: I think you make a great point. I frequently talk about trustworthiness as the foundation of healthy, happy relationships, rather than love. We can love someone a great deal yet not have a good relationship with them. Both people in any relationship need to ask themselves, "Am I being trustworthy today?" Active addicts are not trustworthy. Enthusiastic Twelve Step recovery can transform addicts into trustworthy people. When a family doesn't join the recovery process, they can stay stuck in that place of not trusting, even after the addict is consistently demonstrating trustworthiness. The family remains in fear, which blocks trust. From your experience, would you talk about that a little bit?

James: I had gotten to a point in my addiction, obviously, that my word meant little to nothing. The dynamic in my family of origin had become toxic and sick. I had two parents who were in total opposite schools of thought. My dad was tough love. My mom was a habitual enabler and the one who really took the brunt of my addiction. Today, I have earned back their trust, and my family is, for the most part, good about it. But every once in a while, it gets thrown back in my face. You're not really capable of making good decisions. Many families who are dealing with an addict in recovery, without meaning to do this, have become kind of hooked on the idea that they can control their loved one to some degree. It might be toxic for the family, but you get some degree of control over active addicts because they have an agenda. Families learn how to work with that agenda. Once the addict is in stable recovery, to release that control or completely relinquish those constraints can be difficult. Families don't mean to do it; I'm sure of that. But it happens. It's frustrating to experience, especially as a grown man. I'm forty years old, and I don't want to be directed by my mother and my father. I love them dearly, and I do go to them for advice, but I don't want them running my life. I'm a father now. I'm successful in my recovery program. I have my own responsibilities. Like any other adult man, I'd like to exercise my own free will. I am not saying this too harshly because my parents aren't terrible with controlling behavior. I'm just saying that from time to time, it does come up. I think this tendency exists in every relationship, but in the addiction paradigm, family steps in a lot faster.

Debra: My husband is thirty-eight years sober from alcoholism, having entered recovery in his mid-twenties. Yet his mother every so often still grieves over his addiction and what everyone went through. She speaks of it emotionally, as if it happened yesterday. She'll talk about what it felt like to be sure her son would die. It feels to me as if the pain and fear are still very real to her. I also see how difficult it is for the recovering addict to fully shake the identity of active addict. It's always there, and it frightens families even years later.

James: I think it's a very real scar on the psyche. It's a trauma to everyone involved. As the addict, I certainly suffered my traumas, but in a different way. There is something a lot of people don't understand that's specific to opiate and heroin addiction, for instance. I've overdosed more times than I can remember, and I've been dead more times than I can count. I think most people would imagine that it would be so traumatic to overdose, you would stop using drugs. But I didn't even think about it. Overdosing was just like slipping into a warm bath. You wake up somewhere else, in the hospital or an ambulance, and that's weird, but it's not what people think it would be for the addict. On the other side of that, I've revived people who are dying, and it's horrifying to watch. It's far more traumatic reviving someone than it is to be overdosing yourself. Of course, during my addiction, I've been in horrible places and seen terrible things through all of this. I still carry those memories with me. But I can't imagine—now being a parent myself—having that sense of powerlessness while watching someone you love being destroyed by drugs or alcohol. All of us in the family have suffered a very real scar to the psyche. It can continue to direct our behaviors unintentionally. It's a part of us. But it is something I try to combat daily. I do a lot of work on myself in recovery to try to circumvent the trauma.

Debra: Which makes me think about why it's so important for families to participate in the recovery process—to create support for their addicted loved one, but also for their own emotional sobriety. Families are very affected by the addiction, even though they usually can't see it fully.

James: I think we are all better people for it, when we're properly directed as a whole into family recovery. If we use this as a way to work on ourselves—things we wouldn't have done otherwise—it can end up much better for us all.

Debra: You once talked to me about your experiences in treatment and your struggles. Do you want to elaborate?

James: I realize my struggles in treatment were coming from my inability to make good decisions, but I was still frustrated that some people in treatment would talk about me as if I wasn't even there. The problem is that, after a while, you get so used to it. It was as if I was a thirty-year-old man-child. I had no responsibilities, so I'd just go around and get into my next debauch. Someone would always come and bail me out. "This is my life," I would think. I was used to that kind of existence. It was so familiar. The feeling was as if I was capable of no better. At the same time, as I was going through treatment after treatment, I never saw myself as a bad guy. Even when I was a pain in the butt to everyone around me.

Debra: When addiction becomes the dominant feature in your life, everyone defines you that way. What you are saying makes me consider how Structured Family Recovery works and why it's so important for alcoholics and addicts. Structured Family Recovery reintegrates the newly recovering person, who has been existing under the domination of addiction, back into the family. Working together, the family starts to see their loved one becoming a powerful force for good in recovery. In this way, families come back together in spite of all the past pain.

James: The person in active addiction feels every bit of what is being directed at them, the sting and the burn. All of it has a long-term effect, because the addict remembers it once they are sober. Myself included. People become robotic in their response to addicts because addicts are difficult to deal with and a nuisance. It's so easy to dismiss everything they say and just step in to control. But, by doing that constantly, you are kind of neutering a person. I think treatment is an important thing for anyone who needs help. My problem was that I kept relapsing afterward. As a result, I was sent to treatment over and over again. I became very institutionalized. Consequently, I regressed back into a childlike state, on top of my addiction.

Debra: I would add that repeated relapse also results in a growing sense of hopelessness, for the addict as well as the family. That's a dangerous place. It can cause people to give up. Then the alcoholic or addict becomes even more isolated and vulnerable. How different is it when the family becomes an SFR team? When they invite the alcoholic or addict to join them in weekly SFR meetings before they leave treatment? Everyone moves forward in a positive direction and learns the language of recovery together. The addicted person stops feeling like the identified patient, isolated in that identity, and more like part of a team. How different is that experience?

James: That would be very helpful to someone getting into recovery. When the mind starts to defog a little bit, and the voraciousness of the addicted brain is toned down, that's when the recovering addict needs a voice to talk again. When I was newly in recovery, immediately everything I said was shot down by my father. He thought anything I said was nonsense and useless. It caused me to accept this role as a person who didn't get to say anything. I'm just going to be someone who is told where to go and what to do, I thought. This isn't healthy, and there is no way not to resent it. Because of this, in a sick way, I'd think, well then, I'll show you.

Debra: What you are describing is a continued state of fear-based conflict in the family, rather than recovery team unity. It happens because most families are left with nothing but their fear. We need cooperation and growth instead. Structured

Family Recovery opens up a positive place for addict and family. We can start hearing each other speak from a place of recovery, rather than from the world of addiction. Each is amazed to experience their family members from this new and better place. The strong partnership message from family reduces the probability of a return to alcohol or other drugs.

James: That's huge. In my early recovery, just participating in meetings and having people tell me I was doing a good job or that something I talked about touched them made me feel like I was a contributing member of society again. It was important to have that feeling because I didn't offer anything meaningful to anyone for so long. These meetings made me feel like I had some intrinsic value—and even my past experience, as horrifying as it was, had value too. These little things served as stepping-stones to self-betterment. *Maybe I can accomplish something.* The more families can cultivate this early on, the better the outcome will be, now and in the future. If I can feel valuable to my own family, that's something that tells me I have worth.

Debra: The first time I ever saw you was at a combined Al-Anon and AA meeting. You were about six months sober. Toward the end of the meeting, you shared your thoughts on your recovery journey and absolutely blew me away. I remember thinking, who is this? Your words made such a strong impression upon me. Within the context of the conversation we're having today, it makes me think how important it is to help families experience recovering loved ones in the same way—which can happen, of course, if they come together as family recovery teams.

James: Yes, I agree. I think it's important for family to play a critical part in the recovery process. Although the addicted person needs to follow certain behavioral expectations in recovery, it doesn't help when everything devolves into constant nagging. The passive-aggressive nature of the addict will then kick in, and they will become more resistant. The addict thinks, I'm being talked at all the time, so I'll just create a crisis. But when an entire family engages in recovery, making it their own with everyone a part of it, it brings family to a new place. From day one, as the addict, I am made to feel that I belong.

Debra: How do you experience your recovery now that you have achieved multiple years of sobriety?

James: My recovery today is something I really enjoy doing in this world. When you are addicted, you've been isolated for who knows how long. How are you supposed to get back to having a connection with others? This sense of belonging is imperative. I was reading a study that said the people in Denmark are the happiest people in the world. They attributed this to the fact that most people who live there belong to some kind of social group. I understand this well, because before I participated in recovery—even though I had stopped using drugs—I was thinking of killing myself every day. Once I joined a recovery program, I realized people were listening to me. In recovery, I found my voice. Interestingly, this true enjoyment of participating in recovery came about even though I was initially adamant that I wasn't going to go to AA—for what reason, I don't even know. Today, I am committed to it. I learned how to be a friend in AA and how to be there for other people. I learned not just to take from people, but to actually contribute. My circle of friends has grown far beyond my friends in AA, but it all started there. AA taught me how to properly treat a friend.

What We Need to Do

This section of the book is a road map, providing families with direction on how to put Structured Family Recovery into action. In the upcoming chapters, you will discover details organized in a clear and easy-to-follow manner. Families who begin Structured Family Recovery find meetings quickly feel comfortable and familiar. We begin to see the rewards before much time has passed. By launching Structured Family Recovery, your family is doing something that moves you toward your ultimate goal: being happy again.

While many families may choose to work with an SFR counselor, this section is also written for families who will build a team and engage in Structured Family Recovery without a trained SFR counselor.

14

It Takes a Family

From the beginning, we've had family, sometimes with great joy and other times sorrow. It is our most cherished institution, and the health of the family is a reflection of each member within it. Our definition of family may vary—the one we were born or adopted into or the one we created—but the value of family is uncontested. Our very nature depends on sharing a common life with other people. As author and family specialist David Mace puts it, "Nothing in the world could make human life happier than to greatly increase the number of strong families." If we've lost family to death, divorce, abandonment, or other crises, we can create new families with people in our lives whom we trust and love.

All families face crisis at one time or another; it's how we handle crisis that determines our welfare. While some crises are irreversible, addiction is not one of them. It is the most treatable chronic illness. When we compare addiction to other brain diseases—like Alzheimer and Parkinson diseases—we understand why we have hope. Recovery is not only possible, but those who achieve recovery live full and productive lives.

Structured Family Recovery brings family into the middle of recovery and adds an essential ingredient: love. An SFR family explained it this way: "Structured Family Recovery taught us how to love. It totally changed our perspective and practice of love. We learned to love our addict, each other, ourselves, those who were helping us, and the families out there who were still suffering. Structured Family Recovery removed those things that kept us from fully loving."

Before putting Structured Family Recovery into action, we need to review some key points from the previous chapters. Much of this information is counterintuitive, and without reinforcing these ideas, our common sense can lead us astray. The power of addiction is not to be underestimated. Standing up to it requires that we are prepared.

1. Treatment only addresses the acute stage of addiction.

Treatment plays a very important role for many addicted people who might not succeed without it. It addresses the most severe physical, mental, and spiritual symptoms of addiction. Treatment centers cannot cure addiction, but they can prepare alcoholics and addicts for their return home. The best centers give graduates an aftercare plan, including working a Twelve Step recovery program. Beyond providing aftercare plans, treatment programs do not attend to the chronic nature of addiction. This process begins when treatment ends. It happens primarily in Twelve Step groups and by an addict's work rebuilding relationships at home, at work, in their place of worship (if they are religious), and in their community. Since addicts often don't comply with their aftercare plans or embrace Twelve Step recovery—or do so inconsistently— relapse rates during the chronic phase of the disease are high.

2. Relapse isn't random.

Relapse is a sign that something is missing in a recovery program, usually as a result of underestimating the disease and what it takes to stay sober. Many alcoholics and addicts don't have adequate support in early recovery, and without it, relapse is all too common. We know how addicted people succeed and how they fail—it isn't a guessing game. Addicts who respect the chronic nature of their disease by working a consistent and honest Twelve Step recovery program and restoring key relationships for support at home and in the community have high success rates; those who don't usually drink or use again.

3. A high percentage of addicted doctors succeed, but not because they are doctors.

Doctors are neither easy to treat nor compliant. These professionals are the recovery winners because they engage in a five-year plan of action, called a Physician Health Program (PHP). The expectation of PHPs is that everyone will succeed and consistently work a Twelve Step recovery program. The focus is on supporting recovery behaviors. In the first five years of recovery, 78 percent of doctors with PHPs never have a single relapse. With Structured Family Recovery, we can create a plan of action with similar goals, structures, and supports, greatly reducing the probability of relapse.

4. Motivation and education do not drive long-term success.

As decades of research shows us, our beliefs about the role of motivation in creating lasting change are wrong. Motivation works in the short term, much like a sprint in the long-distance race of recovery. Education is beneficial for breaking through denial, but it isn't a reliable way to change behavior. When we attempt to change attitudes to change behaviors, we have it backward; we change behaviors in order to change attitudes. Social norms—what other people are doing or saying in modeling behavior—are a leading force for change. We win when we keep things simple and doable with immediate rewards and use concrete calls to action that trigger new behaviors. Changed behavior is the key to long-term success in sobriety.

5. Enabling addiction is a misguided strategy.

When families enable alcoholics or addicts, they do so to save themselves. When an alcoholic hits bottom, the family usually does too. Enabling is a way family members try to prevent this from happening. These rescue behaviors are seen as a promise for something better or a guard against something worse. Most people want solutions that heal the family, and enabling is often their well-meaning attempt to help survive the crisis of addiction.

6. Enabling recovery changes the dynamic.

With good direction, efforts that were once directed toward enabling addiction can be redirected to become forces for supporting and sustaining recovery. When families transform themselves into recovery teams, they create new social norms based on recovery behaviors. Everyone in the family begins speaking the language of recovery.

7. Families can make all the difference.

Structured Family Recovery transforms recovery into a shared journey the family takes together with the newly recovering alcoholic or addict. It creates positive social norms, behavioral expectations, tiny tasks, triggers for enabling recovery, accountability, structure, family cohesiveness, and fun, and it serves as a relapse prevention program. It does all this while keeping it simple.

Recovery from addiction is a process of changing behaviors. Changed behavior regularly practiced will change our thinking. Ultimately, it changes us spiritually. There are no magic solutions or pills that can do what we can do for ourselves. I am thankful for that, because if there were, we'd miss out on one of the greatest journeys a family can take together.

15

Begin with a Team

As long as we live and breathe, we have the choice to do something different, to move forward, to embrace solutions. We can't see future results from where we stand at any given moment—especially at the beginning of change. We must live our results one day at a time. With Structured Family Recovery, we do this not in isolation, but as a team.

Alcoholics and addicts do not find lasting, contented sobriety in isolation, either. Treatment and recovery programs are designed to take advantage of the power of peer groups. Intervention works by harnessing the influence of groups. Family (however defined) is the most consistent group in the lives of most people. Those who are addicted are no exception. There aren't enough professionals—or money—to replace family when it comes to securing recovery.

Family is widely understood as the nucleus of civilization. Families are also the social building blocks of societies. When we look at the etymology of the word *family,* we learn that it originates from the Latin word *famulus,* which means servant. As family, we serve each other. In the 1611 publication of the Authorized Version of the Bible, the word was used to mean tribe. Over a 200-year period, from the seventeenth to nineteenth century, the word came to mean "near kin" or what today we call extended family. Structured Family Recovery works precisely because it supports the emotional magnitude and structural stability of family and uses these strengths to establish lasting recovery.

Since the 1950s, families in the United States have been identifying themselves primarily as nuclear families—a mother, father, and children. But, for all of history prior, we lived within extended families made up of a variety of kin. Nuclear families work fairly well—as long as everything stays in good order. When a big enough crisis hits, however, the separate and smaller structure of the nuclear family begins to crack. In an article in *The Atlantic* entitled "The Nuclear Family Was a Mistake," David Brooks writes: "Nuclear families in this era were much more connected to other nuclear families than they are today—constituting a 'modified extended family'. . . a coalition of nuclear families in a state of mutual dependence." Brooks goes on to explain that we increasingly became isolated from other nuclear families and, as a result, the "sheltered family of the 1950s was supplanted by the stressed family every decade since."

The structure of a nuclear family has a hard time holding up when faced with the addiction of one or more of its members. For this reason, when we choose an SFR team, we look beyond the nuclear family as a way to stabilize the family structure. We choose from our grandparents, aunts, uncles, godparents, and close friends with family-like relationships. If these people don't exist in our lives, or aren't reliable in ways that will support recovery, we can assemble our own version of an extended family with significant others beyond family. We go with what we have.

We can directly compare the fundamentals of Structured Family Recovery to a winning sports team. The Association for Applied Sport Psychology's website describes teams at their best: "High-performing teams are high in cohesiveness, shared understanding, and a sense of team confidence . . . even a team full of stars needs to bond, establish coordination mechanisms, and develop a collective belief in the unit's potential to be successful." Winning teams share a sense of purpose with clearly defined goals. Equally important is developing a sense of trust and mutual support. Families accomplish all of these things by simply following the SFR process. The result is a positive family team culture, something dearly needed after enduring active addiction.

Sports psychologists and coaches also identify what causes teams to collapse. A family team is wise to avoid stumbling blocks that include blaming others, individualization, lack of accountability, negative thinking, negative emotions, negative communication, overconfidence, perceived helplessness, and team underperformance. Each member's commitment to the SFR process will help families avoid these pitfalls. As Vince Lombardi famously said, "Individual commitment to a group effort—that is what makes a team work, a company work, a society work, a civilization work." It's also what makes a family work.

Like sports teams, families don't always start out with cohesiveness between teammates. Sometimes the current state of relationships is rocky. Many families who begin Structured Family Recovery have been on that rocky road for quite a while. What matters is not where we start, but where we are going. We are walking away from chaos into the manageable world of recovery. The recovery process itself knits our relationships back together. Many families with relationships complicated and compromised by the corrosive nature of addiction quickly bond when coming together as an SFR team.

Family members rarely refuse an invitation to join an SFR team. If they do object, it's often because they mistakenly conflate Structured Family Recovery with family therapy, imagining that family members will begin pointing out one another's shortcomings. These potential team members need to clearly understand that this does not happen in Structured Family Recovery. We don't tell other people what they feel or think. The experience is positive, forward looking, and collaborative. We don't cross talk. The overarching feeling is constructive and encouraging. We cultivate love and togetherness. As we practice this, we begin to feel secure in our goodness as a family, and our time together reflects this goodness. We begin to experience the liberating nature of recovery. We can finally leave crisis mode behind. This allows our brains to relax and open up. As this happens, our perceptions expand and our thinking clears. Calm brains are good thinking brains.

Team size varies from family to family. Be sure to include people who should definitely be part of the team—typically, this is your inner circle. As a general rule of thumb, these are the people who would feel comfortable sitting in pajamas around the breakfast table together. While an employer might be part of an intervention team, for example, she wouldn't join the SFR team unless she is truly like family. Structured

Family Recovery is different from intervention. If you have an intervention team assembled, select the people from that team who fit the criteria for an SFR team.

Team members are people who have close, intimate relationships with the whole family (including the addicted loved one). For instance, an SFR team for a thirty-two-year-old addicted son who is in treatment or newly recovering could include Mom and Dad (even if they are divorced), a favorite uncle, siblings, and a best friend. In another scenario, an appropriate team for a fifty-five-year-old alcoholic father and husband who is in treatment or newly recovering might include his wife, his adolescent or adult children, his mother and father, and his brother. Teams can be smaller. Sometimes an addicted person has few people in his life—maybe only a spouse and a close friend. In other circumstances, the team may not include any blood relatives, just friends who have become a family of choice. Since meetings take place over conference calls or by using other technologies, people can be located anywhere in the world.

SFR team members don't have to be abstinent from alcohol themselves, but they can't be addicted to any mood-altering substances (including alcohol). As far as the number of people to include, we usually keep teams to six people or less. If you have more people, you can extend your meeting length beyond one hour or keep your sharing time shorter. Whatever you decide, make sure the team agrees on the specifics and sticks to it every week.

If you don't have the makings of a team, you and your recovering loved one can still engage in Structured Family Recovery. Work with a therapist certified in Structured Family Recovery. A professional trained in Structured Family Recovery can help fill out your team and give you the extra substance you need.

One more thought on team selection: if any family member or other person has behaved in any way toward the addicted person or anyone else in the family that is morally and/or legally wrong, do not ever include that person on the team. For instance, someone who is a perpetrator or abuser is not safe as a team member. If abuse is active, contact an appropriate professional for guidance. If vulnerable people are at risk, contact the authorities.

Once you have a team, start by reading the introduction and chapters 1 through 4. (The chapters are short, so it's not a lot to ask.) These first pages prove again and again to be effective at creating team cohesiveness. Ask each person to get the book right away or send out copies to them. People can find the book in public libraries, buy it online, or get it from their favorite bookseller. To make reading simple for team members, use good behavior design. Set a behavioral expectation and pair it with a positive social norm. Everyone on the team is committing to read seven pages a day. Overcome the brain's objection to anything that seems hard. For most people, this takes about twelve minutes. Design for the behavior. "I will be reading my seven pages every day with my morning coffee. I'm keeping my book in the kitchen so it's always handy. When can you read yours?" If you use behavior design techniques with each team member, you will see a higher degree of success. Getting everyone started is what makes everything else possible. Recall what drives the formation of new habits. If we aren't clear about goals and the tiny tasks that actually make change work, then we are subject to daily levels of motivation, which are unreliable. As recovering alcoholics and addicts frequently say, "Action before motivation!"

Sometimes objections will float through your team members' minds. *His problem hasn't really affected me. It's her problem, not mine. I'm too fed up to get involved. I don't have time. I'm done.* Thoughts like these may be the biggest culprit for collapsing teams. They arise from a mindset that sports psychologists and coaches warn their players against: individualization. When participation is viewed as primarily about me, we don't have a team; we have a group of individuals. There is a big difference between the two. All of these objections are focused essentially on ourselves in relation to one person—our addicted loved one (more accurately, the addiction itself). The addiction has victimized us, too, and it's natural to want to back away. When we shift our focus to the big picture—the state of our family—we experience a shift in our emotional response. *This is killing my mother. His children's brain development is being changed by his crack addiction. Her alcoholism is dividing the family. His heroin addiction is bringing our parents to the brink of divorce. My kids are never going to know their grandmother. Dad's death will forever change the legacy of our family. If our child dies before us, we will never overcome the grief.* Structured Family Recovery isn't about any one of us or about the addict alone. It is always about family and who we are as a collective. We each have our individual lives, but we are ultimately defined by family.

16

How Do I Talk to My Addict?

Fresh out of treatment, alcoholics and addicts are often tired of being the center of attention. Although the years of family upset and commotion were symptoms of a disease, most families haven't understood this in a meaningful way. They've connected their hurt and fear to the addict himself—with their anger and frustration directed at him instead of the disease. That difference may seem subtle, but it doesn't feel that way to the addict. *I'm sick of everyone jumping all over me and talking about me behind my back!* This is surprising to families, shocked by the idea that the addict would dare accuse them after all they've been through. To addicts, their family's attempts to survive the onslaught of addiction felt like a war of words and ill treatment directed at them.

So, when an addict returns from treatment, these feelings of anger and resentment still linger. She's been the problem in the family for a long time. Shipped off to treatment, she became "the patient." Now home again, she's the point of contention for the train wreck she left behind and a person under suspicion because the possibility of relapse lurks around every corner. All eyes are on her, always (and for good reason, from the family's perspective). This is emotionally exhausting. She may lash out at the suspicion—not to mention the real and implied accusations—causing more reason for the family to worry and wonder. With both addict and family fearfully focused on each other, and with each harboring unrealistic expectations, everyone can get fed up pretty quickly. The cycle of mistrust and recrimination can build on itself and eventually undermine everyone's recovery efforts. Left unchecked, the family falls back to old enabling ways that provide peace in the moment, giving little consideration about how the problems will grow in the future. Everybody crashes back into crisis mode.

It doesn't have to be like this. There are ways for family members to communicate with the addict that intentionally break this cycle. We can establish terms for our relationships that are different from what they've been in the past. We do this through actions that are transparent and true to ourselves. We demonstrate group support of our alcoholic while simultaneously participating in the recovery process for ourselves. In other words, we attend our SFR meetings and work a Twelve Step family recovery program. The effect on our loved ones can be profound. Initially they may be suspicious of our motives or assume we won't follow through. But if we demonstrate commitment and perseverance, they will notice. They're likely to experience a quiet, growing respect for us and begin to internalize the recovery norms that we are modeling.

Structured Family Recovery is about the family, not the alcoholic. Because we have all shared in the disease, we all need to share in recovery. The message is "This is something we are doing for ourselves as a family. We would really like you to join us because our family isn't complete without you. Recovery is about bringing happiness and fun back to our family by all of us healing together."

Reaching toward positive goals doesn't mean we're ignoring the messes needing attention and the problems that need solving. Addiction can play havoc on every area of our lives. But we can choose whether we sort things out as adversaries or as partners. Alcoholics and addicts emerge from treatment overwhelmed by what they need to do to straighten out their lives. Working the Twelve Steps with a sponsor helps guide them in doing the right things and painstakingly repair the damages to their body, mind, and spirit. Structured Family Recovery welcomes them into a family that joins this journey. Working together keeps us all focused on recovery. By trusting the process, we can feel a little calmer. There is a path to follow. Life will come back together.

With Structured Family Recovery, recovery becomes a two-way street. We share with the family what we've learned in Al-Anon, or our little lightbulb moments during our daily meditation, or the insights we receive by working a particular Step. When these moments are truly for and about our recovery (and not a thinly veiled attempt to influence the addict), they create connection, belonging, and trust. When we share our recovery, we experience feelings that unite us.

Structured Family Recovery invites the addict back into the normal activities of family life. *Do you want to go shopping with me? Would you like to catch a movie? I'm going to run over to Grandma's; would you like to come?* These are the small things that make up our family life. It's important not to underestimate how difficult participating in such activities might be for the newly recovering person, so don't make a big deal out of these invites. Strike a balance between lightly encouraging the addict's involvement in activities and being respectful of the addict's need for space, both of which are important for the brain to adjust to life without the effects of alcohol or other drugs. Remember the Twelve Step slogan "Easy does it."

This process challenges us to examine our family life too. Does it give the impression of a happy place? Have we become frenzied, short-tempered, disorganized, or just plain no fun? Do we all sit around with our faces in screens, television blaring, everyone hunkered down in a private spot? Does everyone grab a bite to eat willy-nilly or by racing to a drive-thru? Do we have ready excuses for why we live this way—each person left to his own devices? Let's take a good, hard look at what the addict is returning home to and what the family "real estate" looks like.

How do you define a healthy family life? How would others in the family answer this question? Are there tiny changes that we can begin making now? What do we need to give up? Let's clean out our cache of unhelpful family life habits like junk from a long-neglected closet. What are we going to keep, throw away, and add? Where can we find guidance to help us do this democratically and effectively? How can we use what we've learned in this book to make lasting changes? As Bruce Feiler, author of *The Secrets of Happy Families*, wrote, "Want to have a happier family? Tinker with it all the time."

Finally, bring fun back into the family. Not just going out to restaurants or shopping, but real fun. Try the novel and new. Have some days that end with "Wasn't that great? Who knew that could be so much fun (interesting, challenging, intriguing, exciting, inspiring)?" Fun doesn't require big and grand and expensive. There's so much out there in the world. Let's open up the windows and doors of our family life. Let the sunshine in and breathe in the fresh air. Let's make it a place where everyone wants to belong.

17

How Do I Talk to My Family?

The following is advice to the newly recovering person from a longtime recovering alcoholic and drug addict. He remembers back on his earliest days in recovery and his attempts to fit back into family life after several years of active addiction and thirty days in a residential treatment program.

When I came home from treatment, it was difficult to talk to my family. I knew what my behavior as an active alcoholic and drug addict had been. I was sometimes kind, sometimes entertaining, sometimes angry, sometimes manipulative, and always dishonest. But what was my role now? How was I supposed to act? Strange as it may seem, in the early days of my recovery I almost didn't know how to communicate. I wasn't comfortable in my own skin and was dimly aware that I'd been letting everyone down for a long time, to put it mildly.

The first thing I realized—and probably the most important thing—was that I needed to win back my family's trust. As an alcoholic and drug addict, I'd shredded their trust again and again until there was nothing left of that precious fabric that binds people together. There's an old saying, "Talk is cheap." That was truer of me than of most people. There's another old saying that provides the remedy: "Actions speak louder than words." If I was going to win back the trust of family and friends, I was going to have to show them I was trustworthy. My actions would prove what my words never could.

I went to a Twelve Step meeting every day and followed through with the rest of my aftercare recommendations from the treatment center. I did what I was supposed to do, whether I felt like it or not. The immediate effect of doing these things was that I never picked up the first drink or drug. I stayed sober, and although my family didn't believe their eyes for many months, my sobriety was something that I could only achieve one day at a time.

The second thing I did was talk a little bit about what I was learning at the meetings, maybe something funny, maybe something insightful. I wasn't trying to prove anything about my meeting, but if something really struck me, I related it to someone in the family.

For example, after the close of one of the meetings, when I was helping clean up the coffee and putting the chairs away, I happened to pass Alan in the hallway. I asked him how it was going. Alan was a short guy with curly hair and thick glasses. I admired the quiet and thoughtful way he talked. He stopped dead in his tracks, as though I'd asked him the most important thing in the world. I stopped, too, just waiting for his reply. After some reflection, he said, "It's going just the way it should. Not that I like it!"

We both had a good laugh over that and then continued on our separate ways. I was so struck by his remark that I repeated it when I went home. My family wasn't sure whether to laugh or scratch their heads, but it made a big impression. And I remember Alan's comment still, these many years later.

The third thing I did was rejoin the life of the family, which I did by asking questions: "How's Aunt Audrey doing?" or "When is that little nephew's birthday?" or "What are we doing for the Fourth of July?" These questions always brought answers and opened the door to conversations that weren't about me, thank God. And they allowed me a chance to offer a little help. "Do you want me to pick up something for the birthday party?"

When I was drinking and drugging, my interest in family was scanty at best. But in the early days of my recovery, I learned that interacting with others and trying to be part of the family gave me less time to be worried about myself and my many self-centered fears.

Twelve Step programs put a great emphasis on service work and for good reason. When we help others, we help ourselves. We find relief from our countless anxieties. We can extend that to our families too. Actions not only speak louder than words, they open the door to real conversation. We find a shared sense of quiet gratitude. We're together again.

Two Recovering Addicts Talk about Structured Family Recovery

Following their time in treatment, Payton and Hunter participated on the same SFR team. Payton's mother, father, and two uncles made up the rest of the SFR team members. Payton and Hunter became friends in treatment, and Payton invited him to join the team.

After completing a full year of SFR meetings, the team decided to keep going. They returned to the beginning, starting over with the meeting for week one. As they described it, they had created something special and were afraid they'd lose it if they quit. As of the time of this interview, they have been doing SFR weekly for over three years.

Debra: How did you first hear about Structured Family Recovery?

Payton: I was in the second half of a twelve-week stay in treatment. My individual therapist suggested, during family week when my folks attended, that we check out the *It Takes a Family* book and consider doing SFR.

Debra: Hunter, what did you think when Payton approached you with the idea of joining the team with his family?

Hunter: I remember talking to Payton when he was still in treatment. He mentioned that SFR was something that had been recommended to him, and he was thinking about doing it. I remember thinking it was a really good idea. I had a couple conversations with my family about trying to get them to do SFR, but they haven't been as interested. I haven't pressed it because I've had Payton's family.

Debra: Both of you had the good fortune of accessing excellent, long-term residential treatment. You know a lot about recovery, whereas the rest of the team didn't have the same knowledge base. I see alcoholics and addicts who join SFR after completing a good treatment program as leaders of sorts because their knowledge is so much greater than the family's. How do you feel that initial discrepancy worked itself out between you and the other teammates?

Hunter: The rate of learning is obviously very different. The people who haven't gone through any sort of treatment are starting from a very different place. But if they are willing to catch up, it's really interesting. Payton and I, throughout SFR, both actively pushed to be less the focus and opened up more space for the others to share. It was important to me that the meetings gave enough space for everyone to share, so we could relate to one another better.

Payton: It's funny, there's a million different things swirling around my head right now. When we really internalized the SFR process, we really unlocked a sense in everyone that this was truly our group and that, fundamentally, everyone is recovering from something. That's a tenet I've really clung to. I've watched my parents' relationship change as well as my relationship with them, individually and collectively, because we weren't just six people in individual therapy. In fact, one of the things I love most about SFR is that it is just Twelve Step enough. The topics are in line with the program itself, but we didn't focus exclusively on my addiction or the danger of relapse. Instead, SFR was the lens through which we approached some really interesting topics, with a range from really joyful to really heavy. I think that was a really great thing. We wouldn't have lasted this long in SFR if every time it was just me talking about my addiction.

Debra: What you are saying brings up a point I'd like to throw out to you both. The way SFR meetings are designed— whatever the topic—is to cool down emotions. Each person shares but in a way that isn't emotionally charged. We can hear each other because we aren't personalizing what we have to say. We aren't threatened emotionally by one another because we just talk about ourselves.

Hunter: The way I would articulate it is, listening to Payton and his parents talk, at first I could tell Payton's parents were his parents. But over time, it was like they were just three adults. It takes the hierarchical structure and makes it almost irrelevant. It forces you to talk to each other as equals. If people are really participating, that's what it really encourages. That's what's so unique about SFR. I think so many families—individuals within families—rely on these crutches of what their constructs should be, based on their title in this hierarchy. It's really detrimental to our ability to communicate. We get stuck in playing this role—who we are in this family—instead of just being a person who can talk to other people. I think SFR is a fantastic mechanism for fostering that. I think it's really helpful, too, for parents to be able to see their children as adults.

Payton: My relationship with my parents as compared to the past is like night and day. It's something we talk about frequently now. It wasn't a thing that changed us externally; it was a set of tools that moved our conversations beyond "Hey, how're you doing? How are things? How's your sobriety?" I still have a really strong identity as my parents' child, but this really has been transformative. Mentally and emotionally, we have now positioned ourselves, in many ways, on the same side of the table. Rather than parents versus child, it's more like parents and child as humans looking out onto a really fascinating world. I've had a big advantage in being an only child, which has played a role in how close I am to my folks. I've always felt I could talk with them. But it is amazingly different now with SFR.

Debra: When would you say, with SFR and working your Twelve Step program, you felt that they began seeing you, once again, as a trustworthy member of the family?

Payton: It's something that's a little hard to pinpoint, but it is something that I've thought about. Also, something we've actually discussed in our SFR meetings—the notion of trust in the context of addiction and repairing the wreckage. Also, the idea that we should try not to indict people for past offenses. Probably about six months in, I had moved to another state and was getting my feet under me again. I remember when the tone of my check-ins (Report, Discuss, Plan) shifted from kind of the culture shock of being back in society post-treatment to a little more forward looking. I used my recovery and the tools in SFR to inform how I wanted to move forward in my life. I don't know if there is one moment in particular, but it seemed like we were talking more from a position of assuming the best rather than fearing the worst.

Debra: That had to have a major impact on how you experienced your relationships.

Payton: I don't know if I give everyone on my SFR team enough credit for just how receptive they've been to adapting. I think, in many ways, it was a lot easier for me to climb up to the level of peer to my parents than it was for them to wrap their head around that. So I give them a ton of credit.

Hunter: I think we were also very blessed by the constitution of the group. Payton's uncles, both very bright guys who had unique perspectives, brought very important voices to our team. They could relate stuff to their families of origin growing up. Having those two voices in the SFR meetings was paramount. It's interesting how different voices change over time, I think really fit for purpose. Then you have another example with my family. They're kind of, "Eh, not really for us." Maybe it's something you, Debra, should consider in your writing—what if you have a family who doesn't want to do this? Even though I haven't been able to work out a lot of stuff with my family like I would have wanted to, having SFR with Payton's family has really helped me in how I communicate with my parents. It's made me much less afraid to talk with them more as peers. Even though I didn't go through the process of SFR with them, it has still helped my dynamic with my family of origin.

Debra: Hunter, has the way you interact with your family after SFR changed how they interact with you even though they never chose to participate?

Hunter: Yes, to a degree. It's a much less noticeable degree than what Payton is experiencing with his parents. But it's definitely helped me. I don't think it's helped my family, but it's helped me. I don't necessarily talk to them more but feel that I have calmer conversations when I need to bring things up. They respond more positively to that.

Debra: Hunter, being married and having children, how do you feel SFR and your recovery program impacts those relationships, even though your wife chose not to get involved in SFR?

Hunter: I find myself so much more aware of my role in inter-personal relationships and the need to be mindful of behaving in a way that sets realistic expectations and reinforces the kind of relationships I want to have with people. I'll be really honest, my relationship with my wife is not really great. We are effective co-parents, we get along really well right now, but I have a really hard time seeing the two of us being married long term. I'm struggling being in a relationship where I feel I'm the only one taking accountability for my side of the street. That being said, I am able to approach conversations with my wife and my children from a much less emotionally triggered place. There are a lot of things that used to make me really angry that I'm now instantly able to understand why that comment wasn't about me, it was about somebody else. Just being able to take a reaction for what it is, understanding it's not a well-thought-through thing. And, also, not being afraid to speak my truth when someone asks me if something is bothering me. So I think SFR and my recovery has helped my interpersonal relationships across the spectrum.

Debra: I often see addicts engaging in the recovery process, but no one else in the family gets involved. It results in out-of-balance relationships. The recovering addict gets healthier, but family members don't change. Am I right to say that you are experiencing this, Hunter?

Hunter: Yes, you grow out of sync. With my wife, this is part of the thing I struggle with—I feel like a very different person than I was when I met her. I'm willing to raise my hand and say, "You know what? Early in our relationship, I very much deceived you. I very much created an image for you that wasn't the authentic me." That's a tough thing to admit to somebody and a tough thing to hear. We've all heard the phrase *growing apart*. I think that we're experiencing the literal manifestation of that. Growth compounds itself, right? So, once there's a small divergence in growth rate between two things, if that divergence remains for very long, it's an exponential gap that starts to develop. It's the antithesis or flip side of the coin to what you have done with SFR. If the family can't grow with the addict, then the family becomes detrimental to that person's recovery. That's a really weird thing to try to address. It's tough to tell a family, "Hey, it's great you put this person in rehab, but if you all don't get your act together, you probably need to put yourself in the problem bucket instead of part of the solution. Families don't want to hear that, but somebody needs to try to tell them.

Debra: The great Earnie Larsen, writing about family, explains that if one person gets into recovery and the other doesn't— lacking emotional sobriety, which is needed for healthy self-regulation—there are only three options in the relationship. The addict relapses and returns to his old self; the spouse joins in the recovery process and meets the recovering spouse at this higher level; or neither of these things happen and the relationship falls apart. Payton, you are in a relationship with someone in recovery who you met after you were in recovery. Can you talk about how this is a different experience?

Payton: It's funny, as you described the three recovery options in a relationship, I was thinking of the breakdown of my first marriage. My behaviors in my addiction might have been prime movers in our breakup, but, in hindsight, I don't think it would have ever worked for some of the intractable reasons you just described. I remember my ex-wife came to family week at my first treatment program. When I returned home seven weeks later, we decided to end the marriage. A big factor in that was, first, that she didn't believe my addiction was real, so that was a fundamental mismatch. But, also, I remember talking to her about SFR and the whole idea being so repellent to her. She didn't feel she needed to do more and felt it was my addiction, so I had to clean up the mess. If nothing else, when it came to our marriage, that would have been the final nail in the coffin, because now that I've gone through SFR and recovery, I know there is no way I would have been healthy in that relationship or any relationship like it.

The fact that my present partner—and soon-to-be wife—and I are both in recovery has become such a unifying factor. She is such a proponent of recovery in living color. We have mutually lived this experience. It's something that no amount of discussions or facilitated therapy sessions could impress upon a nonrecovering partner. I realized that she was often the subject of my SFR check-ins, but so much more than that. Asking her to join our SFR group was a natural coextension of our loving relationship, but it also deepened her bond—and my own—with my family of origin and chosen SFR family.

Debra: Speaking as a family member myself, I can say that family has a very hard time seeing how they become untrustworthy when dealing with the ongoing crisis of addiction. Being in that place of denial, they often see family recovery as a threat or imposition. They sometimes feel the addict has done this to them and can't imagine why they need to get involved in the recovery process.

Hunter: That is my wife to a tee.

Debra: The sad part of this is, most of the time, the spouse or others in a family want the recovering person to make the relationship good for them, without participating in the solution themselves. Of course, as we know, one person alone cannot make a good relationship. This refusal, to use Payton's words, results in the nail in the coffin—the opposite of what most spouses and family members want. They've been hurt repeatedly and are locked down in anger, frustration, and resentment, precisely because they have no good solution for themselves. As it says in the Big Book of AA, "Resentment is the number one offender."

Hunter: Exactly. The longer this goes on, the less I feel like my wife and I have anything in common as human beings. It used to really frustrate me. *Why do I have to look in the mirror and* *she doesn't?* I can't force her to do anything, but it bums me out. I feel like our relationship is really superficial, just about the children. I can still craft a happy life around that, but I'm worried what we're teaching our children in terms of what love looks like. This is where I have the biggest struggle. I guess I'm at a point where I don't care if the relationship makes it or not. It'd be nice if it did and arguably better for my kids. But the longer this goes on, the greater the chasm becomes between our two realities. I can't help but think that she doesn't live in the same reality as I do. You don't have a common universe to ground your relationship. I think it's the same thing with families.

Debra: Payton, could you say a few words about your family's engagement?

Payton: My family is very engaged, supportive, and thoughtful. It's a really fascinating group of people and, I think, if even one piece was different—if there were no uncles, no Hunter, no Mom and Dad—how incredibly different the SFR experience would have been for me.

Debra: Sometimes, families are reluctant to reach out to the extended family—an aunt or uncle or grandparent—because they are still in that secretive or uncomfortable place with the addiction, or they feel they'll inconvenience them. You have experienced the value of including extended family members.

Hunter: I'd like to ask Payton something. Wouldn't you agree that SFR has also fundamentally changed your mom and her brother's dynamic?

Payton: Oh, for sure, yeah. My mom and uncle hit some elements of their really difficult childhood and past relationship that were pretty unexpected. It's allowed them to be more honest and open with each other, which is amazing.

Hunter: SFR allowed them a way to talk about it that's not so wound up and stressful. I think it also breaks down some of the hierarchal stuff between siblings based on their age. It takes some kind of stimulus coming in from the outside to get us off those archetypes that we rely on.

Debra: Do you feel that having this perspective of family through the SFR experience rounds things out? Does it give you a clearer understanding of addiction in a global sense, not just about you as the solo actor in the realm of addiction? Because when we include people, it helps us stay accountable. Did SFR's built-in sense of accountability have a role in your lasting recovery?

Hunter: I would say, absolutely it had a role to play in my lasting recovery. If addiction is associated with unhealthy interpersonal relationships, then the solution is to create healthy interpersonal relationships. That matches up perfectly with something we watched in treatment—the thesis was effectively that the solution to addiction is community. I think that's one thing that is so powerful about SFR. It's different than a Twelve Step meeting. I think SFR is very valuable because it teaches you to be open with people you see on a regular basis. With your family, you are trying to figure out how to make recovery an aspect of that relationship instead of just a tent pole. For people who are being put in the position of doing recovery by themselves, it's kind of scary. Just the demonstration that the family is willing to take part in the journey with you is really powerful. Just the fact that they show up means a lot. They don't need to do it perfectly.

Debra: I'd like to end by asking you, Payton, if your whole concept of the institution of family has shifted somewhat due to your involvement with family in SFR?

Payton: Definitely. I think, as I look at my family of origin, it has changed profoundly largely because of SFR. It's important to the point where, in the last couple of months, my fiancée has joined our SFR group. That's been a really interesting experience as well. I can't imagine going through the last three years without SFR. And to piggyback on what Hunter was talking about, as far as the impact and the interplay between SFR and the Twelve Step program, one of the things I like so much about SFR is that it is an incredible recovery tool and makes sure I'm not hiding in recovery—in other words, not retreating from life outside of my Twelve Step meetings. I think SFR isn't just a stand-alone program but kind of the bridge to the real world. My Twelve Step program is an outstanding space for growth and exploration, but it's more a pocket of reality. It's not that I don't care what a stranger in a Twelve Step meeting has to say—I do very deeply. But it's a whole other thing entirely hearing and watching the evolution of my most beloved family members.

In the next chapter, we hear from Payton's parents.

19

Parents of an Addicted Son Talk about Structured Family Recovery

Caroline called me one day a few months ago. We'd never met before, but she wanted to tell me about her family's experiences with Structured Family Recovery. She invited me to attend two of the family's SFR meetings, where I met the entire team, including her husband, Richard, and their recovering son, Payton. When I asked if she and Richard were open to a conversation that would be shared with other families, she enthusiastically agreed.

> **Debra:** How did you come to decide to do SFR with Payton and other family members? Did you struggle with the decision before you made it?

> **Caroline:** I read the whole book on the airplane on the way home from family week at Payton's treatment center. I would nudge Richard and say, "Listen to this" or "Read this." By the time we got home, I was sure it was one of the only things I could do to help Payton. I felt strongly about that, and after I shared my feelings with Richard, he felt the same.

Richard: The staff at my son's treatment center told us to get the book. One of the counselors we met with spoke very highly of it. We were both caught by the fact that it was an extended approach that goes beyond treatment facilities or professionals. Since we're both medical professionals, I've had some experience with credentialing for several national organizations. When reviewing cases, I've seen success, disaster, and tragedy. With SFR, I remember being uplifted by seeing something that looked like it could work. We had a host of books, but after reading *It Takes a Family,* I was thinking, okay, this one has a program.

Debra: Early in SFR, how did you deal with the need to rebuild trust with Payton?

Richard: I didn't just embrace thinking everything was going to be fine. But I also felt dispirited by the idea, as some people proselytized, that failure is going to happen and you just work around it. As I was trying to rebuild trust, that concept could be quite undermining. When we came back from family week at the treatment center, I felt we were in a dark tunnel, and I was frightened. I felt SFR put a light in my hand. It gave us a place to work together. I have a very different appreciation of fellowship since we've been doing SFR.

Debra: We realize that addiction is a powerful and insidious disease, but with SFR we create an expectation for success. Of course, we still need to plan for relapse. I think of it as analogous to a fire escape plan on the back of a hotel room door. We don't expect a fire, but we need a plan in place.

Richard: I didn't want to walk around with rose-colored glasses, thinking we'll send Payton to the best places for treatment and then just cheer him on. That wasn't going to work. I had to be really honest with myself about that. Having something like SFR was key. At one point early on, we experienced a meltdown. In spite of that, we all attended our SFR meeting anyway. The fellowship of SFR carried us through. That was a turning point for us.

Caroline: We didn't forget that we were invested in SFR. It was a lifeline. It was helpful. It was fellowship. It was all the things each of us needed to continue moving forward. If we hadn't had SFR, I really don't know what would have happened.

Richard: I don't think we would have been successful if we hadn't worked together. I don't think of SFR as linear. I see it more as a mountain climbing analogy, finding different home bases. It helped us create a foundation. It made it possible to do something as simple as ask Payton about his sobriety. Caroline, do you think I could have done that without SFR?

Caroline: No, I don't think so. One of the very first things I experienced was that SFR opened my mind to a new awareness. Instead of focusing on our terrors, there was something we could do. It wasn't always perfect, but we were together, talking, and sharing. I came to realize that the addiction wasn't about me. As family, we have to keep reminding ourselves that we're in this together. We're in this for our addict and our love for that person.

Debra: What does being part of a family recovery team mean to you?

Caroline: It's about what we can contribute to our family member's recovery. If you think about it, as a family member, you don't have a lot of opportunities in life to do something this important. To impact a life is a rare gift.

Debra: As a team, you have all been participating in SFR for three years. Now you're moving into year four. What made your team continue onward after the first year? Why didn't you end SFR at that point?

Richard: Caroline took a really smart approach by throwing out a simple question at the end of our first year: "What do people want to do?" I was very explicit in what I wanted. I found it very reassuring to do SFR. There were many secondary gains. I can be much more honest and direct than I could before. Caroline's relationship with my brother is phenomenally different. When my brother calls, it's often to talk with Caroline, not me. That, for me, is a great gift.

Caroline: For me, the reason to continue was success. I personally changed, everything from self-awareness to self-esteem to decreasing my argumentativeness and judgmental tendencies. I have changed for the good in so many ways. SFR is not anything I want to just do for a short time. This has been a life changer for me. I think it has improved our marriage too. It has enhanced our communication with Payton, and we have seen him become a really different person. It's all been so positive. I can't imagine where we'd be without it; can you, Richard?

Richard: No, I can't.

Caroline: I don't know where Payton would be, either. And here he is embarking on a whole new life as a tremendously changed person. Exactly the kind of person the world wants and needs.

Richard: SFR enhances my relationships with the people I love the most, enhances my ability to communicate with them, and enhances a sense that I am connected to people who matter to me—and I matter to them. Why would I want to give that up?

Debra: When parents have an addicted loved one, the disease can tear at marriages. Can you talk about how recovery has benefited your marriage?

Caroline: I learned that I was taking things for granted in our marriage, that I wasn't fully listening or fully engaging with

Richard. It's easy to cry in each other's arms when something bad happens, like a child's addiction, but then each of you retreats to your own little box. SFR helped me stop blaming others to protect myself. With SFR, I feel recommitted to our marriage, even after so many years.

Debra: You are a family who has made lasting commitments. You made one decision and took the honorable position of sticking with it.

Caroline: Part of it is a matter of honor, part of it is self-preservation, and the biggest part is love.

Debra: What role do you think your involvement with SFR has had in Payton's successful recovery?

Caroline: In my mind, it seemed that Payton was striving for structure in his life. In his addiction, he verbalized he had nothing, was at the bottom of the barrel, and didn't know what was going to happen next. I think, initially, he was holding on to SFR as a rock. Then he began to grow into it and then grow with it. He would take what we did in SFR each week and use it.

Debra: As a mother watching her son grow in this way, how did you react emotionally?

Caroline: Watching him made me feel hopeful and confident, yet I held back because I was terrified of relapse. I was asking myself, "Is this going to work?" Hearing people say relapse is going to happen preyed on my mind. But that didn't last very long. I started to become more and more proud, not just of Payton, but of Richard as well. I could see each of us working together. I hadn't seen that before. It was lifesaving. I decided not to let fear drive me but let progress drive me.

Debra: Many families are afraid to ask their newly recovering loved one about recovery. They often ask: "Are we allowed to ask about their sobriety? What can we say? What should we not say?" They are terrified of having a conversation about recovery.

Caroline: We went through that too. When Payton was in treatment and finally allowed to call us, I remember waiting for that call with Richard. We said to each other, "What can we ask? What should we say?" In SFR, it says that asking someone about their recovery is very important. It's not being nosy. It's not questioning what they are doing day-to-day or minute-to-minute. The question that does nobody any good is "Did you have a drink today?" You have to learn how to make this an expression of love and caring. The first time Richard asked Payton about his sobriety, Richard said it so comfortably and meaningfully. It was much more than a question.

Debra: If no one reaches out, I think addicts would feel isolated. It would create a narrative that the family wants to hide this very important part of their life. How has Payton responded to you when you ask?

Caroline: Many times, since the first time, both Richard and I have asked Payton this question. Sometimes he'll laugh a little bit and say, "Mom, my sobriety is good." He says it in such a warm and embracing way.

Richard: Yes, he's never judgmental of us or reactive.

Caroline: No, he isn't. There is a lot of feeling in his voice. It seems to be an acceptance and almost as if he is saying, "Thank you for asking, I know that you love me."

Richard: Payton came out of treatment needing to make so many decisions: Where should I live, should I get a job, who should I interact with, when am I going to get a Twelve Step sponsor, am I attending enough meetings? At this crucial time, SFR allowed us a place to sit and talk. It certainly helped me build a foundation for trust and communication. The early days after treatment presented some struggles for Payton. SFR had a steadying effect. I've noticed, over time, the ups and downs have really smoothed out.

Debra: Families can have difficulty finding truly helpful resources when someone they love is addicted. What was your experience?

Richard: Caroline and I have resources, so we could pay for Payton's treatment. But I still feel there were limitations to the resources available even to us. My heart goes out to families who have fewer resources. By developing SFR, Debra, you provide an invaluable service to all families. I knew recovery was going to be a lifelong commitment for Payton. Your efforts to give families a year of SFR meetings in *It Takes a Family* is great, but I will cheer whatever you add to this new edition for families who want to continue beyond the year, asking: "What do we do next?" When I received my medical school diploma, for example, I didn't suddenly know everything. I was going to be an intern, a resident, a fellow, a young attending physician. I had to build a foundation for my career. Same with recovery. Because of SFR, our recovery foundation is not built on shifting sand.

Debra: SFR is designed so that nobody in the family is telling the addict or anyone else what to do. How has that worked for you?

Caroline: There has to be a plan. If you want to survive, you have to get yourself into some kind of plan and follow it. In my mind, SFR was that right away. It was doable. SFR isn't hard. The bottom line is just making a commitment. Everyone on our SFR team feels there are no downsides to this program—at least not that we can think of, and we've been doing it for over three years.

Debra: Payton is getting married in a few weeks, and his fiancée has joined your SFR team. Can you share about that experience? It's quite a powerful way to get to know each other.

Richard: I think it's a real credit to her that she has fit into our SFR group quite seamlessly. She clearly conveys how special she finds SFR, while exploring who each of us is in this process.

Debra: You all share the language of recovery. So now, whether it's Payton or your future daughter-in-law, you all speak this language.

Caroline: Yes, and it's a great comfort. I feel loved by her. I feel like she not only loves us but is almost grateful to us for doing SFR with Payton. She is fascinated by SFR. The language has been very important to help us understand each other. Without it, we would be tiptoeing around one another.

Debra: I think the voice of the family is so important in recovery. For many families, they are told so many different things by so many different people, they don't know what to think. In the end, most are excluded from their loved one's recovery journey. If you were sitting with a family, what would you tell them based on the experiences you've had as a family recovery team?

Richard: My experience was that I was frightened, I was overwhelmed, and I had to get over the blame game. I had to draw on the resources I had and look to others for help. This allowed me to participate in SFR and feel like I was contributing something meaningful. I have a better language; I have a better understanding; I have a better ability to deal with my own issues and behaviors. So my suggestion to a family is, if you are wondering what you will do when the addict leaves the safety of treatment and returns home, SFR gives you a road map. If you are fortunate enough to get into a groove with SFR, it's priceless.

Caroline: The first thing I would say is, try it. You have nothing to lose. The structure will help you start, continue, and be successful—if you trust it. The second thing I'd say, move ahead and don't look back. All looking back does is stir the waters. Look ahead. You are looking for change. The third thing is enjoy learning how to love each other again, maybe in a totally different way. Perhaps this is what had to happen for your family to get to a better place. Lastly, be gentle and kind to yourself and to each other.

Debra: I think, sometimes, a newly recovering addict might be wary of joining a family recovery team. Could you speak to the recovering addict?

Richard: I think addicts need to understand that SFR is a bi-directional gift. Family and addict benefit. If people in your life really love you and care for you and want to help in a meaningful way, including them in your recovery journey is precious. This isn't a replacement for your sponsor or meetings and other things that are positive for recovery. SFR is important for rebuilding trust and avenues of communication in a family. It's an ongoing fellowship with an expectation of long-term recovery. As a dad, I am participating because it is my tribe, my most precious people, and I have gained from it.

Caroline: The shame, the fear, the depression—all those negative feelings you may be having—your family is having as well. With SFR, nobody is trying to control you or fix you. That is your job. SFR is here to guide and help, not just for recovery, but to learn about your family all over again.

20

Keep It Simple: Getting Started

More than two thousand years ago, the Chinese teacher and philosopher Confucius wrote, "Life is really simple, but we insist on making it complicated." When we overcomplicate recovery, we can overwhelm ourselves. When we get overwhelmed, we're risking relapse for the whole family. We're tempted to quit, and the addict is tempted to drink. To succeed in recovery, we must do simple things that work. Simple steps change behavior.

Structured Family Recovery is simple. But simple doesn't mean simplistic. It means we find the most uncomplicated solution for a problem. When we oversimplify complex issues, we don't get the results we want. Simplistic approaches underestimate what recovery requires. As family members in Structured Family Recovery, we add two activities (one hour each) to our lives every week, which we will discuss in this chapter. These activities are centered on virtue ethics and role ethics.

Let's start by looking at *virtue ethics*. Virtue ethics asks the question "Who am I?" It speaks directly to my values and morals. It is about who I am as an individual. Are my actions in agreement with my beliefs? If we are honest with ourselves, most of us will admit we're a mixed bag. When addiction enters family life, we often drift further from our ideal self without even realizing it. Fear and feelings of unmanageability lead us to develop a variety of survival skills that help us cope with the ongoing stress and negative consequences caused by addiction. But survival skills are meant for short-lived crises. They aren't healthy life strategies over the long run. In time, as once-helpful survival skills bleed into many areas of our lives, they harden into habits and character defects. What was meant to be a temporary solution has now become permanent behavior. We need to be perfect all the time. We allow no space for making mistakes. We try to control all the people, places, and things around us. We're filled with resentment and anger—sometimes below the surface and other times unhesitatingly out in the open. We are overwhelmed with self-pity. We become martyrs. We puff ourselves up with a false sense of importance. We beat ourselves up over and over. We begin to use dishonesty to manage our circumstances. We become critical. Nothing is ever good enough. We make everything a joke. We take on an "I don't care about anything or anybody" attitude.

One of the weekly activities in Structured Family Recovery is designed specifically to address this question—Who am I?—and the gap between who we want to be and how we so often behave. The activity calls for us to attend one Al-Anon meeting each week. These Twelve Step programs for families are brilliantly designed to deal with how individuals are changed by another's addiction (often without knowing it). In practical ways, they help us become the person we were meant to be. In Structured Family Recovery, these Twelve Step family meetings connect us to the greater recovery community, which includes our addicted loved one. By attending one meeting every week, we are taking steps to improve ourselves as individuals. We will become better people in ways that may later surprise us. With each member of the family working a recovery program (and our addicted family member in AA or another Twelve Step group), we are all learning how to bring a greater and better version of ourselves back to the family. In doing so, we literally redefine how we live together. We begin to build a more solid family structure. Engineers will tell you that if you want to build a structure that can carry a heavy load without collapsing, start with a triangle. The triangle is the strongest and simplest structure in geometry. It's no wonder the triangle was chosen as the image representing Twelve Step programs.

The second activity is a weekly SFR meeting. This brings family together in recovery. After all, no one person alone can build a solid structure for the family, no matter how strong his personal recovery plan might be. It takes every one of us. A family isn't only two-thirds or a half of its members. It is everybody—including the alcoholic or addict. While our Twelve Step recovery is for us as individuals, Structured Family Recovery moves the individual into the whole.

SFR introduces the family to *role ethics*. Role ethics asks, "Who am I in relation to you?" That's a powerful question. If I'm filled with fear or anger or controlling behavior or perfectionism or martyrdom or grandiosity, I'm not consistently safe around other people. These character defects hurt others in all kinds of ways and push people away. The irony is that character defects often feel like virtues while we're using them. But they're not. Virtues lift us up; character defects tear us down. We can't have a conversation about role ethics without also talking about virtue ethics. Who am I in relation to you is determined by who I am. One relies on the other. They overlap and they interconnect.

Role ethics remind us that we do not live in a void. We are not silos existing side by side. Our individual growth is put to the test only in relation to others. Role ethics is a way our virtue ethics are tested. It is in the improvement of ourselves as individuals that we transform the answer to the question asked of us by role ethics—Who am I in relation to you? As a recovering addict said of his family's SFR experience: "We were always close as a family—even through my addiction. But SFR brought us closer than we ever imagined possible. It changed everything."

Role ethics are about family unity. Rather than draining each other, our interactions can be changed to nourish each other. We build trust. This doesn't happen magically. It happens because we are each engaged in the rewarding work of recovery. *When I am only focused on me, I don't really see you. When I am overly focused on you, I don't really see me. When I am focused on "we," I see you and me.* This is the one of the most important results of our SFR meetings—becoming fully and positively engaged with one another. To get started, we simply make a commitment to Structured Family Recovery. From there, the process naturally does the job of moving us toward our destination.

Getting started with Structured Family Recovery asks us to build these two simple things into our lives on a weekly basis: an SFR meeting together with our team and an Al-Anon or other Twelve Step meeting for ourselves. Each one occurs once a week for an hour and, combined, betters who we are and who we are to others. Our addicted loved one will follow all the recommendations of her aftercare plan, including attending multiple Twelve Step meetings each week—sometimes attending ninety meetings in the first ninety days. Families who work their Twelve Step program of recovery by making a commitment to their weekly meeting now share a common experience with their addicted loved one. If we struggle to schedule one hour of Al-Anon into our week, we have a new appreciation for our alcoholic or addict who is jump-starting recovery with a meeting every day for those first critical months of early recovery.

As we begin seeing the benefits, not only for our family and our addicted loved one, but in all areas of our lives, we'll be surprised at how this small time commitment can bring rewards of such magnitude. After just four weeks of Structured Family Recovery and Al-Anon, the sister of an addict said, "I was experiencing so much anxiety due to the pressures of my graduate studies, but now all of that anxiety has vanished. I have the same pressures, just not the same reactions to those pressures. I'm amazed how this is changing my life outside of my family." The wife of another addict had a similar report: "This has changed how I parent my children and the kind of supervisor I am at work. I even heard two employees talking about how their interactions with me have improved—quoting things I said that truly inspired them. What they didn't know is that those inspirational thoughts came straight from my Structured Family Recovery and Al-Anon programs."

Simplicity is key to success. We keep SFR meetings simple by using conference calls or other audio technologies. For Structured Family Recovery, audio is simpler than video technology. It is easier to use on our phones wherever we might be. Any decision that makes participating in Structured Family Recovery even a tiny bit harder makes it more likely people will skip meetings or drop out entirely. Conference calls mean no one has to drive anywhere, no need for child care, no worries about clothes, makeup, or hair. Family members can participate from anywhere. If you're on vacation in Florida, for example, and your family is in New York, you can easily attend. If you are at your daughter's soccer practice or in bed with a head cold, no problem. A sister of an addict attended her family's SFR meeting from the hospital after having a baby. Everyone on the call could hear the gurgling of the newborn. With conference calls, the meeting comes to you.

Most family members coping with a loved one's active addiction were never told about Al-Anon or had discounted the importance of attending. It's not unusual for most people in a family to have never before stepped into a Twelve Step meeting. With our loved one now embarking on the rocky road of early recovery, it is perhaps even more urgent that we engage in family recovery. Our mutual accomplishments in Structured Family Recovery depend on it. We cannot strengthen our relationships with one another without making necessary changes within ourselves, and this is afforded by Twelve Step involvement.

Al-Anon is the most common Twelve Step group for families. However, there are other excellent options, such as Families Anonymous, Adult Children of Alcoholics, and Nar-Anon. Families Anonymous is popular with parents of addicted children of all ages. Adult Children of Alcoholics consists primarily of grown children of addicted parents. Nar-Anon is specifically for family members of addicts who use drugs other than alcohol and who attend Narcotics Anonymous. Find meetings by searching online. In choosing your meeting, keep it simple. Select the best day and time for you. Is a lunch meeting best? Or a meeting after work or dinner? Maybe Saturday morning is easiest. Pick a convenient location. If you have to drive a long distance or struggle with traffic, you are more likely to start skipping your meeting. Choose from meetings located near your home or workplace. You can try different meetings to see which ones you like best. Always ask yourself, "Will my choice keep this simple over time or will it begin to feel hard?" Always go for simple.

Once you've found a meeting to attend, make it even simpler by designing for it. B. J. Fogg, PhD, knows that behavior change isn't random, it's systematic. In his book *Tiny Habits,* he explains that when we aspire to change but fall short of our aspirations, "It's a design flaw— not a personal flaw." We have to make change easier. We discussed how behavior design works in chapter 8, "Tiny Tasks." It's a good time to use that guidance.

However, before anything else, we have to figure out what we're trying to do. To what are we aspiring? Is attending Al-Anon meetings our end goal? Probably not. Maybe we're willing to go because we can't bear how addiction is tearing our family apart. Maybe we are terrified our addicted loved one will lose everything, even die. We are tired of all the worrying and fighting. We are all struggling to get along. There are so many problems. But are these things aspirations? No, they're not. These might be the forces driving us to Structured Family Recovery and Al-Anon, but they are not aspirations.

Dr. Fogg tells us we need to get clear on our aspirations. Why are we considering doing these recovery things with our family? What's the answer? Aspirations are usually simple and direct. In fact, when most families drill down, they come to the same conclusion: I am doing SFR and Al-Anon because I want us to be happy again. Happiness is definitely an aspiration.

Once we know our aspiration, we can determine the behaviors that will take us there. But, as Dr. Fogg cautions, just guessing at what to do won't work. So what exactly do we want? What is our true aspiration? We need a methodology for change. Going on the internet and searching for random inspiration isn't a good plan, either. Change requires following specific behaviors designed to make aspirations into reality. Action steps must be doable—in other words, simple. "Matching yourself with the right behaviors is the most critical step in the Behavior Design process," writes Dr. Fogg. When it comes to family affected by addiction, if happiness is our aspiration, achieving it is dependent upon group change. Fortunately, today, families coping with a loved one's addiction can utilize SFR and Al-Anon—two models designed precisely for group change, including specific behaviors and a process for implementing them.

The only design we need to create for ourselves is a mechanism for getting us to show up. We need to identify a trigger for going to our Al-Anon meeting. Regular and predictable triggers help establish consistency. The time our chosen meeting is scheduled will often reveal our trigger. If it's in the morning, we'll go after breakfast. If it's during our lunch hour or after dinner, we'll be triggered by those meals. When we link the day and time of Al-Anon to something we already do, attending the meeting will naturally flow from that triggering activity. For example, every Wednesday after I get off work, I go to my Al-Anon meeting.

21

Getting the Right Support

Once we have a team, we want to put Structured Family Recovery into action with a sense of immediacy. It's in taking action that we begin to see changes materialize. It's important to maximize support as early as possible for our newly recovering loved one. So how do we do this? Families have several choices. We're going to take a tour of several ways families can move forward, paying close attention to different circumstances and needs.

Before we look at these different options, though, it is important to point out a significant and often-overlooked fact that affects all families with an addicted loved one in treatment. If your loved one is in a residential treatment program, he is learning about recovery from morning to night every single day. If she is involved in an intensive outpatient program, she is receiving a less comprehensive level of care but is still involved in regular programming with a specific treatment plan. Addicted loved ones who are attending Alcoholics Anonymous or other Twelve Step programs, working the Steps with a sponsor, and making friends with other people in the program are rapidly learning about recovery. They are already beginning to see changes in their thinking and behaviors. As family members, we get very little or none of what our loved one is experiencing. They have entered an entirely new world, with its own language, and we are left behind in the old world. We need to catch up.

Most families think relationships will be better simply because our loved one is in recovery. Obviously, their sobriety is a huge positive achievement. However, newly recovering alcoholics or addicts cannot fix everything for everybody, and we cannot expect them to. Our old-world thinking won't mesh with their new-world thinking. Standing in two different worlds, we find it difficult to reconnect. Over time, either the addict will move back into the old world (relapse) or we will move into the new world (family recovery); another possibility is that the divide will grow wider as no one moves. Until we are all living in the new world of shared recovery, the family will remain out of balance, with strained relationships and ongoing mutual misunderstandings. Structured Family Recovery brings us into the new world together.

The easiest way to catch up with our recovering loved ones is to work with a trained and certified SFR counselor. While this book is written to make it possible to do SFR without professional help (more on that later), we are going to start our discussion about options by describing the highest level of support and then moving to the lower levels of support. Most (but not all) who choose to move ahead without an SFR counselor do so because of financial concerns. Many families have put everything they could afford into accessing treatment services for their loved one. As a result, these families often believe a lower level of investment and support is their only option. But there are ways to access higher levels of support even when financial resources are limited.

An SFR counselor is a skilled guide, offering the highest level of support. Moving families through each weekly meeting, SFR counselors keep everyone in the recovery lane, preventing us from slipping back into the disease lane. Most of us have been practicing crisis thinking and rescuing behaviors for a long time, and we are prone to returning to familiar patterns. The pathways in the brain that were built while dealing with addiction are strong and well formed. Slipping into this negative brain is much easier than building new pathways for recovery. A skilled SFR counselor will correct our courses, quickly bringing us back to this new world of family recovery. Our brain is redirected to right thinking. Staying on track, we will continue to create new pathways. By using our old pathways less and less, they will begin to atrophy. We begin experiencing growth in emotional sobriety while our loved one is practicing chemical sobriety. Together, we start to share this new language of recovery and a better family life.

We're not blind to the possibility of relapse—both by the addict and by the family. We all understand the dangers of a chemical relapse, but we rarely think about the dangers of an emotional relapse. When a family member has a major emotional relapse, it can trigger a cascading relapse effect among the other team members, including the newly recovering alcoholic or addict. For this reason, SFR calls for everyone on the team to complete a Recovery Plan. This is a success plan for each member. In Structured Family Recovery, the expectation is always success—never relapse. Recovery Plans are much easier to create under the guidance of an SFR counselor, who brings a knowledge base and skill set that makes everything simpler—and simple is good. We want to get this very important plan of action right.

Families need to demonstrate confident participation in their SFR meetings before inviting their loved one to join the team. Creating a positive social norm, which simply means setting a good example, is one of the most powerful things we can do to sustain lasting change. When our loved ones are in treatment, we are already working together. We want to be ready as a team to ask them to join Structured Family Recovery, preferably by week three or four. We can't ask our alcoholic or addict to join wavering family members and a disorderly meeting. We need to be operating smoothly and with conviction. This not only helps our addicted loved one feel comfortable, but it signals that we know what we're doing. An SFR counselor is trained to bring us to this place of confidence quickly.

If your team can work with an SFR counselor, your family will find it advantageous. Of course, working with a professional always comes with a fee. This can be an obstacle for some. Let's explore ways SFR teams who would like to have the added support of an SFR counselor can access help while minimizing costs. We're going to look at some realistic solutions families have found to be budget friendly. As we do, remember, families always have the option to use this book as a guide without an SFR counselor.

If a family wants to access the highest level of support, but cost is an issue, one solution is the *splitting costs method*. Family members simply divide responsibility for the professional fee among team members. SFR teams frequently make this work. For example, one family team included the addict's parents, grandparents, and uncle. They split the professional fee three ways, making it affordable for all. By doing so, they were able to work with an SFR counselor every week. Remember, your entire team receives this help for the same cost as an individual session. The professional fee remains the same no matter how many people are on the team—two, four, six, or more.

Another option is to start out with an SFR counselor and a plan to wean off professional help, with the family members eventually doing SFR on their own. This is called the *baby bird method*. Families typically work with an SFR counselor weekly until team members complete their Recovery Plans. Then, they begin alternating weeks, one week working with an SFR counselor and the next on their own. Once this feels comfortable, they work with an SFR counselor one week out of four. If all is good, the family then flies out of the nest and proceeds on their own. The SFR counselor is still available if they need some advice or extra help. To make this approach even more affordable, it can be combined with the splitting costs method. You should have the option to pay for this service week by week, so you won't need to come up with a large amount of money up front.

Families who want the extra support of an SFR counselor but who can't seem to find space in their budgets with the above methods might do an exercise called *competing positives*. This concept originates from the Positive Psychology Center at the University of Pennsylvania. It helps us build awareness around how we make choices between a variety of positives in our lives. Some of these positives are free (quiet time with a book), and some cost money (buying clothes or going out to eat). Most of us experience ongoing competing positives. *If I buy this expensive purse, I can't go out to eat for a month. I can afford this new car if I don't move into a bigger apartment.* We weigh each positive and assign a value to it. Positive psychology experts suggest we make more deliberate decisions when faced with competing positives. We ask ourselves,

"Between these two positives, which one will have the greatest positive effect on my future?" We can use the competing positives exercise when our team wants to access the extra support of an SFR counselor, but the cost is a strain on the wallet. The process may reveal that we can replace some positives that cost money with positives that don't. There are things we may decide we can do without, at least temporarily.

The competing positives exercise can be creatively combined with the splitting cost method and the baby bird method to put professional help within reach. If none of these are enough to increase a limited budget, make a commitment to become serious students of this book, trust your team, and embark on SFR on your own.

This edition of *It Takes a Family* is intended to make it clearer and easier for families to work together as SFR teams without professional help. We don't want family members who love an alcoholic or addict to feel they cannot participate in Structured Family Recovery because resources are tight. After all, addiction can cause strains on a family's financial security, and getting treatment comes with its own costs. This shouldn't prohibit anyone from gaining the benefits of SFR.

Doing it on your own, however, requires using this book as your recovery bible. *It Takes a Family* charts the course for you and contains all the tools you need. But you must read carefully, follow directions, use the checklists, be diligent, and make an unwavering commitment as a team. Drawing from the wisdom of AA's founders, your motto is "Half measures avail us nothing." If you hit a bump in the road, most SFR counselors will help by making themselves available to consult with your team for an hour or so. They will answer your questions and steer you in the right direction. It's a good idea for any SFR team going it alone to have identified an SFR counselor who is willing to consult with the team members from time to time. That relationship can prove to be invaluable and will cost very little in the scope of things.

As Dwight D. Eisenhower, thirty-fourth president of the United States, said, "Our real problem, then, is not our strength today; it is rather the vital necessity of action today to ensure our strength tomorrow." Put together a plan that works for your family team and begin. We don't get anywhere until we get started.

Finding Professional Help

Since Structured Family Recovery takes place over conference call, you can work with an SFR counselor located anywhere in the United States. If you live internationally, technology makes it possible to work with SFR counselors anywhere in the world. Do an internet search for a certified SFR counselor or go to lovefirst.net.

22

Put the Basics into Place

We lay the groundwork for family recovery even before our first SFR meeting. The structure we put into place at the beginning is particularly important for setting us on the right path. We build a recovery program by working a recovery program. Just like our addict, we jump in—sometimes kicking and screaming but, ultimately, we begin by relying on hope and faith. Recovery is a learning process. Every moment of resistance, doubt, questioning, and resentment that we experience as we start out has a lesson for us. Our struggles parallel the struggle our addict is having with making a commitment to recovery and sobriety. This shared beginning, rough as it feels at times, is a marvelous recipe for empathy.

Knowing that behavior creates change, we don't need to rely on our thinking or our feelings. We trust that our recovery behaviors will lead us to right thinking. We move our feet first. It is perfectly acceptable, even normal, to feel reluctance to doing something new as long as it doesn't stop us from taking that first step forward. Feelings adjust themselves to our actions. As with the addict in recovery, the world around us changes only when we change ourselves.

Good behavior design starts with putting the basics in place. This chapter outlines the things each member of the team needs to do before your first SFR meeting. Sometimes, one member of the team coordinates with everyone, making sure these things have been completed.

Materials You Need

There are a few items that each team member will need prior to the first SFR meeting. First, everyone needs a copy of this book, *It Takes a Family*. Read at least the first four chapters before your first SFR meeting. If you are engaging in Structured Family Recovery without an SFR counselor, read the entire text. The book educates all of the members of the team to a level similar to what their loved one is learning in treatment. It is a full family curriculum on the disease of addiction and how it becomes a family disease. It takes a deep dive into a nuanced and advanced understanding of recovery and what is required for success. The final section of the book includes a detailed program for a year's worth of SFR meetings for the entire family, including the newly recovering alcoholic or addict.

Second, team members will also need a daily reader. These little books are used for selecting the Daily Reading for SFR meetings each week. For this reason, all members on the SFR team need a copy of *Courage to Change* by Al-Anon Family Group. Additionally, the newly recovering alcoholic or addict needs a copy of *Daily Reflections* by Alcoholics Anonymous World Services. They can be purchased at most Twelve Step meetings or from booksellers. Daily readers for other types of Twelve Step programs (such as sex addiction) are also available. There are many recovery daily readers and meditation books available through various publishers; Hazelden Publishing has the most extensive catalog.

Third, everyone will need a notebook and pen for jotting down notes as well as journaling insights from SFR meetings and short weekly assignments. Most families come to value their notebooks as a recorded history of the journey they take with SFR. Keep everything handy, perhaps in a canvas bag, so you're not searching for things before your SFR meeting. Then it's all together and ready to go.

Make a Group Commitment

Start with a group commitment to meet on a specific day each week and come fully prepared to participate. If every week requires a decision from the team members as to whether or not they will attend, your group will be unstable and your progress sketchy. Families who achieve the greatest success are families who make this commitment together. If you have this book, you've already started this commitment piece. Once there is commitment, meeting every week becomes automatic. As one family member put it, "As a team, we just had to say let's go!"

Some families may not be ready to make a big commitment right away. In this case, the family can still make a commitment, but a smaller one. Your family will do well to commit to at least twelve SFR meetings before reevaluating. If the family decides to move forward, that's a good time to make a bigger commitment. Management consultant and author Peter F. Drucker put it best: "Unless commitment is made, there are only promises and hopes . . . but no plans." How your family moves forward will speak volumes to your newly recovering loved one.

Make a Decision: Choose an SFR Counselor or SFR Chairperson

Decide as a team what level of support you need. Before making a decision, review the previous chapter, "Getting the Right Support." There are different ways a team can proceed.

Working with an SFR counselor makes the startup process easier and smoother for all. Some families choose to work with an SFR counselor throughout all of the weekly meetings. When you are not planning to work with an SFR counselor, select a member of your team to act as the SFR chairperson. Choose someone who is highly respected by everyone on the team—especially by the addict. This is a person nobody wants to disappoint and who usually will have the least amount of emotional baggage with the addicted person. Think of the chairperson as the team diplomat. Most families know right away who best fits this role. The chairperson is someone who has a cool head and the ability to gently keep people on track. If there is no one who comes close to fitting this description, it may be a sign that family relationships have deteriorated to a point where there is a significant breakdown of mutual respect. In this case, when at all possible, work with an SFR counselor, at least until family relationships are repaired enough to move forward on your own.

If a team decides to work with an SFR counselor on a bimonthly basis rather than weekly, an SFR chairperson moderates the off-week meetings. When a family team feels working with a professional is no longer necessary, the chairperson takes on the role of moderator full time. A checklist for the SFR chairperson can be found in chapter 26, "Structured Family Recovery Checklists."

Select an SFR Secretary

The SFR secretary is the team detail person. The position can rotate among team members, each taking the job for a number of weeks. It's beneficial for everyone to take a turn, since service positions cultivate a greater sense of team cohesiveness. The SFR secretary is responsible for scheduling weekly meetings, setting up conference calls, and taking brief minutes at each meeting. The secretary will email these minutes to team members as well as the SFR counselor, if you are working with one. Chapter 26, "Structured Family Recovery Checklists," provides a checklist for the SFR secretary.

Choose an Accountability Partner

Until you have a Twelve Step sponsor, select a member of your SFR team as your accountability partner. This is the person you will call during the week to report on your recovery progress. For example, "I have trouble keeping my commitment to attend meetings, so I will call you before and after each meeting." We all do much better when we promise to be honest with another human being. Accountability increases our sense of belonging. *When I belong to you, and you to me, we are accountable to one another.* Accountability is about working together, being open and honest, staying focused on our goal, and creating trustworthiness. Serving as an accountability partner comes with its own set of expectations. *I must be accountable before I can talk to you about your accountability. I must create a safe place for you. I must make myself available to you.* Each person on the SFR team can act as an accountability partner, working with one teammate at a time. Avoid one or two people taking on this responsibility for the entire SFR team. Keep it simple.

Simple Weekly Assignments

While in treatment, our loved ones get a treatment plan, listing a number of reading, writing, and sharing assignments that they work on throughout their stay. They also attend daily lectures and groups. By engaging in these activities, they are gaining a considerable amount of knowledge and insight. In the beginning weeks of Structured Family Recovery, the family team has its own plan, including assignments to make sure everyone reads this book in its entirety, guaranteeing that everyone is fully up to speed. Additionally, each SFR meeting ends with a short assignment for the following week. These assignments are neither laborious nor time consuming. "Simple, simple, simple" is our motto. But we do need to do certain things to gain the right recovery base. We develop a capacity to speak with our newly recovering loved ones with a high degree of confidence. We want to know what we are talking about when we speak of recovery.

Three-Second Celebration

In *Tiny Habits,* B. J. Fogg points out that most of us have many ways of telling ourselves that we did a bad job, but very few ways of saying we did a good job. Dr. Fogg understands how the brain responds to the power of celebration. He calls it a superpower. Celebration isn't empty praise for doing nothing, but a way to make your brain pay attention when you've accomplished something. Dr. Fogg explains: "When you celebrate, you create a positive feeling inside yourself on demand. This good feeling wires the new habit into your brain. Celebration is both a specific technique for behavior change and a psychological frame shift." When we celebrate, we create positive emotions, and "emotions create behaviors." Positive experiences and celebrations accumulate over time, changing what we do and how we feel. Dr. Fogg, explaining his own experience with celebration, says, "It was like a warm space had opened up in my chest where there had been a dark tightness. I felt calmer and even a little energized. And this made me want to feel that way again."

Each SFR team selects a three-second celebration that everyone agrees to. Whenever someone meets a recovery goal, the team celebrates together. You can even choose a team cheerleader to initiate celebrations. *I went to my first Al-Anon meeting! Awesome!* Celebrate as a choir of enthusiasm. A lukewarm celebration isn't a celebration. The brain will barely notice these, because lukewarm doesn't make anyone feel good. So don't be shy when celebrating. Belt it out with emotion! As Kay Redfield Jamison writes in her book *Exuberance: The Passion for Life,* "[T]he quick dispersal of exuberant or triumphant emotion accelerates the spread of the news of victory. . . . When there is cause for celebration . . . infectious fervor will further a swift dissemination." She goes on to point out that the transmission of emotions is rapid, and we are capable of spreading and catching joy. Just think what happens when someone is having a hearty belly laugh, tears running down his face, rocking forward in his seat, slapping his knees. We may not even know what the person is laughing about, but without much delay we are laughing too.

Celebrations happen during the Report, Discuss, Plan portions of the meeting, as families share what went well in their recovery over the past week. Decide what celebration works for your team. It might be *Awesome! Victory! Boo-yah! You rock! Hip, hip, hooray! Yes, you did it! You're a star! Woo-hoo! Hallelujah! Brilliant! Excellent! Wow, wow, wow!* Once you choose your celebratory exclamation, practice around the house until it's yours. Then belt it out whenever someone accomplishes a recovery goal. As one family member told me, "At first, I really thought the celebration thing was silly, but I grew to love it. When I accomplished a milestone, I couldn't wait for SFR and hearing my family shout out, 'You rock!'" As your team learns to celebrate in your own unique way, you will create the feeling Dr. Fogg calls "shine." Let's all shine together.

Schedule Your First SFR Meeting

Just get a few basics in place: date, time, and who will set up the conference call. Setting up conference calls is easy. You can choose from several services. We use freeconference.com, and schedule all our calls online. By email, each family member receives an invitation with a telephone number connecting them to the conference call and a passcode that allows them to join the meeting. Simply follow the prompts. These services are free and easy to set up with smartphones. If you are working with an SFR counselor, that person will take care of scheduling.

Attempting to plan meetings that change from week to week can be time consuming and confusing. It's far simpler to hold meetings at the same time every week. Making an unwavering commitment to that date and time also keeps it simple. As one family told me, "No other activity ever comes between us and our SFR meetings. Every one of us made a commitment to always be on the call." In fact, one family member changed his departure date for international travel plans to keep from interfering with his family's SFR meeting.

Double-check that everyone has a copy of this book, so all team members are following along and participating fully during the SFR meeting. Confirm that they have read the first four chapters. If so, and if you are working with an SFR counselor, get started. Remember, if you are proceeding without an SFR counselor, everyone needs to read the entire book first. Otherwise, you won't know what you are doing, and it will be impossible to get the most out of the process.

Family Members Start First

We cannot say it too often: begin your SFR journey with family members first. Do not include your newly recovering loved one in the first meetings. It's imperative that, by the time you invite the alcoholic or addict to join the team, you are capable of leading by example. Your loved one should be sober, enrolled in a treatment program, or faithfully working a recovery program by attending Twelve Step meetings on a regular basis. The family members should all be able to say they've been to at least one Al-Anon or other Twelve Step family meeting before your addicted loved one is part of your SFR meetings.

You need to be comfortable with the format of SFR so meetings run smoothly. If your team appears disorganized, unsure, or confused, you will send the wrong message when your newly recovering loved one joins you. She may even refuse to continue as a team member. You don't need to be an expert on addiction and recovery, but having a good handle on how to proceed with Structured Family Recovery creates a positive experience for everyone. Positive experiences lead to continued involvement. Team cohesiveness and confidence in what you are doing establishes a positive social norm. Remember, positive social norms are the most powerful way to bring about change—and norms are contagious. Left to our own devices, we often unwittingly create negative social norms. What we demonstrate through our actions has a forceful impact on our loved one's behaviors. When the SFR team exudes confidence, the recovering alcoholic or addict will sense it immediately.

When your team is ready to invite your recovering loved one to join SFR, you can do so as early as the third or fourth week, but not before. The first two meetings are designed for the family members without the addict present.

Share Your SFR Recovery with Your Loved One in Treatment

If your loved one is stable in his treatment program (or sober in AA or another Twelve Step group), you can talk with him about the family's participation in Structured Family Recovery and the recovery process. Here is an example of a good way to share this information:

> Jack, we have terrific respect for what you are doing in treatment and recovery. We can only imagine how hard you are working and some of the difficulties you face. But we also trust that you are experiencing a lot of really good moments and personal insights, and having some fun. We're proud of you and hope you are proud of yourself. We also have come to learn that this is a family disease. We all played a part in the addiction, so it is only right we play our part in recovery. We love you and we value our family, so we've made a commitment to Structured Family Recovery and our own Twelve Step work. Our SFR team meets over conference calls, so it would be easy to include you while you are in treatment. Our meetings focus on the positives of recovery and are very encouraging and constructive. This is not therapy. You'll see how good it is when you experience it for yourself. Would you join us for our third (or fourth) meeting?

Sometimes newly recovering loved ones think that family involvement means they are going to be chastised verbally, or their past behaviors will be thrown in their face. They imagine anger, blame, and disappointment. Who would want to join such a group? Be clear that SFR is about building a future in recovery. It's a "positive brain" experience that will bring the family back together. Together, we'll start to have fun again.

23

How to Navigate an SFR Meeting

Structured Family Recovery is precisely what it says—a structure for recovery as a family. It isn't random; it is built to function in a very specific way. The process creates a spiritual connection within the family. Before long, family members begin to see significant changes unfold. As one member of an SFR team put it: "I always loved my family, but I thought we were supposed to stay in our own lanes. Sure, we were close, but we were essentially operating as a group of individuals. Before SFR, I never realized it could be different. Now we experience each other as something greater—a family. It's a much better way."

Each SFR weekly meeting is part of a larger design that moves everyone forward into a spacious recovery. The SFR meeting structure creates a path forward, out of the grips of addiction. Rather than restricting us, adhering closely to the structure allows us to expand. The structure is a canvas we fill with our unique visions, personality, spirituality, and warmth. One mother told me she always begins her family's SFR meeting by saying, "You are valued, you are loved, you are worth it." Many families, after completing all the SFR meetings in the book, love it so much they start all over again.

Before we begin, we must remember that Structured Family Recovery is not group therapy. It is not a place to air grievances. Giving a voice to our hurts, resentments, and anger can feel like a positive for the individual in the moment, but it is a negative for the family. Families have been hurt enough by the addiction. We do not need to continue doing this to each other in recovery. Instead, we choose what is optimal for family cohesiveness. This includes taking our problems and negative emotions (which we all have) to our Twelve Step groups. The Steps and our sponsors will help us discover appropriate solutions.

Let's learn about the elements of Structured Family Recovery and how to navigate a meeting.

The Elements of an SFR Meeting

Before starting each weekly meeting, the SFR counselor or the SFR chairperson selects the order in which the members of the team will take turns reading and sharing. This makes the process go smoothly, avoiding confusion and awkward silences. A smooth process doesn't waste time, increases engagement, strengthens cohesion, and makes everyone feel more comfortable. By knowing the order, the members are able to follow the person before them. No one waits for an invitation or needs an introduction before speaking.

Opening Statement

The Opening Statement is an important ritual every week. It tells us we're moving into a different space and what is expected of us while we are in this space. We leave behind agendas that don't belong in Structured Family Recovery. Each week, we read the Opening Statement to recommit ourselves to the process, reinforcing the trustworthiness of this space and the hour we share together. Group expectations also support mutual respect and safety.

We read the opening round-robin style, following the order of readers selected each week. For example, Marie, Clark, Teresa, Stephen, Paul, Kelly. Each member is checking in to the space by taking a turn to read. This is a ritual of joining our voices together. It ensures participation of everyone in the group. Equally important, team members are hearing everyone else's voice. Neuroscientists have found that listeners have an easier time focusing on the spoken word when it is being expressed by a familiar voice. The voices of those closest to us activate the brain in unique ways, arousing emotional and creative responses.

Daily Reading

Each week, a team member is prepared to read from a Twelve Step daily reader, such as *Courage to Change* or *Daily Reflections.* The opening reading sets the tone for the entire hour. The chosen reading is about the meeting topic of the week. Each meeting's reader is selected the week before, so she will be prepared with a reading she believes best reflects the team. People take choosing the week's reading very seriously. It is a significant act of service to take the time necessary to diligently review all of the possible readings for a particular topic and find a reading that will be meaningful to the entire team. One father of a newly recovering addict took two hours looking for just the right reading. His wife explained that they had purchased numerous Twelve Step daily readers and meditation books. Her husband pored over each book and every reading on the topic before deciding what to bring to the group. Imagine how his newly recovering son felt, knowing that his dad took recovery so seriously. Do you think that addicted son paid close attention to what his father chose to read?

After reading, the week's reader shares with the team why he chose that particular selection. Hearing the reasons why someone chose a reading or reflection is a very powerful experience. After the reader is done reading and sharing, the other team members all offer their insights. Everybody learns something from each person's thoughts.

Report, Discuss, Plan

Families love this part of the meeting: Report, Discuss, Plan. It's the place where everyone on the team shares and celebrates personal milestones—going to a first Al-Anon meeting, finding a home group, faithfully reading a daily reader, getting a sponsor, signing up for working the Steps with a sponsor, chairing a meeting. When we share our recovery progress, we set a positive example for everyone on the team, including our newly recovering loved one. This has a powerful effect on team members who may be lagging behind. They will instinctively want to catch up. One family had a team member who hadn't yet attended a family Twelve Step meeting. He said he would but never managed to do it. One week, the team accepted a challenge for the upcoming week: "Let's make our family a 100 percent family—everyone makes an Al-Anon or AA meeting this week. No one person can reach the 100 percent goal for the rest of us. It's going to take every one of us to succeed." The fellow who was dragging his feet surprised everyone. By the time they gathered for the next meeting, he had not only gone to his first meeting, he had found a sponsor as well. This was cause for one big celebration during that week's Report, Discuss, Plan.

Report, Discuss, Plan consists of three check-in items. Each is self-explanatory. The first asks us to refer to our Personal Recovery Checklist as we report what went well in our Twelve Step recovery over the past week. Note that this is very specific to recovery. We are not talking about general self-care, which is beneficial and encouraged but different from recovery. In Structured Family Recovery, we want to speak specifically about what we are doing for our Twelve Step program. The Personal Recovery Checklist informs us about what we've done well and what needs improvement. We are accountable to ourselves with these questions. The checklist is designed to help us answer the questions.

Within this first check-in item, "Do I need someone's insight?" is an optional question. We use this question when we know we need to improve our recovery program in a certain area but feel stuck. We ask this question of a team member who is having more success in that area. *Tamara, I'm struggling getting a sponsor, and you've been successful getting one. Could you share some of your personal insights on how you did it?* Tamara isn't going to tell her what to do. Instead, she is going to share what she did and how it led to finding a sponsor. If someone asks any team member this question, the correct way to respond begins with "This is what worked for me . . ."

The second check-in item invites sharing about the insights we gained from last week's SFR assignment. Each meeting ends with a small assignment that directs us back to our Twelve Step community. When we share our insights, we provide the rest of the group with something important. Although we've all done the same assignment, we get to see it through the experiences of each other, learning something from our team members that we hadn't seen. Everyone brings something valuable to our group—no matter how simple—and that's what strengthens our sense of belonging and pulls us closer together.

The third check-in item challenges us to tell the team exactly what our recovery goal is for the upcoming week. It's easy to break promises to ourselves, but not so easy to break our word to these important people in our life. Naming our goal aloud in front of others makes it a sacred promise. How likely are we not to keep our word under those circumstances? The Personal Recovery Checklist once again helps us choose our goal. Then we make one more commitment. We state how many times we will contact our accountability partner in the upcoming week. An accountability partner is a team member whom we commit to calling to talk about our recovery progress or to share something interesting we learned in a meeting. These calls typically take five or ten minutes.

Family Recovery Discussion

This discussion portion of the meeting is composed of three parts, each of which is read aloud by a different team member. The first section is read. The reader then shares her insights. After that, team members share their insights, round-robin style. No one interrupts or makes a comment when another is speaking. We show respect by listening quietly. This same process is repeated for each of the remaining two paragraphs.

Learn Something New

Learn Something New provides information supportive of the weekly topic. The information is not necessarily from Twelve Step recovery literature. However, it supports recovery by offering a particular perspective, sometimes scientific, philosophical, or spiritual. It directs our thinking in a manner appropriate to where we are on our recovery journey.

Steps

The Steps information focuses on one of the Twelve Steps. SFR meetings in this book, from first to last, go through all twelve of the Steps. Each week, this section provides deeper understanding of each Step and how it works. While most people know something about Twelve Step programs in general, they rarely know much about the actual Steps. Recovering loved ones are typically far ahead of the family when it comes to the Steps due to their experiences in treatment and AA. These sections provide insights and offer an opportunity for all team members to share their thoughts. This deeper understanding is especially important for family members as they build their recovery vocabulary. The Steps section also provides the team members with something they can talk about at their Twelve Step meetings.

Working a Recovery Program

Working a Recovery Program clarifies the difference between going to a meeting and working a recovery program. Here we find practical suggestions and insights on how to work a recovery program in a way that leads to positive change in relationships and everyday life. As a wife of an addict said,

> I thought addiction was my husband's problem and once he was sober everything would be all right. But that's not the way it worked out. So I relented and went to Al-Anon, but I just sat in meetings and never got involved. Of course, in those days, I didn't think Al-Anon was doing anything for me. I didn't understand that it was me not doing anything for Al-Anon. Then my husband relapsed and almost died. While he was in treatment, I was losing my mind. That's when I realized I needed to go back to Al-Anon, get a sponsor, and begin working the Steps. After my sponsor and I completed all Twelve Steps, I changed in ways I never expected. I am a much better person today, and my husband has been sober for several years now. We both share a language of recovery, and we use the wisdom to navigate our lives together. It's the relationship I always hoped for, but I had to do my work to get here.

Assignment

These are short assignments that direct us back to our Twelve Step recovery communities. Use your notebook to journal and jot down insights. Doing weekly assignments is something practical that we do. It is a bridge from one week's SFR meeting to the next. It's also the way we weave together our SFR and Twelve Step meetings. We bring what we learn in SFR to our Twelve Step program, and vice versa. When we share insights from our assignments, the wisdom we carry from one meeting to the other enriches our entire family team. Everything learned by every team member is amplified when we bring it to Report, Discuss, Plan.

Closing Statement

We conclude each meeting as we started it—with another positive ritual. Our Closing Statement is "The Promises" from the Big Book of Alcoholics Anonymous. The Promises are a beloved part of the Big Book for alcoholics and addicts all around the world. Through SFR, more and more families are coming to know them and love them too. The Promises remind us of the benefits we can expect to come true in our lives by working this program one day at a time. We are a family group engaged in recovery. As the individual team members experience the Promises coming true in their life, the entire family is elevated and freed of burdens. We change together, and family is a reflection of our betterment.

The entire team participates in the reading of the Promises, using the round-robin style. It's beautiful to hear the voices of those we love speak these words.

For more information on the weekly meeting process, consider listening to *The Best Minds Podcast* titled "The Structured Family Recovery Experience," a discussion with three SFR counselors, at lovefirst.net /best-minds-podcast.

24

Don't Drop Bombs: Red, Yellow, Green Light

Structured Family Recovery doesn't allow us to wallow in problems; it immerses us in solutions. SFR is structured, offering a particular course to follow that will move us in a very specific direction. We don't wrestle with the many problems caused by active addiction. Everybody has been doing that for a long time to no avail. Here's a little-known secret: with active recovery, most problems actually work themselves out. We simply do the next right thing. SFR is designed to keep families moving forward from one right thing to the next. Red Light, Yellow Light, Green Light is a gatekeeping tool that helps us do just that. This technique keeps the group focused on its singleness of purpose, steering us away from old patterns and conflicts.

What happens if a team member drops a bomb—inserting some outside issue that doesn't belong in SFR into the meeting? *I think we need to talk about how much money our brother has cost Mom and Dad. How is he going to pay them back? I really think we should all be concerned about this!* We simply say, "That may be important, but it's a Red Light issue." Without argument, this swiftly signals that the topic is inappropriate for an SFR meeting. There is no discussion, the meeting isn't hijacked, we aren't eating up precious time, and the team members are allowed to keep their focus where it ought to be.

"Bomb drops" are cognitively stressful for the team. The control centers of team members' brains have been depleted by years of coping with active addiction. Bomb drops tax them further, triggering disturbed emotions and setting the stage for conflict. The family system starts heating up again. In that instant, our thinking, emotions, and behavior begin to shift away from Structured Family Recovery as attention moves to some unmanageable problem. This is not a benign distraction. Effects can linger into the next few meetings. Everyone is tense. *Will there be another bomb this week?* We need to let our brains relax inside the safety of our structure. We need to know what to expect every week. No surprises.

For these reasons, we build separate outlets for family members' concerns. Once our addicted loved one has agreed to accept help, much of the chaos and residual wreckage of addiction still remains. It takes time to put a life back together, clean up the messes, and pick up the pieces. The mess has been around for a long time. We cannot and will not suddenly fix all the problems and right all the wrongs. We need a way of categorizing our concerns. We want a quick way of determining importance, urgency, and strategy. Red Light, Yellow Light, Green Light does that for us. It's simple and direct. Is this a Red Light issue, a Yellow Light issue, or a Green Light issue? Let's take a look at how it works.

Red Light means the issue is not appropriate to address. Yellow Light means we don't know if it is or isn't appropriate, so we're going to give it time or get more information. Green Light means it is appropriate. Once we identify the correct light, we know if we should or shouldn't take action or wait and see.

Let's use the bomb-dropping example above. A sister is very agitated about the money her parents have given her brother during his addiction. She's been angry about his financial irresponsibility for years. She decides the SFR meeting provides an opportunity for her to draw everyone's attention to this problem. With the best of intentions, she drops a bomb about her brother's irresponsibility and her parents' financial enabling. She stresses that her parents could ill afford the money they've spent. She doesn't understand that she is hijacking the meeting. It feels like a critical issue to her. The team members are suddenly confronted with an emotionally charged situation. They are not sure how to react or what to say. There may be stunned silence or a contentious discussion. The parents may feel embarrassed and chastised. The brother's defenses go up. However it goes, the team is no longer engaged in their purpose for meeting—Structured Family Recovery.

How could this be handled differently? First, the team must agree from the beginning that outside issues will be addressed outside of SFR. These issues are always a Red Light for SFR. Certain concerns need to be addressed elsewhere. To see how this works, let's walk through the correct way for the sister to address her concerns.

If the family is working with an SFR counselor, the sister can arrange a case management call with the counselor separate from the normal SFR meetings. After discussion, the SFR counselor determines that the money issue is a Red Light for SFR because it strays from the content and focus of SFR. If the SFR team members were to address the brother's past irresponsibility, they would alienate him. Structured Family Recovery is a catalyst for recovery, not a mediation session for outside family issues.

During the case management call, the SFR counselor redirects the sister to the Green Light venues for addressing these concerns. Perhaps the sister needs to sit down with her parents to discuss these concerns outside of the SFR meeting, then turn the matter over to her parents to decide for themselves, since this issue is really between her parents and her brother. The SFR counselor explains why it's a Red Light for the sister to take on the problem as hers—it isn't her money. The parents decide in their own time if it's productive or helpful to address this issue while their son is jobless, broke, and in treatment. Their immediate concern may be different than their daughter's—that their son finds a job and a place to live after treatment. The SFR counselor suggests that these concerns would be a Green Light issue for their son's treatment counselor. The parents share their thoughts with the counselor, who then addresses these issues in the son's aftercare plan, recommending a sober house that helps residents find employment.

So the sister's concerns about her parents' money are a Red Light for SFR. A conversation with her parents outside of SFR is a Green Light. The parents' sharing of their concerns with the counselor in treatment is also a Green Light. The treatment team's decisions to add recommendations in the aftercare plan to address these concerns is a third Green Light.

Let's look at another example. An adult son was in treatment for crack cocaine, meth, and Xanax addiction. He joined his family's SFR team while still in treatment and has now been home for two months. He has a high-pressure job, and some of the team members are concerned that his long hours at work may be a relapse warning sign. Although he has been getting to some AA meetings, it is hit or miss. The team schedules a case management session with the SFR counselor. They review the son's Recovery Plan (which was created by the son), including his aftercare recommendations from the treatment program. In his plan, he asked that his dad and his best friend approach him with any concerns about relapse warning signs. The SFR counselor gives the Green Light for the dad and friend to talk to the son outside of the SFR meetings. They meet, sharing their concerns in a very loving manner, and review the Recovery Plan together. After the conversation, it is a Green Light for the son to share the results of their talk in the next SFR meeting during Report, Discuss, Plan. *I talked about my relapse warning signs with my sponsor. He and I set up an AA meeting schedule, daily phone calls, and time for the two of us to get together weekly. He suggests I discuss working fewer hours with my boss and, if that doesn't work out, find another job.*

For families who are not working with an SFR counselor, it is appropriate to set up a time to discuss issues of concern with the chairperson and team. To help sort out what concerns are appropriate for SFR, ask, "Is this concern directly related to relapse warning signs or relapse?" If it is, then it's within the realm of Structured Family Recovery. The Recovery Plan is consulted and followed separately from the SFR meetings. If it isn't, then it is a problem that needs to be addressed elsewhere.

Sometimes a concern feels like a relapse issue, but it isn't. *Our sister's boyfriend is an alcoholic. We're concerned the relationship will lead her to relapse after treatment. This is a Red Light issue for SFR but a Green Light issue for her counselor in treatment. We bring this to the counselor because the boyfriend is currently the issue, not relapse.* In treatment, the counseling staff can work therapeutically with the sister to address her problematic relationship.

Yellow Light can sometimes be the hardest to determine. Here is an example of a family using a Yellow Light approach. Ken and Katie's college-age son wanted to go back to school three months after getting out of treatment. They felt uncomfortable about his readiness and the idea of him living in the dorms. The SFR counselor correctly determined it was a Red Light issue for SFR, but a Yellow Light issue for the family. Making school a point of contention in the weekly recovery meeting could cause bigger problems. The son could gear up his defenses and position himself against his parents and the SFR team. The Yellow Light helped the parents take a slower approach while including their son in the decision making.

Ken and Katie decided to talk with their Al-Anon sponsors, who presented them with a series of questions: *Is this an emergency?* "No," they said. *For your son, is this a need or a want?* "It's a want," they said. *Should he get what he wants whenever he wants it?* "No, that's what happened in his addiction," they said. *What Twelve Step slogans could help you right now?* Ken and Katie chose "One day at a time" and "First things first." They discussed using the first three Steps of their Twelve Step program for guidance. The sponsors didn't make their decision for them but helped them clarify thinking by using recovery principles.

Sitting down with their son, Katie and Ken told him they understood why he thought going back to college was a good idea. "But first things first," they said, using a recovery slogan that he understood. "You'll get back to college, but let's do this right. Let's start by researching universities and colleges." By taking time to explore possibilities with their son, they discovered collegiate programs for recovering students. They learned that these programs required a minimum of six months of sobriety before admission, which solved the problem of going back to school too soon.

Eventually, their son was accepted at a college that had a highly successful and engaging collegiate program. He would be actively involved with a group of students in recovery. The son was happy to go back to school, and the parents felt comfortable knowing his recovery would remain a front-burner issue. By using the Yellow Light, they gave themselves more time to work out a good solution and avoided conflict.

When a family member has a serious emotional relapse, you can follow the same steps. All of the SFR team members may experience a moment when they start slipping off track. Slips can come in many forms, including complacency or overconfidence. When working with a team, we have an advantage. The loving people who are engaged in recovery with us can gently guide us back on course. As Marcus Tullius Cicero, Roman statesman and philosopher, wrote: "*Non nobis solum nati sumus* (Not for ourselves alone are we born)."

A Red Light, Yellow Light, Green Light Decision-Making Checklist is available in chapter 26, "Structured Family Recovery Checklists."

25

We Use Checklists

Checklists are both simple and powerful. They reduce complexity into small steps and then remind us exactly what we need to do. In an essay on human fallibility, philosophers Samuel Gorovitz and Alasdair MacIntyre identify two reasons why we fail when we are capable of success. The first is ignorance. Sometimes we simply don't have the required knowledge to do the job. The second is ineptitude. We have the knowledge but apply it incorrectly.

Dr. Atul Gawande, a U.S. surgeon and expert on optimizing health care systems, writes in his book *The Checklist Manifesto*, "Checklists seem to provide protection against such failures. They remind us of the minimum necessary steps and make them explicit. They not only offer the possibility of verification but also instill a kind of discipline of higher performance." He goes on to say that bad checklists are imprecise and too long, making them impractical. He recommends checklists that are precise, covering the most important steps without trying to spell out everything. The best checklists are quick and simple to use. Once again, we see simplicity touted as a precursor to success.

There are two types of checklists. First there is the "Do–Confirm" checklist. Once a task is completed, you reference the checklist to determine if you did everything properly. This is a good choice when you are well practiced at a task. The second is the "Read–Do" checklist. This walks you through the essential steps of an endeavor, checking each item off as you go. For beginners, or when engaging in complex activities, this is particularly helpful. Structured Family Recovery uses the Read–Do checklist.

Dr. Gawande found that physicians, on average, take up to seventeen years to adopt new treatments in their practices. This long timeline isn't because of unwillingness, but because "the necessary knowledge has not been translated into a simple, usable, and systematic form . . . distilling the information into its practical essence." I think we can say the same is true for addicts and their families. When it comes to engaging in recovery and achieving lasting sobriety, nobody has ever before translated family recovery into a simple, usable, and systematic form that makes it understandable and doable. Structured Family Recovery does exactly that.

Aviation specialists, who create checklists for pilots, have refined lists into the most usable form. The recommended number of items on an aviation checklist is five to nine. By adding more, we're apt to overtax the limits of our working memory. Language is simple and explicit. The list fits on one page. Colors or patterns are a distraction. All of these suggestions are incorporated into SFR checklists.

Dr. Gawande describes why we humans benefit from this kind of organization, "Discipline is hard—harder than trustworthiness and skill and perhaps even selflessness. We are by nature flawed and inconsistent creatures. We can't even keep from snacking between meals. We are not built for discipline. We are built for novelty and excitement, not for careful attention to detail. Discipline is something we have to work at." Checklists, he says, can make discipline a norm, something reliable we can depend on.

Checklists prevent common mistakes and omissions. They act as triggers for what actions we need to take (Read–Do). Checklists keep it simple, preventing us from complicating things and making tasks harder than they need to be. Checklists prevent patterns from our past returning to cause failures.

The checklists in the next chapter are a reflection of what you've learned reading this book. They're not intended as an outline of every detail. Remember, our brains turn off when we see complex, lengthy checklists. Short and simple is the rule. When we need more information about a specific step, we use the book or talk to our SFR counselor, chairperson, or teammates. Checklists are simply reminders.

The brain can work against us. Our inherent faith in ourselves often trips us up. We believe we'll remember things we don't, and we trust that the motivation we feel in the moment will extend to next week or the week after. But it often doesn't. We may feel gung ho today but be totally uninterested later. Our brains give us the benefit of the doubt when we really don't deserve it. Checklists help us avoid the disconnect between what we believe we will do and what we really do.

Checklists are designed for consistency. Consistency leads to family transformation. An SFR team member who had the role of team chairperson says, "Before we have our SFR call, I always pull out my SFR Chairperson Checklist. I go through every step on the list, which I think of as short reminders. In the beginning, I did this so I knew what I was supposed to do. After a while, I knew what to do, but I used the checklist so I wouldn't forget anything. Now, I know the checklist by heart. But I still use it because it centers me. I feel ready for our SFR meeting."

The checklists in the next chapter helps us stay on our path to recovery.

26

Structured Family Recovery Checklists

All SFR checklists are located in this chapter, making them easy to reference. Each is designed as a "Read–Do" checklist. We're asked to simply read through the checklists and follow those we need, when we need them. These checklists reduce steps to their simplest form by organizing information for the purpose of taking action. Read–Do checklists are perfect when doing something new and unfamiliar.

The following SFR checklists will help keep your SFR team on track:

- SFR Overview Checklist
- Red Light, Yellow Light, Green Light Decision-Making Checklist
- Personal Recovery Checklist
- SFR Chairperson Checklist
- SFR Secretary Checklist
- Recovery Plan Checklist

You can download and print checklists at lovefirst.net/sfr-resources or hazelden.org/web/go/ittakesafamily.

SFR Overview Checklist

☐ Read the book *It Takes a Family*.

☐ Begin SFR meetings and attend Al-Anon before inviting the recovering person to attend week 3 or 4.

☐ Select an SFR counselor or chairperson.

☐ Select a team secretary.

☐ Review the SFR meeting format and prepare before meetings.

☐ Use checklists as a simple way to stay on track.

☐ Practice optimism and the spirituality of kindness.

☐ Add fun to recovery.

☐ Review the "Red Light, Yellow Light, Green Light" method of decision making.

☐ Explore guidelines for developing a Recovery Plan. Refer to chapters 27 and 28.

Red Light, Yellow Light, Green Light
Decision-Making Checklist

☐ No surprises: We don't drop bombs in the middle of SFR meetings.

☐ We bring concerns to the SFR counselor or team chairperson outside a meeting.

☐ We ask: "Is this concern directly or indirectly related to relapse warning signs or symptoms?"

☐ Decisions are made upon reviewing the concern and its appropriateness for SFR.

☐ Red Light: A concern may be legitimate, but it's not appropriate for an SFR meeting.

☐ Yellow Light: A concern may be legitimate, but we're not sure if it is or isn't appropriate for an SFR meeting. We give ourselves more time to contemplate.

☐ Green Light: A concern is legitimate and is appropriate for an SFR meeting.

☐ We follow the guidelines in our Recovery Plans when approaching teammates who are demonstrating relapse symptoms or who have relapsed.

☐ We demonstrate flexibility, giving teammates reasonable time to make better recovery decisions, unless they are in imminent danger. We then act quickly, engaging professional services as needed.

Personal Recovery Checklist Reminders

Choose a Twelve Step Meeting for Family Members: Al-Anon, Adult Children of Alcoholics, Families Anonymous, Nar-Anon, Codependents Anonymous, S-Anon, or Gam-Anon, and others. Celebrate Recovery is a Christian Twelve Step program. Families begin by attending at least one meeting per week. Select a home group; this is the group you always attend. You can find meetings online.

Choose Twelve Step Meetings for Recovery from Addiction: Alcoholics Anonymous, Narcotics Anonymous, Gamblers Anonymous, Sex Addicts Anonymous, Overeaters Anonymous, and others. Follow recommendations from the treatment staff or your Twelve Step sponsor for weekly meeting attendance. Ninety meetings in ninety days are often recommended. Select a home group; this is the group you always attend. You can find meetings online.

Choose a sponsor. The person who helps you work the Twelve Steps is called a sponsor. Sponsors are typically same gender.

Service work. Accepting a volunteer position to help out at your home group is called service work. These are small tasks such as setting out the literature, making coffee, arranging chairs, or greeting people at the door.

Fellowship. Socializing with people from your Twelve Step meetings is called fellowship. Several people may get together after a meeting at a restaurant or coffeehouse, for instance.

Personal Recovery Checklist

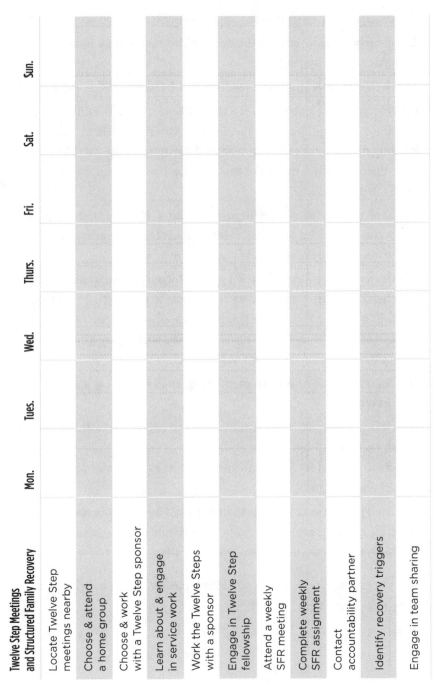

Twelve Step Meetings and Structured Family Recovery	Mon.	Tues.	Wed.	Thurs.	Fri.	Sat.	Sun.
Locate Twelve Step meetings nearby							
Choose & attend a home group							
Choose & work with a Twelve Step sponsor							
Learn about & engage in service work							
Work the Twelve Steps with a sponsor							
Engage in Twelve Step fellowship							
Attend a weekly SFR meeting							
Complete weekly SFR assignment							
Contact accountability partner							
Identify recovery triggers							
Engage in team sharing							

SFR Chairperson Checklist Reminders

The chairperson moderates, starting and ending meetings on time.

The chairperson designates the order team members will share. The order changes weekly.

The chairperson prompts the reading of the Opening Statement.

Daily Reading (selected prior to the SFR meeting). The chairperson introduces the topic and asks the team member who selected the Daily Reading on the week's topic to read and then share about it. Next, each team member shares his or her thoughts on the reading following the designated order for sharing.

The chairperson introduces Report, Discuss, Plan. Team members follow the designated order for sharing. Each team member shares on all the questions before the next team member shares.

The chairperson moderates the Family Recovery Discussion. The chairperson selects a different team member to read each of the three readings in this section. After reading, each reader shares his or her thoughts. Then the rest of the team members share their thoughts following the designated order for sharing.

The chairperson asks a team member to read next week's SFR assignment.

The chairperson selects a team member to choose a reading for next week's Daily Reading. Use the index of any variety of daily Twelve Step readers to look up the topic and choose from a number of readings offered on that topic.

The chairperson asks the team to read the Closing Statement. The closing statement is read round-robin style by the entire team. The team follows the designated order for sharing.

Note: If you are working with an SFR counselor, he or she will assume these responsibilities.

SFR Chairperson Checklist

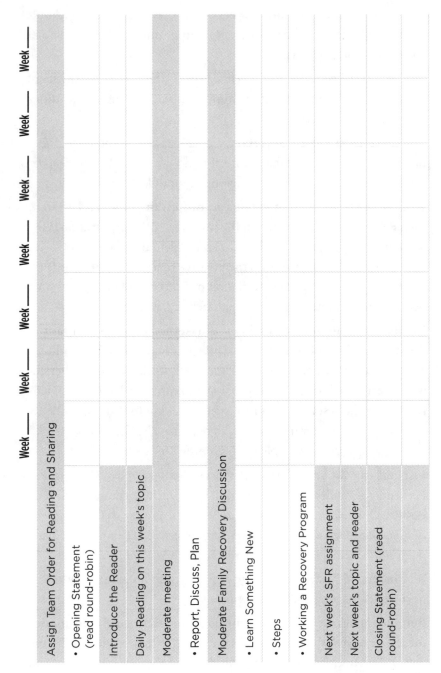

	Week ___	Week ___	Week ___	Week ___	Week ___	Week ___	Week ___	Week ___
Assign Team Order for Reading and Sharing								
• Opening Statement (read round-robin)								
Introduce the Reader								
Daily Reading on this week's topic								
Moderate meeting								
• Report, Discuss, Plan								
Moderate Family Recovery Discussion								
• Learn Something New								
• Steps								
• Working a Recovery Program								
Next week's SFR assignment								
Next week's topic and reader								
Closing Statement (read round-robin)								

SFR Secretary Checklist Reminders

The secretary keeps minutes for each SFR meeting. Creating minutes for every SFR meeting helps keep everything simple. Reading minutes creates an orderly feeling.

The secretary keeps the minutes brief. Everything works best when we keep it simple. By keeping the minutes brief, creating and reading minutes is an easy task.

The checklist guides the secretary. Checklists keep us on track. We don't have to remember what we need to do. Use checklists to keep this service position simple and an ongoing labor of love.

Remind the team when someone's accomplishment was celebrated. Include every SFR celebration in the minutes—*We celebrated Booker for finding a home group!* Add your team's celebratory shout-out— *Awesome!* Celebrating lights up the positive brain. The brain needs five positives for every negative. Addiction produced a lot of negatives. We need positive meaning in our lives; that's why we celebrate.

Remind the team which member was assigned to select the Daily Reading on the topic for the next SFR meeting. The Daily Reading sets the tone for the entire SFR meeting each week. Team members who select a reading take it very seriously, searching Twelve Step daily readers for the best reading for the team. It's kind to add a short thank-you in the minutes for the past week's reader—*Thanks, Hanna, for the reading you chose on the topic "Easy Does It" this week.*

List goals for the upcoming week voiced during Report, Discuss, Plan. A friendly reminder of goals is helpful. Don't include names. Present a Positive Outlook List—*Great week ahead! Here are our goals: Attend my Al-Anon meeting, call my accountability partner, read* Courage to Change *daily, start working the Steps with my sponsor. Good job, everybody!*

Reminders. If this week's meeting requires us to prepare something for next week's meeting, include a reminder.

Remind the team of the date, time, and conference call information for the next SFR meeting. Always include this information in the minutes. It benefits everyone to be reminded and to know where they can find the conference call information.

SFR Secretary Checklist

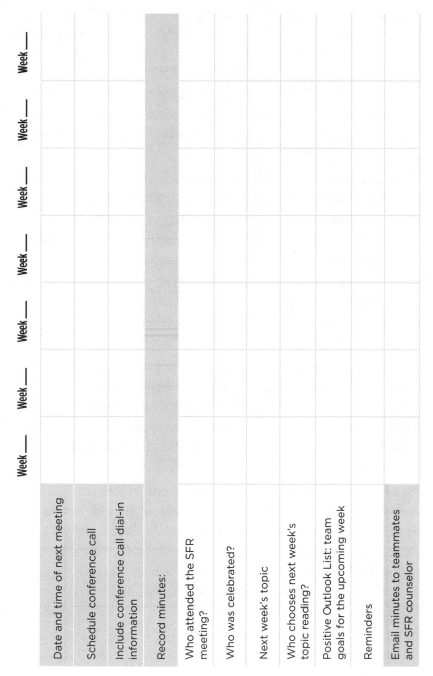

	Week___	Week___	Week___	Week___	Week___	Week___	Week___	Week___
Date and time of next meeting								
Schedule conference call								
Include conference call dial-in information								
Record minutes:								
Who attended the SFR meeting?								
Who was celebrated?								
Next week's topic								
Who chooses next week's topic reading?								
Positive Outlook List: team goals for the upcoming week								
Reminders								
Email minutes to teammates and SFR counselor								

Recovery Plan Checklist Reminders

Using the SFR Recovery Plan, we each make a pledge. In the past, it was only the newly recovering addicted loved one who made a pledge, based on an aftercare plan devised while in treatment. Families were not given an opportunity to participate in this solemn promise of recovery. With the SFR Recovery Plan, we come together to make this promise for the welfare of the family and each member in it. We pledge that we are committed to the best in each of us, to successful recovery, and to long-awaited family healing.

We launch ourselves into recovery. There are two Recovery Launch Plans: one for family members and one for the newly recovering loved one. Easy to complete, our plans point us to our recovery pathways. Launching ourselves into recovery has the added benefit of uniting family in this common pursuit.

The Treatment Aftercare Plan is added. Treatment teams create individualized aftercare plans (also called continuum of care plans) for their addicted patients. This plan is important and is always included in the Recovery Launch Plan.

We make ourselves aware of relapse warning signs. Emotional relapse among family members can knock the entire family off balance. For the newly recovering person, relapse may include return to use of alcohol, drugs, or other addictions. Completing the Relapse Warning Signs Checklist helps us identify our warning signs and share them with the team.

We make a Recovery Reconnection Agreement. When family members or addicted loved ones relapse, they often can't see it as problematic. They may resist accepting help. That's why we make decisions now, creating a plan to reconnect with our recovery. We clearly state how we want to be helped and by whom (our Recovery Ambassadors). We also write a letter from our present sober self to our future relapsed self. We do this not because we expect relapse. We do it because preparation is always smart.

As a family, we are transparent. We share our plans with one another. Addiction lives in the shadows; recovery lives in the light. Our goal is to build trust as we move away from fear.

Recovery Plan Checklist

Recovery Plan Goals	Date:	Date:	Date:	Date:	Date:	Date:	Date:	Date:
Recovery Launch Plan								
Treatment Aftercare Plan								
Relapse Warning Signs								
Three-Second Celebration								
Recovery Reconnection Agreement								
Letter to My Future Self								
Statement to My Family								
Choose Recovery Ambassadors								
How to Approach Me								
Invite Feedback on My Recovery Plan								
Provide Copies to Others								

27

Everyone Creates
a Recovery Plan

The SFR Recovery Plan has a job to do. This detailed, easy-to-read document helps prevent relapse (emotional and chemical), creates behavioral expectations (essential for lasting change), and, if there is an emotional or chemical relapse, outlines clear steps to nip it in the bud.

Our Recovery Plans lay out actions that support lasting, contented sobriety. Each member's plan becomes a sacred promise to herself and everyone on the SFR team. We are pledging to each other that we are committed to recovery and the family healing that follows. This is an exercise that is potentially lifesaving, and certainly family-saving. It is not to be taken lightly. Every team member needs to engage in the simple and straightforward process of developing a plan appropriate to his recovery situation and role in the family. Each Recovery Plan puts in place all the elements necessary for lasting change: make it simple (but meaningful), create a positive social norm (contagious behavior), and set behavioral expectations (accountability to our actions).

Our Recovery Plan is a blueprint for change-producing actions. We can't think our way out of problems we behaved our way into. If change were easy, we wouldn't be in the spot we're in right now. Sustained, positive change isn't random, but systematic. Wanting change doesn't make change. Knowing better doesn't do it, either. We need to admit we need help. We need to be willing to ask for help. Then, we need to accept help.

When we do these things, change begins to happen, and things start turning around quickly.

Everyone knows the negative consequences of chemical relapse and that it's never good. Rarely, however, do we discuss the dangers of emotional relapse. The power of emotional relapse shouldn't be underestimated. A return to enabling behaviors can endanger an addict's sobriety. Emotional relapse spreads toxic emotions and behaviors throughout the family system, dismantling unity. Emotions are not benign. Just as positive emotions support and stabilize recovery, negative emotions disrupt recovery and often lead to relapse.

A Recovery Plan consists of six sections (mostly checklists) and two short letters. Each section begins with an explanation and instructions. Additionally, three of your weekly SFR meetings will focus specifically on completing Recovery Plans. The majority of newly recovering alcoholics and addicts will join SFR prior to these recovery planning meetings, so they participate in completing the Recovery Plan with the family. If your loved one's participation in Structured Family Recovery is delayed, circle back when your loved one comes on board.

SFR counselors are excellent guides throughout the Recovery Plan process. If you are not regularly working with an SFR counselor but feel some extra help would be valuable, utilize an SFR counselor on a short-term basis until everyone on your team completes a Recovery Plan. To locate a trained and certified SFR counselor, do an internet search or go to lovefirst.net.

Further Information
A Recovery Plan Checklist is available in the previous chapter, "Structured Family Recovery Checklists."

28

My Recovery Plan

Actions speak louder than words. When every team member completes an SFR Recovery Plan, then every team member has brought his commitment to life. When everyone completes these assignments, each person will experience a sense of shared mission and a unity of purpose that is entirely new. This work awakens the very soul of the family and gives each of us a share in its life. As the mother of a recovering addict put it, "The Recovery Plan, for me, is an organized mind plan." She adds that no family needs to be afraid of the Recovery Plan, saying, "There's nothing scary here, just the basics."

We will all be doing inspiriting work on these plans, putting our intentions in black and white. They also include contingency planning, so we're prepared for any eventuality. Take the time to complete your Recovery Plan thoughtfully with your team. Share about the work you are doing during your SFR meeting's Report, Discuss, Plan.

We will complete our Recovery Plans during specific SFR meetings.

Recovery Launch Plan

Recovery Launch Plan for Family Emotional Sobriety
The Recovery Launch Plan details the specific actions we will take to build our personal recovery programs. It fulfills several functions at once. First, it is our personal commitment to the activities we will participate in weekly. Second, it shows how a modest time commitment can

turn the family into a powerhouse for recovery. Third, it underscores our solidarity with each other, including our newly recovering loved one. When everyone on the team engages in recovery together in a democratic fashion, we will begin to see real change.

- ☐ Starting right away, I will go to _____ family Twelve Step meeting(s) a week. I will find meeting choices at al-anon.org or search online for other Twelve Step family groups.

- ☐ I will devote two minutes to my daily reading in *Courage to Change* at this time during my day _____. I will share insights gained with my SFR accountability partner _____ time(s) a week.

- ☐ I will choose a home group by SFR week _____.

- ☐ I will get a Twelve Step sponsor by SFR week _____.

- ☐ I commit to completing the first three items on this Recovery Launch Plan in time to invite our recovering loved one to join SFR by week _____ (usually week three or four).

- ☐ I will start checking off my accomplishments using my Personal Recovery Checklist (found in the previous chapter).

Family Twelve Step meetings include Al-Anon, Adult Children of Alcoholics, Families Anonymous, Nar-Anon, Codependents Anonymous, S-Anon, and Gam-Anon. Celebrate Recovery is a Christian Twelve Step program. All offer meeting lists that can be found online.

Recovery Launch Plan for Sobriety

As a newly recovering alcoholic or addict, I will follow specific actions detailed in the Recovery Launch Plan to stay clean and sober and build a solid program. I can't think my way into sobriety. Instead, I must take the actions that lead to lasting recovery. I may have a continuing care plan from a treatment provider (see the next checklist), but the Recovery Launch Plan is where the rubber meets the road. In a few short weeks, I know the surprising by-product of these actions will begin to appear: joy. I will have new friends and a new purpose. Completing the Recovery

Launch Plan also keeps me in solidarity with my SFR team members, who are building their own programs of Twelve Step recovery.

- ☐ Complete the Treatment Aftercare Plan Checklist when I receive it from my treatment team.
- ☐ Commit to the goal of attending ninety meetings in ninety days (Twelve Step group of my choice).
- ☐ Choose a home group within two weeks.
- ☐ After choosing a home group, choose a Twelve Step sponsor within one week and begin working the Steps.
- ☐ Get five telephone numbers from sober (same-gender) members of my Twelve Step group. Call and talk to one person a day.
- ☐ Spend at least ten minutes each day reading recovery literature, starting with the AA **Big** Book or the NA Basic Text.
- ☐ Spend two minutes every morning reading my Twelve Step daily meditation book, *Daily Reflections* or *Twenty-Four Hours a Day*.
- ☐ Talk with my sponsor the number of times he or she recommends, _____ times a week.
- ☐ Volunteer to set up the meeting or clean up after meetings.
- ☐ Engage in fellowship (going out for coffee or a meal) with other recovering people after a Twelve Step meeting or other social interaction.
- ☐ Start checking off my accomplishments using my Personal Recovery Checklist and talk about these in Report, Discuss, Plan (see chapter 26, "Structured Family Recovery Checklists").
- ☐ Sign up for monitoring (random alcohol and drug testing) to rebuild trust with my family and create accountability for myself.

Twelve Step meetings include Alcoholics Anonymous, Narcotics Anonymous, Sexaholics Anonymous, Sex Addicts Anonymous, Gamblers Anonymous, Overeaters Anonymous, Food Addicts in Recovery Anonymous, Nicotine Anonymous. Celebrate Recovery is a Christian Twelve Step program.

Treatment Aftercare Plan

Check each item that was included on your Treatment Aftercare Plan.

- ☐ Attend _____ Twelve Step meeting(s) per week.
- ☐ Get a Twelve Step sponsor within _____ weeks after discharge from treatment.
- ☐ Attend intensive outpatient treatment or other continuing care program at _____.
- ☐ Follow up with a primary care physician for _____ _____.
- ☐ Follow up with _____ for ongoing mental health, psychological, or other services.
- ☐ Follow up with sober house (transitional housing) at _____ for _____ months.
- ☐ Work with a recovery mentor or sober coach at _____ for _____ weeks or _____ months (circle one).
- ☐ Sign up for monitoring (random alcohol and drug testing) at _____ for _____ months.
- ☐ Other: _____ _____ _____

Relapse Warning Signs

Relapse Warning Signs Threatening Family Emotional Sobriety

Everyone experiences emotional relapse warning signs from time to time. Check off the items in this list that could apply to you. Note that you do not have to be currently experiencing these warning signs. If you know you have experienced them in the past, you know what to watch for—and what you're asking your team to watch for. Honesty is the key.

- ☐ I allow my daily activities to interrupt my recovery schedule (my Twelve Step meetings, daily readings, time with my sponsor).

☐ Temporary issues, such as an illness, keep me away from recovery activities, and I do not resume them.

☐ I've stopped enjoying or doing the little things I do for myself.

☐ I have an inability to set appropriate limits with others. I'm either too lenient or too rigid.

☐ I'm obsessive in needing to take on all responsibility and still feel I'm not doing enough.

☐ I mentally ruminate over old resentments.

☐ I've returned to old controlling behaviors, trying to control people, places, and things.

☐ When anyone points out the unhealthiness of my behaviors, I become defensive.

☐ I fall into self-pity, complaining to others about all that is wrong in my life.

☐ I engage in the blame game, avoiding responsibility and making others the scapegoat for all my problems.

☐ I'm nervous or worry chronically. I may not know the source of my worries and feel a free-floating anxiety.

☐ I've lost faith in my understanding of a Higher Power.

☐ My attendance at Al-Anon or other family Twelve Step groups is sporadic; I always come up with excuses not to go.

☐ I'm overly emotional (crying or raging or manic) with no understanding of why.

☐ I lose control over my temper with my spouse, children, or other family members.

☐ I have extreme mood swings without warning. My feelings are exaggerated.

☐ I have deep feelings of loneliness or isolation. I've stopped reaching out to friends or family.

☐ I use dishonesty to manage my world. I create lots of little lies to control others or hide what's going on with me or my addicted loved one.

☐ I medicate with alcohol, other drugs, food, or overspending.

☐ I feel hopeless and helpless. I don't believe anyone can understand or help me.

☐ I have an apathetic, "whatever" attitude.

☐ I believe everything must be perfect at all times, and, as a result, no one meets my standards.

☐ I don't make time to read recovery literature, such as *Courage to Change* or other daily readers.

Relapse Warning Signs Threatening Sobriety

Relapse warning signs are often subtle and easy to miss. As an addict, you may discount their importance and rationalize them away. But dismissing warning signs is one of the biggest warning signs of all. Making an exhaustive list now is good preparation for a day when you might be feeling unstable. Check off every item that could possibly apply to you, being excruciatingly honest. Share this list with your sponsor.

☐ I doubt my ability to stay sober but keep this a secret.

☐ I think I can be abstinent without working a program of recovery.

☐ I am overconfident.

☐ I avoid talking about problems.

☐ I am secretive about my recovery activities with my family.

☐ My life is out of balance. I work too much or too little. I exercise too much or too little.

☐ I overreact to stressful situations.

☐ I am isolating physically or emotionally. I don't connect with my Twelve Step sponsor.

☐ I am making unrealistic plans.

☐ I never do anything to have fun.

☐ I can't relate to people in my Twelve Step meetings.

☐ I am easily angered or irritated.

☐ I am blaming others for my problems or the past.

☐ I lack structure in my days.

☐ I live with people who drink or use other drugs.

☐ I spend time with "wet faces in wet places," setting me up for relapse.

☐ I've lost faith in my understanding of a Higher Power.

☐ I don't make time to read recovery literature.

Three-Second Celebration

Many people celebrate their successes easily and with great enthusiasm. You just have to watch a professional football player after a touchdown or a child on his birthday. In his book *Tiny Habits,* Dr. Fogg writes: "When you celebrate effectively, you tap into the reward circuitry of your brain." Dr. Fogg's research shows that celebrations are essential in helping people encode positive change into their brains, fostering lasting results. In Structured Family Recovery, we recognize that celebration is a serious part of solidifying recovery. Therefore, we generously cheer on and celebrate our teammates' admirable accomplishments.

☐ By week _____, my team and I will select an exclamation of celebration to use for our Three-Second Celebration (see chapter 22, "Put the Basics into Place").

☐ I commit to celebrating my SFR teammates' milestones with enthusiasm (Report, Discuss, Plan).

☐ I commit to bringing my recovery milestones to the SFR meetings for celebration (Report, Discuss, Plan).

☐ I commit to celebrating my SFR experiences by expressing my gratitude for my SFR teammates' commitment.

☐ I celebrate using team sharing, telephoning a team member to share an inspiration or an aha moment from my Twelve Step meeting or daily reader (see chapter 33, "We Cultivate Trustworthiness").

☐ I celebrate by enthusiastically welcoming our newly recovering loved one in beginning to attend SFR meetings.

☐ Every time I engage in a recovery behavior for myself, no matter how small, I use the Three-Second Celebration to celebrate myself.

Recovery Reconnection Agreements

By reconnecting to our recovery, we reconnect to self-worth, trust-worthiness, and the respect of others.

Recovery Reconnection Agreement for Family Emotional Sobriety

When I have a recovery relapse, my behaviors are based in fear. Relapse is an emotional barrier between me and other people. I am disconnecting myself from the people I love. Even when unintentional, my behaviors keep others from feeling comfortable around me. While I'm protecting myself, I'm unwittingly isolating myself. This is not part of my recovery plan. The Recovery Reconnection Agreement gives me a way back to the solution. I agree to take the following steps to reconnect with my recovery, my family, and myself and to minimize unintended consequences.

- ☐ I will immediately discuss the current situation with my Twelve Step sponsor, attend a meeting with my sponsor, and follow my sponsor's recommendations.

- ☐ I will share in a Twelve Step meeting the exact nature of my emotional relapse and how I am using the program to move back into emotional sobriety.

- ☐ I will attend three Al-Anon meetings in the next seven days. If I don't have a sponsor, I will ask someone from my Twelve Step group to sponsor me.

- ☐ If I have a sponsor, I will ask about completing a good Fourth and Fifth Step. If I have already completed these Steps, I will talk to my sponsor about doing a daily Tenth Step.

- ☐ If I am having serious emotional relapses while working a good recovery program, I will determine if there are issues that need to be addressed by a licensed counselor or psychologist specializing in working with family members with addicted loved ones.

- ☐ If my emotional relapses are frequent and severe, I will consider attending a residential program designed to work through persistent problems experienced by family members of an addicted person.

Recovery Reconnection Agreement for Sobriety

If I relapse, I need to take action before consequences pile up. Having a plan that I've agreed to in advance makes it easier. Experience shows that creating a specific plan is a powerful tool to avoid relapse in the first place. My Recovery Reconnection Agreement puts all the elements in place for managing a challenging situation and getting back into the solution. I no longer need to isolate myself if relapse occurs. Instead, I can ask: "Which person do I want to be involved? How do I want them to approach me? What actions will I take and under what circumstances?" I can prove my trustworthiness by being thorough and courageous now, when I'm sober.

Although the expectation is always for lasting sobriety, if I have warning signs, a slip, or a relapse in the future, with this plan, I'll know exactly how to reconnect to my recovery—and my family—and get myself back on track.

- ☐ If any member of my SFR team is concerned about my sobriety, that person must first go to our SFR counselor or SFR chairperson.

- ☐ The SFR counselor or SFR chairperson consults my Recovery Reconnection Plan to know how to help me.

- ☐ The Recovery Ambassadors I've selected in my Recovery Plan should come to me with their concerns, following my plan for the best way to approach me.

- ☐ I give my Recovery Ambassadors permission to contact my Twelve Step sponsor. Name:_____ Telephone number: _____.

- ☐ If I am having relapse warning signs, I will work with my sponsor to develop an appropriate recovery plan, including attending an appropriate number of meetings per week, meeting with my sponsor, calling recovering people from my Twelve Step groups, getting involved in service work, and reading recovery literature every day.

Choosing the Appropriate Level of Support

Small Slip

If I have a one- or two-day slip, not requiring detox, I will do the following:

- ☐ I will get honest with my SFR team, starting with our SFR counselor or chairperson.
- ☐ I will follow my Recovery Reconnection Agreement together with the Recovery Ambassadors I have named to work with me.
- ☐ I will get honest with my Twelve Step sponsor and my home group.
- ☐ With my sponsor, I will develop a Twelve Step recovery plan with more support, including ninety meetings in ninety days. I will share the plan with my SFR team during Report, Discuss, Plan.
- ☐ If I don't have a Twelve Step sponsor, I will get one immediately and talk with this person daily.
- ☐ I will use my SFR accountability ___ times a week, and I will use my Personal Recovery Checklist to keep me on track with my Recovery Plan.
- ☐ I will sign up for monitoring. This includes random alcohol and drug testing or scheduling a future polygraph test for sex addiction or gambling addiction, if I haven't already.
- ☐ If I still can't stay sober, I will use my full relapse plan.

Full Relapse

If I have a full-blown relapse (didn't stop using after one or two days), I will work with my sponsor, SFR counselor (or other addiction professional), and my Recovery Ambassadors to determine the following:

- ☐ Do I need detox?
- ☐ Do I need a professional assessment?
- ☐ Do I need day treatment or intensive outpatient treatment?
- ☐ Do I need inpatient or residential treatment?
- ☐ Is a Twelve Step immersion residential program the best choice for me?

☐ Do I need a halfway house or professionally monitored sober house?

☐ I will review and restructure my recovery program to provide greater support with the help of my Twelve Step sponsor, Recovery Ambassadors, and SFR counselor or other addiction professional.

☐ I will sign up for monitoring. This includes random alcohol and drug testing or scheduling a future polygraph test for sex addiction or gambling addiction, if I haven't already.

Letter to My Future Self

I will write this letter with great seriousness. I am reaching into the future, to an unforeseen day when I find myself struggling. If that day comes, hearing my own calm and insightful words will be a priceless gift. I know myself well, so my guidance will be trusted. I know best how to counsel my future self, who may be in need of good advice. I will also remind myself of the recovery activities I am doing now that are making my life work so much better. Through this letter, I can be a beacon of hope when I need it most.

Examples of Letters to My Future Self

Sober Alcoholic/Addict to Relapsed Self

> Dear James,
>
> It's me, the person who knows you best—your sober self. I hope you'll never have to read this letter, because if you're reading it, it means you've relapsed.
>
> I know what you're thinking: "It's not that bad!" Yes, it is that bad. You might almost believe your rationalizations, but not quite. Underneath it all, I know you wish you hadn't picked up.
>
> You're not going to control your drinking and drugging. Not just because you can't control it, but because you can't even want to control it at this point. Once the

addiction is reawakened, you can't stop it on your own. And you don't want to stop it. Before you know it, you're back to full speed—ninety miles an hour into a brick wall.

I know what you're going through, the desperation and the sickening feeling that goes with being obsessed with needing to get high. You may not want to admit it to others, but I know how awful it feels. I know you don't really want to throw your family and your sober friends away. You don't want to toss away your dreams, your life, your promise.

You may not know it, but everybody is pulling for you. Think of how amazing it has been having your family doing Structured Family Recovery and getting into recovery with you. There's never been anything like this in our family. The drinking and drugging aren't worth it. There's too much to lose.

I know you don't want all the consequences that come with ongoing addiction. I sure don't want to go through it again. Do you think you can throw all the good things away and hope the fates will smile on you anyway? It doesn't work that way, and we both know it. The pain always gets worse and, as much as we drown it out with booze and drugs, it never goes away.

Everyone is on your side. Your family, your sober friends, your AA group. You can't change the fact that you've relapsed, but you can change how you handle it. Maybe you were overconfident, maybe you thought one drink wouldn't matter. That's water under the bridge now. Forget it. Just do the next right thing.

You're an honorable person. I know that about you. You love your family. You're smart. You have what it takes to make a good life. So, don't let this go any further. Put a stop to it. Start with a clean slate. Get honest. Get help. I'm asking you to follow the advice of your sponsor, your family, and me. Everyone will welcome you back with open arms. You have family and all the people in AA in your corner. With help, you will get through this, and it's going to be all right.

Finally, I want you to do it for me. I want me back— the sober me who was returning to a life of happiness and respect. I refuse to give up on us. Let's get back to what we were doing that made our successful sobriety possible: our meetings, working with our sponsor, working the Steps, and engaging in weekly SFR meetings. We can do this together. Without a doubt, it will all work out.

Love,

Your sober self,

James

Emotionally Sober Husband to Relapsed Self

Dear Tom,

If you are reading this letter, you are probably in danger of an emotional relapse. Please take what I write below very seriously because this could be the difference between a life of happiness and one of misery.

Since I am committed to working my Al-Anon program, I don't think I would have stopped going. So, it can only be one thing: if I have relapsed, Sara has relapsed. I know I can't trust myself when she relapses. I am her biggest enabler. I can't say no to her. So, right now, I have to declare myself untrustworthy. In this letter, I make a solemn promise to Sara and our family to recuse myself and let others in the family make decisions about how to help her. I will support whatever the family and professionals decide. I will also double my Al-Anon meetings and work more closely with my sponsor. I know that my enabling of Sara makes me a friend to her addiction and a danger to her. I love her too much to let that happen.

Sincerely,

Your emotionally sober self,

Tom

Emotionally Sober Wife to Relapsed Self

Dear Amelia,

This is your emotionally sober self writing to you, my future relapsed self. Things were going along so beautifully for us while we were going to our Al-Anon meetings and working with our sponsor. Since you are reading this letter, I know we are in a major emotional relapse. I think I have an idea of how that transpired, so let me take a guess at how things are going today. Here's the relapse scenario I am imagining we are now living:

We became complacent. We believed we had everything under control, which worked for a while. But then, our thinking gradually started changing. Pretty soon we were having ruminating thoughts about many negative things. We became obsessed with our husband's recovery program while ignoring our own. While worrying about his sobriety, we were simultaneously jealous of the time he was spending going to his AA meetings.

Then the controlling behaviors kicked in. We were trying to control everyone and everything. Of course, that didn't work out well, so our anger and resentment started bubbling up. We vacillated between self-pity and passive-aggressive behaviors. All our old patterns started to re-emerge. It felt oddly familiar and comforting, but it never led to anything good.

Then, our husband started going to even more meetings. That led to huge blowups. We would scream at him. We called him names. We accused him of not loving us. When he'd leave for his meetings anyway, we'd break down hysterically crying. When he told us his sponsor said he needed more meetings because things weren't stable at home, we became hateful toward his sponsor. Then, our husband came home from his AA meeting one night, after we'd had a particularly big argument, and said he didn't think he could live in the house and stay sober unless I got back into Al-Anon. Well, we couldn't believe our ears. He's the problem, he's the addict. We grabbed the car keys and left in a rage.

Maybe I didn't get all of the details right, but I'm sure I got the essence of what's been going on. I know the routine. We lived it for a long time. I like recovery and emotional sobriety a whole heck of a lot more. I also want to keep my husband. We both love him. We don't want to mess this up. Let's go back to Al-Anon. Let's call our sponsor. We have a good story to tell about what happens when you drift away from your recovery. We'll laugh at ourselves for all the craziness. Our sponsor will be happy to see us. Let's do it for each other, for our marriage, and our future.

All my love,
Your emotionally sober self,
Amelia

Statement to My Family

In SFR, we always expect lasting sobriety, but we still prepare for the unexpected. In a crisis, the Statement to My Family gives family fortitude and a clear vision forward. Family members don't listen to the disease talking; they get their loved one the help that is needed. If their loved one becomes combative, family members lovingly share the Statement to My Family, promising to follow through with the message's wishes.

Newly recovering loved ones can use the sample statement below as an example for writing a similar statement specific to their situation. Family members write one appropriate for emotional sobriety. A signed copy stays with the SFR team, in care of the chairperson, SFR counselor, or other trusted member.

Sample Statement to My Family

"I ask my family to act as quickly as possible if I am in danger of relapse or in relapse. I may be difficult to deal with while I am in such a bad place, but do not let me persuade you not to help me. The sooner you help me, the less damage is done by this insidious and powerful disease. Regardless of what I may say or do, remember, I love you."

Choose Recovery Ambassadors

I choose my Recovery Ambassadors, the two people who I want to approach me if I'm exhibiting relapse warning signs or relapse. Recovery Ambassadors are usually members of my SFR team but can also be selected from my recovery world.

Person 1 _____

Person 2 _____

How to Approach Me

Following are the ways I'd like to hear my Recovery Ambassadors' concerns.

- ☐ Approach me with love, patience, and understanding.

- ☐ Use an outreached hand, asking me to reconnect to my recovery and my family.

- ☐ See me as someone suffering from a disease that causes an overwhelming compulsion coupled with denial, not as a bad person who doesn't love my family. I love my family even when it doesn't look that way.

- ☐ Remind me that I can reconnect—with SFR; with my Twelve Step group, my sponsor, my family; and with my healthy self—and everything will work out.

- ☐ Remind me that I can trust my family. Addiction is never trustworthy.

- ☐ Remind me that my family always loves me. Tell me that addiction has never loved me. Addiction is nothing more than a trickster and a thief in my life.

- ☐ Come to me with my Recovery Plan in hand. I need a plan I can say yes to in this moment—a plan that I committed to when I was strong in sobriety.

☐ Read me the Rapid Relapse Response message that I wrote as part of our SFR team. It will remind me that I asked you to help as quickly as possible.

☐ Remind me that I am worthy of having good relationships, a fulfilling life, and happiness.

☐ Tell me that I am worthy of sobriety and that everyone on our team will walk the path with me to help me find my way back.

☐ Remind me that I am not alone.

☐ I now make a promise that I will love you back and hold your outstretched hand. Even if addiction is telling me not to reconnect with you, the no of addiction will not stop me from saying yes. After all, you are the people I love most in this world.

☐ Other: _____

Invite Feedback on My Recovery Plan

I will choose one SFR team member to read my Recovery Plan and give me honest feedback. Does my plan include the necessary elements for successful recovery? My first job is to listen without comment.

If I hear things that I am not in total agreement with, I will choose among the following individuals to get additional feedback: my sponsor, my Recovery Ambassadors, my SFR counselor, and/or an addiction counselor. I can then compare the feedback I've received from multiple trusted sources and make the best choices for my lasting recovery.

Feedback Sources

☐ SFR team member _____

☐ Twelve Step sponsor

☐ Recovery Ambassadors

☐ SFR counselor

☐ Addiction counselor

Provide Copies to Others

Once you have received and incorporated feedback, copy and email your entire Recovery Plan to the individuals you've selected below:

- ☐ SFR chairperson
- ☐ SFR counselor
- ☐ My Twelve Step sponsor: _____
- ☐ Recovery Ambassadors and other SFR team members:

  _____

  _____

- ☐ Others: _____

  _____

Signed: _____ Date: _____

29

Understanding AA and Other Twelve Step Groups

Beginning in 1935 from a little spot on the map, in Akron, Ohio, Alcoholics Anonymous (AA) has spread around the globe, reaching millions of people in more than 170 countries. Each meeting is autonomous, self-supporting, and nonprofessional. There is no leader to direct the activities of the group. Each individual meeting is supported by the dollar-in-a-basket contributions of the members, if they have it to spare. Each group pays its own rent, provides its own coffee, and buys its own literature.

AA spread throughout the world for one reason: it worked. No commercial interest built a chain of AA meetings, like Starbucks or McDonald's. Every meeting was started by one alcoholic talking to another and was sustained by attracting others who wanted what they have—contented sobriety. There are no promotions, fundraising campaigns, or sales pitches. But in every hour of every day, alcoholics and addicts attend these meetings around the globe, sharing their stories, laughter, and tears and sustaining each other in the fellowship of recovery.

The Twelve Steps are at the heart of Structured Family Recovery's success, just as they are with the Physician Health Programs (PHPs) that provide help for addicted doctors. The Steps are also at the core of the most effective alcohol and drug treatment programs. Some programs are designed as Twelve Step immersion programs, such as The Retreat in Minnesota. These centers establish a solid foundation of recovery based exclusively on the principles of AA.

There are various Twelve Step fellowships, including AA, Narcotics Anonymous (NA), and Cocaine Anonymous. Each is similar in structure. There are also programs for process addictions, including Gamblers Anonymous and Sexaholics Anonymous. The opening and closing statements for meetings may be somewhat different, but the Twelve Steps are basically the same. There are open meetings and closed meetings. Anyone can attend an open meeting, including supportive family members and friends. Open meetings are typically speaker meetings, in which someone tells her story. Closed meetings are exclusively for people who identify as an alcoholic or addict, providing confidentiality for members. These meetings give alcoholics and addicts a safe space for sharing openly and honestly.

When a newly recovering person begins attending Twelve Step meetings, following a few guidelines can help build an effective program of recovery.

1. *Go to meetings every day.* It's often suggested that newcomers have a goal of attending ninety meetings in ninety days. The obvious reason, of course, is the high potential for relapse in the first three months of sobriety. More meetings equal more safety. But frequency also creates familiarity. Attending every day, the new person gets to experience a number of different meetings and chooses his favorite meeting for a home group. He gets to know a variety of recovering people and ultimately find a sponsor. He begins feeling comfortable with the routine. When walking through the doors of a meeting, there's nothing better than hearing, "Hey, Bill, good to see you!" Psychologists have found that people need up to eighty-three days to develop a new routine. Addiction creates habitual negative behaviors and thinking patterns; ninety meetings in ninety days ingrains new, positive ways of living life.

2. *Choose a home group.* This is the meeting recovering alcoholics and addicts never miss. They see their sponsor here, know all the regular members, and volunteer for a service position. When sober long enough, they might begin chairing meetings. The home group is just

what the name implies: home. Walking into this room is so comfortable that alcoholics and addicts look forward to it. They come to trust and rely upon their home group members. They laugh and joke together, but conversations can also be dead serious. These are people who often become lifelong friends.

3. *Get a sponsor.* Sometimes alcoholics tell me they only need their families to help them stay sober. If family members alone couldn't keep the alcoholic sober before treatment, it isn't likely they can do so after treatment. Nobody understands an alcoholic like other alcoholics. They can see through the blather and speak knowledgeably from personal experience with successful recovery. As one AA member's sponsor told him, "I drank for twenty years, and I've been sober for twenty years. There's nothing about this stuff I don't know."

4. *Follow the directions.* An old-timer in AA once said, "Something crazy happens to people after they've been sober about fifteen minutes. They think they're recovery experts. Well, they're not. They're drinking experts." Twelve Step programs offer suggestions about how to live in sobriety based on hard-won experience. Alcoholics and addicts who follow these suggestions tend to stay sober; those who don't are likely to relapse.

5. *It works if you work it.* If you talk to someone in the middle of a relapse, you almost always hear the same thing: "AA didn't work for me." But AA doesn't work for you, you work for AA. This is comparable to the student who flunks out of school saying, "College just didn't work for me." Did you go to class? Read your textbooks? Study for exams? No? Well then, it's *you* who didn't work out. The same applies to recovery.

Terminal uniqueness is a term for a dangerous delusion experienced by people suffering from addiction. They think their situation is different and they are unique, and that regular rules don't apply to them. They believe programs that help others could never help them. They can't imagine they could be helped by Twelve Step groups. *Well, it might work for you, but not for me.* Never mind that a hefty percentage of people coming through the doors of AA or other Twelve Step groups all have the same thoughts and doubts. They sit in the meetings skeptical and with an air of superiority. No matter how dire their circumstances, they are dismissive of these recovering people. They act as if they know more than anyone. Usually, this is their way of covering up the gut-wrenching fear that they won't ever be free to live without alcohol or other drugs. Secretly, they believe nothing could overcome the power of their addiction. They are in a place of hopelessness—a place where all addicts eventually end up.

Twelve Step meetings work for anyone who has the capacity to become honest with herself and others. AA and other Twelve Step meetings are found across all cultures, continents, and people. When the focus stays on recovery principles, differences in personality, circumstances, and culture fade away. We're all human, and we're more alike than we are different. As alcoholics and addicts continue attending meetings, they begin to understand this important point. They hear other people tell their story and begin to grasp the similarities in addiction and in recovery. In time, they begin to absorb the power of the group and appreciate the wisdom of a collective experience that goes back many decades.

Not only are Twelve Step programs the recovery method of choice for the largest majority of people, repeated clinical trials comparing these programs to other treatment methods (such as cognitive-behavioral therapy) have shown the Twelve Steps to be the most effective approach. The latest Cochrane Review's findings show that Twelve Step facilitation in treatment centers improves success rates. When treatment programs implement AA and Twelve Step Facilitation designed to increase AA participation after treatment, it "reduces healthcare costs substantially." The review also states, "The authors found high certainty evidence that . . . programs designed to increase AA participation can lead to higher rates of continuous abstinence over months and years, when compared to other active treatment approaches."

There are other recovery programs besides those based on the Twelve Steps. We often hear people say, "There are many ways to recover," but they are rarely specific as to what those other ways are and the efficacy of the programs. This is when revisiting the concept of competing positives is helpful. Newly recovering people sometimes become confused when given a choice between a number of different support programs, including those that disregard the Twelve Steps. Let's assume all of these other programs have positives. To families, a loved one's willingness to attend one of these other programs may feel like a positive. When we are looking for long-term success in recovery, however, we are not just looking for a positive. We are looking for the optimal way to create lasting sobriety. That's why Structured Family Recovery incorporates the Twelve Steps into SFR meetings, and not some other recovery option.

Alex's First AA Meeting

Alex was twenty-six years old when he went to treatment for chronic alcoholism. He didn't know anything about AA or recovery, but he went to a couple of meetings while in treatment. Arriving home, he learned his parents were attending Al-Anon. "Seeing my parents go to Al-Anon rocked my world," he said. "My dad was a very busy attorney, and for him to make time for those meetings for me, well, what could I do but go to AA?" Now many years sober, Alex thinks back on his first meeting out in the world.

> I wasn't sure I was ready for sobriety, and I didn't know what my life would be like without alcohol. I had asked my counselor how many AA meetings he thought I should go to every week. The counselor looked at me and asked, 'How many days a week did you drink?'
>
> That shocked me, because I was a daily drinker. So, I tried to go to ninety meetings in ninety days. It seemed a bit much, but then everyone thought my drinking was a bit much too. I actually went to more than ninety, as it turned out.
>
> I was discharged from treatment on a Monday, and I went to a meeting that same night. I was nervous about going, but truthfully, I was glad to get out of the house after dinner. Everyone was walking on eggshells on my first day home.

Since I'd been to AA in treatment, it wasn't totally foreign, but this was going to be my first meeting in my hometown, and I'd be walking in alone. Would I see someone I knew? What would the people be like? Was I really going to sit around for an hour with a group of strangers? The whole thing seemed surreal.

The meeting was at a church a few miles from my home. It was early evening and already dark. There were cars in the parking lot of the parish hall, so I figured I was in the right place. Two minutes before the appointed hour, I got out of my car and walked in the door.

People were sitting around a table in one of the rooms off a long hallway. It was a small meeting, maybe a dozen people. They were men and women, and all of them were older than me. I couldn't imagine them getting together under any other circumstances.

They greeted me very warmly when I walked in the room. Needless to say, with such a small group, the newcomer stood out. They offered me a cup of coffee and some cookies from a side table. They were an affable bunch, and I could tell they were genuinely pleased to have me join them.

I don't remember what was said during that meeting, but I remember the feelings. First, there was kindness. They weren't roughnecks and they weren't holier-than-thou types. They were thoughtful and seemed to understand my discomfort. They made me feel at ease and immediately accepted me as one of the group.

Second, I could feel their sympathy and their precise knowledge of my situation. They understood me, even though we were different, because we had the same problem. They didn't learn it out of a book, that's for sure. They had lived it, and now they were living in the solution. Their experience made them ideal teachers, even though they didn't try to teach. They just shared their experience, strength, and hope. It was amazing.

Third, they had something I wanted (or maybe needed). They had a great sense of humor, and I could tell they were comfortable in their own skin. They believed in themselves and something greater, too, and whatever it was, it was working for them. They made me feel that I could have it too. I was part of the club, and, as one of the older guys said, 'This club has the highest initiation fee in the world.' I laughed out loud.

I understood their jokes, and they understood how fragile I was. The hour went by quickly. I got a couple of names and phone numbers, along with tips for good meetings around town. They told me to keep coming back, and I did. It sounds corny, but one day at a time, I just kept doing it. I kept staying sober one day at a time, and the days turned into weeks and the weeks turned into months. But it was always one day at a time."

Alex has been sober many years now and has helped other people find sobriety through sponsoring newcomers to the Twelve Step program. He often talks about those first meetings when he was a newcomer and the kindness of the people he met. What would have happened if he'd postponed his first meeting? What if he had decided he needed a vacation or time to relax after treatment rather than the immediate support of other recovering alcoholics? Alex was fortunate that the treatment program he attended emphasized getting involved in AA right away. Fortunately, for Alex and his family, he didn't delay a single day.

30

Understanding Al-Anon and Other Twelve Step Groups for Families

Family members can feel unsure about going to their first Al-Anon meeting (or Families Anonymous, Adult Children of Alcoholics, Co-Dependents Anonymous, Nar-Anon, S-Anon, or Gam-Anon), as does their addicted loved one when attending that first AA or other Twelve Step meeting. Nobody knows what to expect. It can feel overwhelming for some—even intimidating. If you're nervous, remember: Al-Anon has spread around the country since the 1960s, without any promotion. That didn't happen because people were having a bad experience. Like all the groups grounded in the Twelve Steps, it's a program of attraction, and people keep coming back for one reason—it works.

Members of SFR teams sometimes wonder why they need to go at all. After all, the family is engaged in Structured Family Recovery. *Shouldn't that be enough?* Of course, it's a positive step forward for everyone to come together as a recovery team. But just because something is positive doesn't mean it will get us where we want to go. Structured Family Recovery is built as an equation. The elements of the equation— Structured Family Recovery and Twelve Step groups—add up to a big move forward. If we're to get the outcome we want, we need them both. Think of it in terms of an apple pie. While having a bushel of apples might be a good thing, we're not going to get the pie without flour and sugar and butter.

Your First Al-Anon Meeting

The easiest way to get started is to go online and search for Al-Anon in your town or city. In most locations, you will find a number of choices, with different days, times, and locations. Select a meeting near you at a time that best fits your schedule and make a commitment to go. Remember: everyone is attending Al-Anon for the same reason, and everyone was anxious about their first meeting. Don't think about it, just go. You will find that people are welcoming and will be glad to have you at the meeting. There are no dues or membership lists. No one places expectations on you.

At your first couple of meetings, listening is a good way to start. There is never pressure to speak in Al-Anon. You'll soon notice that people who've been going to Al-Anon longest rarely talk about their alcoholics. They attend Al-Anon for their own benefit, because their loved one's addiction has affected their mental, emotional, and spiritual well-being. If we stop to think about it, alcoholics attending AA focus on themselves and their issues. We wouldn't want them focusing on us. Family members and friends need to do the same in Al-Anon. This can be confusing for newcomers who initially want to talk about their addict. This is a natural starting point for newcomers, and a little bit of information about addiction in the family sets the stage. But Al-Anon is for *you*. You need to move the focus back to you. When asked how they are, many family members often respond by explaining how their addicted loved one is doing: *Well, Joe got his third DUI. I think he'll be losing his license, and I'll be driving him everywhere. It's going to be an extra burden on me, but he'll need someone to drop him off and pick him up from work every day.* When we begin focusing on ourselves, our response is more like this: *I've been talking with my sponsor to better deal with the latest crisis in my alcoholic's life. Today, I know he will have to experience his own consequences. If he's not willing to get into recovery, then he'll have to figure things out on his own. I am working my program one day at a time. I can handle that much. I choose to focus on what I have to be grateful for today.*

During Twelve Step meetings, members share their experience, strength, and hope. This means we talk about ourselves. We don't tell others what they should or shouldn't do or feel. When we listen to others share, we learn from their experiences. We don't have to agree with everything they say. We take what we like and leave the rest. While we may not relate to everything being said in a meeting, more often than not, we will hear something we needed to hear.

Janice grew up in a home with an alcoholic father. In her twenties, she came to realize that all her boyfriends, no matter how promising, were alcoholics. She didn't see the pattern at first, but over time it became apparent. "I had a serious relationship with a successful financial manager," she said. "I thought I had finally met the one." On a lovely Saturday morning, they arranged to meet at a favorite Chicago restaurant. "I found him chugging Manhattans on the rocks at eleven o'clock in the morning," she said. "He ordered me one, and when I refused it, he started belittling me. That's when I knew I needed counseling to figure out me. Why was I always dating alcoholics?" Janice found a therapist who worked with adult children of alcoholics.

"My counselor told me I needed Al-Anon," she said. "But the thought of it confused me. I didn't know what to expect or how to find a meeting. After six weeks of counseling—and always admitting I hadn't yet gone to a meeting—I forced myself to find an Al-Anon meeting." Janice described entering the church basement where the Al-Anon meeting was being held: "The meeting had already started, and the clip-clop of my high heels seemed to echo throughout the room. I wanted to turn and run, but I knew they all saw me. I thought it'd be rude to leave," she said, laughing. Janice sat down at a table with eight other women. As she looked around, she realized none of the women could possibly have anything in common with her. "At this particular meeting," Janice said, "everybody was much older than me, and I could tell these women had lived hard lives."

Once Janice began listening to the women share, she was spellbound. "The wisdom and spirituality in that room was like nothing I'd ever heard before," she said. Janice went on to explain that with all the hardships these women had experienced, they found a serenity she deeply longed for. "Without knowing it, I was given a lesson in principles before personalities," she said. "I prejudged these women as different than me, when they had so much to offer me."

In Al-Anon, it's said, "Though you may not like all of us, you'll come to love us in the same way we already love you." This saying addresses the idea of "Principles before personality." In Al-Anon, we focus on the principles of the program, not the people at the meeting. The Steps and the principles remain constant. Personality speaks to the members' individual differences. We learn to look beyond personality. We accept each person as a gift—an opportunity for us to practice patience, tolerance, and forgiveness. The principles of the program stand steady, while personalities come and go.

Most Al-Anon meetings are held in church meeting rooms, not because of religious affiliation, but because churches are numerous and have available meeting spaces. You'll also find Twelve Step meetings of all kinds in hospitals, community centers, and other places with space to share. Some towns have Twelve Step clubhouses that offer meetings for alcoholics, addicts, and their families seven days a week, from morning to night. Some have a coffee bar and socializing areas so people can meet with friends or with their sponsor.

There are women's meetings, men's meetings, and mixed meetings. There are meetings for beginners, discussion groups, Twelve Step study groups, and speaker meetings. It's fairly easy to find an Al-Anon meeting scheduled at the same time as an AA meeting, but held in separate rooms. Family members can go to their respective meetings and then get a cup of coffee or a bite to eat afterward.

"My wife is in AA and our family is doing Structured Family Recovery," says Jorge. "Every Saturday morning, my daughter and I go to our Al-Anon home group together. It used to be that I hardly ever saw my daughter, as busy as she was with her career and social life. Now, every week, we have our morning meeting. Then we go out for coffee and a bagel. It's our quality time. We talk about everything."

In Al-Anon, people don't counsel each other. There is no cross talk in meetings, which means you don't get unwanted advice. Members learn how to solve their common problems by listening to others share about themselves. We work the Steps with a sponsor. There are no leaders or professionals in charge of Al-Anon. Members volunteer to chair meetings. There is an opening and closing statement. Al-Anon is not group therapy, and there is no facilitator. Nobody takes attendance, and there's never an obligation to attend. Al-Anon asks members not to discuss therapy techniques, psychology, religious affiliations, intervention, non-Al-Anon literature, and treatment programs during meetings. These boundaries keep Al-Anon pure.

Al-Anon is anonymous, so members use first names only. Discussions are confidential, which affords safety and trust. Newcomers sometimes worry they'll see someone they know at an Al-Anon meeting. A woman told me she saw a married couple she knew from church at her first meeting. Horrified that they might see her, she scurried to the back of the room. "After the meeting, they came up to me and gave me a hug," she said. "They told me their son was addicted to heroin. I started to cry and told them my daughter was a heroin addict too."

When we walk into Al-Anon, we'll notice that members look like people we see in the grocery store, at work, in school, and around our neighborhoods. They come from every walk of life. We find a mix of retired people, young people, middle-aged people—rich, poor, and middle class. Some have been attending meetings for years and others just a short time. Everyone comes because they have been affected by someone else's addiction. While Al-Anon was started for family and friends of alcoholics, the program applies to all addictions. We all share a common problem.

Faced with the prospect of going to Al-Anon, family members sometimes react in ways much like alcoholics and addicts when they are first told to attend Alcoholics Anonymous. One of the most frequently heard objections is *I don't have time.* For many people, this is not just a dodge. They really are busy. But when we sit down and look at our schedules, we can always find time to fit one Al-Anon meeting into our week. If anything, it gives us time to pause and reflect—a positive activity that's often rare in our lives. Plus, every struggle we have with fitting Al-Anon into our schedule is an opportunity to understand our alcoholic's struggles with attending AA. It's easy to be judgmental—until we have to do it ourselves.

Elaine worked for a nonprofit organization in Washington, D.C. "My job was all-consuming, and then I went home to my kids," she said. "When my husband, Marc, was in treatment for his drinking, I was told to go to Al-Anon." Elaine was so overwhelmed with taking care of responsibilities while her husband was away, she couldn't find a free minute. "When he came home, he was going to AA every night. I didn't know when people thought I'd go to Al-Anon," she said.

But then Elaine learned about a noontime Al-Anon meeting close to her office. "I ran into an old friend and told her about Marc's treatment, and she told me about an Al-Anon meeting a few blocks from my work. Now I bring my lunch there twice a week. It's just what I need in my hectic life. I cope with everything better."

When looking for Al-Anon meetings, remember, try to find those closest to your home or workplace. Make it easy to get there. What's the best time? Right after work, in the morning, in the evening, or on the weekends? Try several Al-Anon meetings and choose the one that fits best. Ask the people in Al-Anon for recommendations on other meetings to attend. Look for people who are working an enthusiastic Al-Anon program. If you think, *I want what these people have,* you are in the right place. Attend a meeting several times before you decide if it's right for you. When you finally make a choice, consider that meeting your home group.

You'll most likely find a sponsor at your home group. It's the place where everyone knows your name. Get involved. Make the coffee or put out the literature. As one Al-Anon member said, "I've made a commitment to always show up at my home group. I greet newcomers and make myself available to them. My sponsor is there, so we always have this meeting together. It's a place where I know I'll find support and friendship."

Let's imagine for a moment what it is like to walk into an Al-Anon meeting for the first time.

If we want to turn around and go home, think of what we'd say to our addict: "Stick with it!" Walk up to a few people who look like they know what they're doing and introduce yourself. When we let people know it's our first meeting, they are welcoming and helpful.

When the meeting begins, the volunteer chairperson or another member reads an opening statement, which gives an overview of the purpose of the group. Introductions are made, beginning with the chairperson. "Hi, my name is Sofia, and this is my home group," followed by others saying things like, "Hi, I'm Willie, and this is my first time at this meeting," or "My name is Geena, and this is the first time I've attended Al-Anon." The group responds, "Hi Geena, welcome." It may sound corny, but in practice it creates a sense of warmth and belonging. When we share our names and welcome each other, we begin to connect.

The openness of the group is contagious. In most meetings, everyone gets a chance to share. There is an invisible power that comes from so many people sharing their experience, strength, and hope. A feeling of renewal fills the room. We learn that when we change ourselves, the world around us changes. Mother Teresa could have been speaking of the benefits of Al-Anon when she wrote, "None of us, including me, ever do great things. But we can all do small things, with great love, and together we can do something wonderful."

31

The Twelve Step Sponsor Relationship

Each of us needs someone who can help us figure out how to navigate these new waters, someone who comes without emotional baggage and isn't related to us. We need someone who can share hard-earned wisdom and who understands our struggles because she's been where we are. We need someone who has worked all Twelve Steps and has a sponsor of his own.

An Al-Anon member describes her experience working with a sponsor:

> I was sitting there . . . with someone who knew who I was and accepted me for who I was. I felt connected to the world in a completely new way. I no longer had to go it alone as I had done for so many years. To have the unconditional love from another human being without being judged, without feeling ashamed, was a great turning point for me in my recovery. I had been working long and hard, but always alone. Now I was connected. . . . The fear I lived with (because of my secrets) had changed to hope, because someone took the time to care. It gave me the courage to move forward in my recovery with confidence.

Our sponsors will listen to our story and our daily struggles. They will be available for us and walk with us on our journey of recovery. They will help us work all Twelve Steps. Although Twelve Step sponsors serve as mentors and guides, they are not members of our SFR team and do not attend SFR meetings. Sponsors play a specific role in recovery, and sponsorship must remain pure to preserve the integrity of AA, Al-Anon, and other Twelve Step groups.

What we experience in our Twelve Step meetings, what we hear from our sponsors, and what we read in the literature are the things we bring back to our SFR meetings. It's a partnership that keeps moving us upward. As the individual SFR team members share what they have learned and experienced, everyone in the family gains insights and a richer recovery experience.

AA literature includes much about sponsorship, which applies to other Twelve Step groups:

> Whether you are a newcomer who is hesitant about "bothering" anyone, or a member who has been around for some time trying to go it alone, sponsorship is yours for the asking. We urge you: Do not delay. Alcoholics recovered in A.A. want to share what they have learned with other alcoholics. We know from experience that our own sobriety is greatly strengthened when we give it away!

The same goes for Al-Anon and the other Twelve Step family groups.

Whether your fit is AA, NA, Al-Anon, or another Twelve Step program, choose a group that exudes enthusiastic recovery. Enthusiastic members make for enthusiastic recovery. The key to success is the willingness of members to take sponsorship seriously. If group members don't offer sponsorship, you may need to find another group.

A great way to get an initial feeling about a group is to tell people that you're new and then say, "I'd like to get some feedback on sponsorship and working the Steps. I need to understand what it means to work a program." This is an ideal way to share during a meeting when you first start going. It puts you in a position of listening and learning. Pouring out your troubles isn't your priority; learning to work a program is.

Choosing a sponsor is an informal process with only a few guidelines. Choose a sponsor who has what you want and has worked through all of the Twelve Steps with a sponsor. Your sponsor should be the same gender (those in the LGBTQ community may select sponsors of the opposite gender). "Stick with the winners," as the saying goes. We need someone who works a confident recovery program.

When asking someone to be your sponsor, you are giving that person a great compliment. Anyone you ask will typically say yes, unless she doesn't have adequate time to give you. Most people in the program who meet the qualifications for sponsorship know that being a sponsor gives them an opportunity to work the program in a special way. When you ask someone to be your sponsor, you are giving him a gift. People will accept the gift only if they know they can do it justice.

We Practice the Spirituality
of Kindness

A friend of mine recently celebrated twenty years of sobriety. Remembering back to the day he became sober—twenty years ago, in detox and very sick—he said, "I woke up and there was a man from AA sitting next to my bed. He gently put his hand on my shoulder and said, 'It's going to be all right.' I didn't believe him at the time, but he's here tonight, all these years later, to help me celebrate." Kindness comes in small packages, little acts that mean so much we never forget them.

True kindness doesn't sit in judgment asking, "Do you deserve me?" Kindness is an identity we choose for ourselves. When we are kind, we have chosen not to be critical. When we are kind, we have chosen not to be angry. When we are kind, we are saying, "You are valuable to me." Small kindnesses are so powerful that when we choose them, we can change a family. Some families are filled with so much hurt, they can no longer find kindness in their hearts. But AA has a saying, "Act as if." Act kind, and you will become kind. Aristotle said it too: "Acting virtuous will make one virtuous."

This doesn't mean we deny and repress feelings of anger or hurt. It simply means we choose to act on our positive feelings and values with each other. We've been battered enough; bringing more anger to the family does not help us. It's far better to take responsibility for our hurts and harms by working through them in a setting where they can be processed and healed. That's what the Fourth through the Tenth Steps are for, and we should lose no time in working through these Steps with our sponsor after completing the first three Steps.

David Brooks, columnist for the *New York Times,* wrote, "The manners and mores of a community are a shared possession. When you violate social norms, you are not only being rude to people around you, but you are making it more likely that others will violate the norms in the future. You are tearing the social fabric." Verbal slights and discourteous remarks, which accelerate when addiction inhabits a home, tear at the fabric of our families too. If we believe that the manners and mores of a family are a shared possession, wouldn't it then be terribly wrong to trample over them? If kindness belongs to everyone, do I have the right to extinguish it with unkindness?

During active addiction, much is not beautiful and many things hurt us, and we, in all likelihood, hurt others. Kindness is hard won after so much injustice and pain. It's born of an experience that offered us little hope. Yet once we're delivered into recovery, we are given the opportunity to repair and strengthen the fabric of our families. It takes working together, and that cannot happen without kindness.

Poet Naomi Shihab Nye, in her poem "Kindness," writes, "Before you know what kindness really is you must lose things, feel the future dissolve in a moment like salt in a weakened broth. What you held in your hand, what you counted and carefully saved, all this must go so you know how desolate the landscape can be between the regions of kindness. . . . Then it is only kindness that makes sense anymore, only kindness that ties your shoes and sends you out into the day to mail letters and purchase bread, only kindness that raises its head from the crowd of the world to say, *It is I you have been looking for,* and then goes with you everywhere like a shadow or a friend." Living in the aftermath of addiction, kindness makes perfect sense.

We Conduct Ourselves with Gentleness

Funny thing about our brains—they don't take constructive criticism well. Someone once said, "First we're ticked off, and then we're enlightened." Neuroscientists tell us our brains are naturally defensive. Don't be defensive, we say, but our brains just are. One of the most important functions our brains have is to protect us from harm, both physical and psychological. When we feel criticized, our brains often protect us by resisting negative information—even when it is constructive. We change the information rather than changing ourselves.

AA and other Twelve Step programs have bypassed this particularity of the brain by discouraging cross talk—giving each other advice or feedback. In Twelve Step meetings, people share their experience, strength, and hope. Others take what they like and leave the rest. It's a great system because it works in a way that doesn't summon the defensive brain to the rescue.

In meetings, we follow AA's lead for the most part, choosing to share about ourselves instead of talking about others. We are doing recovery, not family therapy. In fact, unless the family is so broken that members are unable to work together in an SFR setting, family therapy at this juncture can be unhelpful. The risk is that the addicted loved one will begin focusing on relationships (a code word for other people) rather than himself and his recovery. Addiction has created so many hurt feelings that stirring the pot just pulls up resentments, poisoning the waters. Instead let's use the Twelve Steps to rid ourselves of resentments, get into a place of positive spirituality, build sturdy sobriety (emotional sobriety for the family), learn to focus on ourselves, and build some trust. By doing these things, most family problems fall away. Unless there are compelling reasons to do so earlier, contemplate family therapy after a year of good, strong recovery.

Our impulse is to do the opposite. We often feel an urgent need to get to the bottom of our problems, air things out, tell each other exactly how we feel, and get things off our chest. "Whew, I feel better now," we say after telling everyone exactly what we think—but it's usually a fleeting feeling of relief. Feeling better in the moment doesn't mean we're better off. Too often, it's a lot of talk (mostly about our reactions to other people) and very little action, and it rarely offers much in the way of making change. A far more effective way to change our attitude is to work a Twelve Step program to change our behavior. In the words of the thirteenth-century Sufi mystic and poet Rumi, "Yesterday I was clever, so I wanted to change the world. Today I am wise, so I am changing myself."

Our struggles start making sense when we understand that our survival-oriented brains are built with a negativity bias. We are prone to remember our negative experiences more strongly and in more detail than our positive experiences. We generally judge our families with a brain that zeroes in on the negative. We even process negative and positive experiences in different hemispheres of the brain. In a *New York Times* article entitled "Praise Is Fleeting, but Brickbats We Recall," Alina Tugend writes, "Negative emotions generally involve more thinking, and the information is processed more thoroughly than positive ones . . . we ruminate more about unpleasant events." In other words, bad events wear off more slowly than good events.

This may be evolutionary—a way of remembering events that threaten survival and reduce the likelihood of passing on one's genetic material. But this adaptation of nature has its drawbacks. As George Vaillant, MD, writes in his book *Spiritual Evolution,* "Negative emotions are often crucial for survival—but only in time present. The positive emotions are more expansive and help us broaden and build. . . . They help us to survive in time future." Dr. Vaillant explains that our negative emotions are in service of the "I," whereas our positive emotions are supportive of the "we." This raises our understanding of why Twelve Step recovery focuses on freeing ourselves from negative, isolating emotions and increasing positive emotions that establish human connection.

We must be cognizant of the fact that our brains aren't always trustworthy. All that bad stuff—and no one is denying that there's bad stuff—is likely to be remembered more strongly and keep circling around in our brains, while the good stuff is often bleached out over time. We seem to be built to fret, which prevents us from giving each other a fair shake. Forgiveness often seems impossible. Lasting negative emotions serve to isolate us rather than unite us. Understanding this helps make sense of why heaping complaints on others keeps the circle of pain going. We can reliably predict that the recipients of our unburdening of negative feelings are bound to react strongly to our criticism, ruminate about what was said, and have difficulty forgetting it—creating an endless cycle of hurt and retribution.

Does this mean we never bring up anything negative? Can we approach difficult issues, such as relapse warning signs in our addicts or family members, without tripping the cerebral wire that closes the door to criticism? Do we just give up and, as some suggest, never use any form of intervention when we see our loved ones veer off the rails, lest we appear confrontational? Do we restrict ourselves instead to a neutral position with questions such as "How is that working for you?" We need to understand that criticism doesn't always have to be critical.

Let's begin by neutralizing criticism without neutering it. At its best, criticism is how we define the merit of something—usually through serious examination and review. "Is my involvement in my recovery program substantial enough to support lasting sobriety, or do I need to do something more?" *Criticism* is a noun. On the other hand, *critical* is an adjective, describing an action or a person. *Critical* suggests finding fault and calling attention to flaws in something. "I'm always being told I'm not doing it right, but I don't see how you're much better." It's easy to see the benefit of one over the other. When criticism is used as evaluation and is about the event, rather than the person, it can be very helpful. When an entire team is working toward success—believing in progress not perfection—criticism is welcomed as something supportive and helpful if there is a threat of relapse.

So how do we talk to one another when we need to say we're worried or scared? What can we say when we see something that doesn't look like recovery but rather the return of the insidious beast of addiction? How do we point out behaviors that seem like recovery sabotage? We are often as uncomfortable offering criticism as we are receiving it. We worry that if we bring up anything negative, we'll be seen as judgmental and be accused of putting our nose where it doesn't belong. We address this by choosing the people we want to approach us with relapse concerns and exactly how they should talk with us.

Preparation is the key to this. When we are completing our Recovery Plans, we choose Recovery Ambassadors, the people we want to approach us if we are in relapse. We complete a checklist that communicates clearly how we'd like our ambassadors to talk with us. We can more easily listen to people we invited to come to us with concerns. We can more easily accept their help.

We can then report the decisions we made with our ambassadors in the next SFR meeting (during Report, Discuss, Plan). We explain our plan for reconnecting with our recovery. By making it safe, we can—if necessary—give important and meaningful feedback to any of our SFR team members whose recovery is in a slump or a slip.

Since our brains go on the defensive, we want to be honest about what's going on with us when we're receiving feedback from our Recovery Ambassadors. We might say, "Jack and Oliver, I hear what you're saying, but my brain is doing its thing right now, getting sort of defensive. I know it's a normal reaction and has nothing to do with the value of what you are telling me. Let me take a minute for the defensiveness to die down, so I can respond to you honestly and openly."

When we have been connecting to one another with positive experiences in SFR, we aren't primed to be as defensive as we otherwise might have been. We are more able to listen. We know the people who are reaching out love us. We have all become more trustworthy, kind, and gentle with each other. Relationships are different now. In the words of author E. A. Bucchianeri: "An acquaintance merely enjoys your company, a fair-weather companion flatters when all is well, a true friend has your best interests at heart and the pluck to tell you what you need to hear."

Because we regularly attend SFR meetings, problems are unlikely to grow out of proportion before anyone notices. Most challenges will be small and self-reported. For example, during Report, Discuss, Plan, someone might say: "I put recovery at the bottom of my list this past week and skipped my Al-Anon meeting. I need to contact my SFR accountability partner this week to help me keep my recovery priorities straight." Of course, a team member could be untruthful about completing recovery activities, but a group can sniff out dishonesty because of its dissonance with recovery goals and values. The very attitude of the person begins to shift to a negative place. Recovery and dishonesty project distinctly different energies. If we're concerned about someone, always go back and review that person's Recovery Plan.

33

We Cultivate Trustworthiness

Scottish author and poet George McDonald wrote, "To be trusted is a greater compliment than being loved." Addiction preys on trust. It is by the misuse of trust that it survives. It gets its way through lies and subterfuge, using for its purposes the sweetest and dearest qualities of the person whose body, mind, and spirit it has invaded. When that doesn't work, it turns to wrath.

As alcoholics and addicts gain even the smallest foothold in recovery, and the fog lifts and the brain begins to clear, they begin to realize they've lost their most precious possession: the trust of others. Addiction has ripped apart their most important quality: trustworthiness. As a result, civility is at its lowest ebb. Acts of compassion dry up. When no one trusts them, no one has faith in them. We love one another, but if we cannot trust one another, it's impossible to have healthy, happy relationships. Love gets us into a relationship, but trust keeps us there.

Most alcoholics and addicts want to know how to get trust back. When I worked with alcoholics and addicts in treatment, it was one of the first questions they'd ask me. "How do I get my family to trust me again?" They urgently want to find a way back into the fold, because living without trust is painful. But trust cannot be reclaimed by apology or promise; it must be earned.

Alcoholics and addicts must realize that they no longer have the right to ask, "Do you trust me?" The only question they can properly ask is "Am I being trustworthy today?" Being trustworthy in recovery is demonstrated—evidenced by specific daily actions that include working a recovery program, establishing a habit of honesty, treating others with courtesy and kindness, and remaining sober. When they fall short of the mark, those in recovery make amends. Taking responsibility for mistakes and shortcomings is an act of trustworthiness. Family members must ask themselves this same question. It's hard for families to see—as they try to survive one crisis after another—how they become untrustworthy too. It's no one's fault. It's simply the trust-corroding assault of the disease upon our thinking, emotions, and spiritual self.

In recovery, trust is measured in twenty-four-hour increments. *Am I being trustworthy today?* As time progresses and the addict stays true to his program of recovery, people in his life come to believe that the answer to that question is yes. But every early recovery comes with a warranted uncertainty. Each day must speak for itself. The disease is close to the surface, and recovery is still finding its footing. If a newly recovering person strays from the program and holds on to dishonesty, trustworthiness isn't earned. Untrustworthiness is the disease of addiction in action.

Paradoxically, a trustworthy addict knows that she can't be trusted on her own to maintain sobriety. She's aware that the disease is always in the wings waiting. Protection comes not from the addict's thinking, but from the wisdom of the greater recovery community. As it's said in AA, "My head is like a dangerous neighborhood; I should never go in there alone."

When families ask, "How do we know he won't relapse?" they are really asking, "How can we trust again?" Families stay focused on the addict's every move, trying to determine at what point in time their loved one becomes trustworthy.

Families often fixate on how little trust they have for the addict—reminding her at every opportunity. This is never helpful. A family's lack of trust should not be articulated in a way that is punitive or humiliating. We're better served supporting recovery and setting appropriate limits. The addict needs limits to know what it takes to move beyond them. Families need limits to protect themselves from the disease. These actions are best guided by empathy, always remembering the addicted person is suffering from a disease, while the family suffers from its secondhand effects. If we as family do not engage in the recovery process, we don't change and grow with our recovering loved one.

After she stole from them repeatedly, selling their valuables for drugs, Catherine, a young heroin addict, was no longer allowed in her parents' home. When she finally agreed to treatment, she thought she'd be welcomed home again. Her parents, however, remained firm. They knew it took more than treatment to stay sober. They helped her move into a professionally supervised sober house, where she lived and worked for the next eighteen months. When Catherine celebrated her first year of sobriety, her parents invited her home for a celebration. She was bubbling over with delight. She knew what it meant to earn the right to go home for a few days and spend time with her parents. It made her proud of her recovery. By learning to live within a structure imposed by her mother and father, she learned what she needed to do to grow beyond those limitations.

Catherine's parents didn't wrestle with how much they could or couldn't trust their daughter. Instead, they asked themselves another important question: "Can Catherine trust us?" If they allowed themselves to be fooled by false hopes or empty promises, the answer would be no. So they made tough decisions, setting necessary limitations using love. In doing so, they were saying, "Yes, we are being trustworthy parents." Being trustworthy in this way required them to support only their daughter's recovery, regardless of Catherine's bitter feelings. They endured emotional tantrums and abusive language from her in the beginning but stood firm. When she reached one year of sobriety, they celebrated this important milestone with her, but they also understood that it was still just a beginning.

Team Sharing

In Structured Family Recovery, we do something called *team sharing*. Throughout the week, members contact each other to share something about recovery they've found truly inspiring or that has challenged their way of thinking. This kind of sharing builds trust. An alcoholic might call his sister and say, "I was reading my AA meditation book this morning and had such an aha moment, I had to call you. For the first time, I realized that not having to take a drink today is a freedom, not a struggle. I wanted to share that with you." Team sharing isn't scheduled or expected; it's something we're moved to do by discovery. We share something we find impactful, exciting, or surprising with someone on our SFR team. It's an intimate connection that allows us to know one another on a spiritual level.

Since our brains tend to react more strongly to the negative than the positive, we need to create many more positives in recovery. We do this to overcome the negatives we lived during the addiction, and we can't accomplish it without the other people on our teams. The mutual experience of sharing good things produces positive experiences. It's estimated that it takes five good experiences to overcome one bad. Team sharing creates trust and a sense of belonging to one another.

We Have Fun in Recovery

Play lights up our brains. It generates many positives most alcoholic families can use more of: trust, empathy, optimism, a sense of belonging. According to Dr. Stuart Brown, pioneer of innovative studies on play, "If you want to belong, you need to engage in social play." Signals learned and practiced during play are the basis for building trust among humans.

Throughout the disciplines of neurophysiology and developmental and cognitive psychology, there is significant research on play. Research shows that the brain doesn't develop normally when it suffers from play deprivation. Without the restoration and capacity-building benefits of play, our brains begin to atrophy. Dr. Brown tells us it isn't work that's the opposite of play; it's depression. Play has a biological place in our lives, he says, just like sleep and dreams.

In addicted families, there hasn't always been much fun while our lives are overrun with negatives. We need to create more play in our families with laughter, enjoyment, and happiness. Play helps heal relationships. By playing together, we feel closer to one another, experience greater empathy, increase our sense of belonging, and have healthier immune systems. We rebuild what stress has damaged.

Play refreshes our relationships, especially when we're willing to try new and novel ways of having fun. It activates our reward center and creates an altered state of mind. Play activates good brain chemistry, which is what an addict needs after having a drug-soaked brain for so long. Families need to rejuvenate brains that have been assaulted with unrelenting stress.

Recovery needs to be fun. We get to learn how to enjoy each other's company again. Fun is also essential in preventing relapse. If the addict is bored out of her mind, she's more likely to drink or drug. If family members feel their relationships are stale, they're less likely to bond. As human beings, we are designed to play throughout our lives.

So be creative. Sing. Dance. Play games. Bike. Picnic. Swim. Make popcorn and watch old movies. Go bowling. Make an apple pie. Go to the zoo. Check out the free things to do around town. Make cookies and package them for friends. Have soup night and invite the whole family over. Play charades. Go sledding or make a snowman. Make paper snowflakes. Take a tour of an art museum. Plant something. Make an old family recipe together. Start a family book club. Look at old family photos or videos. Shoot hoops. Visit garage sales. Take a field trip to an interesting part of your state. Write and direct movie shorts using your smartphone. Go thrift shopping. Organize a talent show. Plan random acts of kindness. Watch comedies. Cuddle and share your favorite memories. Learn something new together. Join a bicycling club. Visit small farms to pick berries or apples. Go to a park or a conservatory. Attend an auction. Fly a kite. Make a fort. Help at a soup kitchen. Start a family tree. Raise butterflies. Learn about an interesting topic together. Learn how to say *I love you* in ten different languages. Play croquet or badminton. Start a family photography club. Read a book out loud to each other. Go out, lie in the grass, and stargaze.

Do something, anything that is new, different, fun. And laugh.

34

Recovery Makes Everything
Else Possible

Eric Clapton writes about his life in sobriety. "The last ten years have been the best of my life. They have been filled with love and a deep sense of satisfaction. . . . I have a loving family at my side, a past I am no longer ashamed of, and a future that promises to be full of love and laughter. . . . If I were anything but an alcoholic, I would gladly say that [my family is] the number one priority in my life. But this cannot be, because I know I would lose it all if I did not put my sobriety at the top of the list."

As is true with any other alcoholic or addict who achieves lasting sobriety, Clapton explains, "I continue to attend Twelve Step meetings and stay in touch with as many recovering people as I can. Staying sober and helping others to achieve sobriety will always be the single most important proposition of my life."

I go back to these words again and again, drawn to the power of them. Here is a man of great success, talent, and wealth. One doesn't often reach such pinnacles without also being smart and savvy. Yet, for him and his family, recovery comes first. He understands most clearly that, without this central commitment, all else is lost. If recovery comes second or third on his list of priorities, he will no longer be "going to any lengths" for recovery and will eventually slide back into the disease, taking his family with him.

Make recovery the most important thing for your family. Claim your right to the gifts that come with sobriety—both chemical and emotional. Begin now and take it one day at a time. Schedule your first meeting for Structured Family Recovery and follow the guidance for weekly meetings. Get professional help from an SFR counselor if you need it or if you feel better having it. Move forward in a direction that takes you to a place worth going. Choose to no longer follow the disease of addiction. If we do these things, we not only save the addict, we save us all. We make something better for our family and our communities. We change the future.

Ultimately, with all we learn and know, we move onward by way of the heart. It's a bruised heart, no doubt—whether we're the family member or the addict. We're all in tatters after our tenure with addiction. Our hearts may be wounded, but we cannot move forward led by our wounds. We must move forward led by our hearts.

As the Irish playwright George Bernard Shaw noted, "Those who cannot change their minds, cannot change anything." If we define ourselves by where we are now, how we feel in this moment, believing more in the old fight than in new possibilities, it isn't addiction that holds us back; it is ourselves. It's far better to turn toward the best in us and gently forgive our worst.

When we come together with Structured Family Recovery, we leave our reasons for anger outside the door. Not that the pain and disappointment and hurt aren't real—they just ultimately are not helpful. They perpetuate the past. The urge to relive these memories over and over again brings nothing new to the table. Better to bring our sufferings to our Twelve Step work and leave the pain behind. In Structured Family Recovery we are focusing on how to get to that better place. So, let's unshackle ourselves, stop licking the wounds, stand up straight, and put our focus where it belongs: squarely on ourselves. We then make a commitment to work together to create lasting change.

As Tom Brokaw, television journalist and author, said, "If we are not put here for anything else but to help each other get through life, I think that's a very honorable existence."

Epilogue
The Hero's Journey

The American mythologist, writer, and lecturer Joseph Campbell discovered in his studies that myth, storytelling, and religions around the world share a fundamental narrative, or *monomyth*. He calls this basic and universal story "the Hero's Journey."

Campbell describes this journey in his book *The Hero with a Thousand Faces*: "A hero ventures forth from the world of common day into a region of supernatural wonder: fabulous forces are there encountered and a decisive victory is won: the hero comes back from this mysterious adventure with the power to bestow boons on his fellow man."

Every person who enters into recovery from the disease of addiction, I believe, embarks on the Hero's Journey. He begins an ordinary life, thinking nothing threatening or life-altering lies ahead. He goes about his business—home and family, work, and friends—unaware that something is brewing.

Once addiction begins creating a negative pressure on his life, he is already standing on the extremity of change. He is being coerced to pay attention—both from external forces and deep internal disruptions. He will be changed one way or another, and he now must make a choice.

But, as the hero faces the unknown, he refuses the call. He turns away from the adventure he is meant to take. As his world continues to crumble, he comes upon a mentor who shares wisdom, teaching the hero courage and good judgment. It is only then that he agrees to leave his ordinary world and cross into this new, unfamiliar territory of sobriety.

Once in the new world, it isn't easy for the hero. He second-guesses himself. He is tested and feels the cold breath of fear on his face. He can turn back or push forward. He must decide.

By providence and good fortune, new allies stand by his side, preparing him to rise to the challenge. This is the time in which the hero must confront his greatest trials and tribulations. He must be willing to go beyond what he believes is possible. Out of this ultimate struggle, like the phoenix rising from the ashes, comes a new life.

This is when our hero discovers the treasure—recovery. He knows he must bring this treasure home. The road to home isn't an easy one, with much to overcome along the way. But when he finally arrives, it is as someone who has been transformed, bringing with him a power that changes the world from which he began.

As family, we go with our addict on this journey. We are tested all along the way. But, together, we find the treasure, and we bring it home.

PART 3

Structured Family Recovery
Weekly Meetings

This section includes the Opening and Closing Statements for your SFR weekly meetings and templates with suggested topics for a full year, broken into four quarters with agendas and topics for each week.

Here is a guideline overview for conducting your weekly SFR meetings.

- Read and share in round-robin style. For each meeting, select an order for team participation.

- Begin each weekly meeting by reading the Opening Statement.

- Ask the assigned team member to read the Daily Reading for the week that she chose and then to share why she selected that reading. Then ask the other team members to share their thoughts.

- Have all of the team members read and answer, for themselves, the Report, Discuss, Plan questions.

- Choose a reader for each of the three sections of Family Recovery Discussion. After each reading, ask the reader to share his thoughts. Then have the other team members share their thoughts.

- Ask a team member (asked by the SFR counselor or chairperson) to read next week's assignment.

- Choose a Daily Reading reader for next week's topic.

- End each meeting by reading the Closing Statement.

Opening and Closing Statements
for Structured Family Recovery Weekly Meetings

Use round-robin style reading for both the Opening and Closing Statements as determined at the beginning of each SFR meeting.

SFR Opening Statement

1. Our team meetings are confidential. We are bound not to disclose what is said here to nonparticipating family members, friends, or other persons. Observing confidentiality, we create an atmosphere of trust and safety.

2. We join and start conference calls on time. By doing so, we show respect for team members and their schedules. If someone is late, we do not stop to go back and explain what was missed. We continue with our agenda.

3. We speak only about ourselves, using "I" statements. We do not use "I" statements as thinly veiled "you" statements. We do not tell others how they feel or think, or what they should do. By keeping the focus on ourselves, we learn what is within our power to change: *I have the power to change myself.*

4. Negative emotions often linger well into early recovery. Turning anger, resentment, or blame on our family members results in multiplying our problems. We work through negative emotions, working the Steps with our Twelve Step sponsor and during Al-Anon, AA, or other Twelve Step meetings.

5. We follow the "Red Light, Yellow Light, Green Light" protocol. We don't drop unexpected issues or "bombs" into the middle of SFR meetings. We contact our SFR counselor or chairperson outside of the meeting to decide how to proceed properly or whether to proceed at all. If someone inadvertently drops a bomb, we simply respond, "I think that's a Red Light issue."

6. We are active listeners. We treat one another as we would like to be treated. We are tolerant of others' limitations and honest about our own. We celebrate our successes. We remember that none of us is perfect, but we are all deserving of love.

7. This is our group and our time. We use it wisely for our mutual benefit. We focus on how the Twelve Steps are implemented in all our affairs.

SFR Closing Statement: The Promises

We've divided The Promises' paragraph into its individual sentences, for your ease in reading this round-robin style.

1. If we are painstaking about this phase of our development, we will be amazed before we are halfway through.

2. We are going to know a new freedom and a new happiness.

3. We will not regret the past nor wish to shut the door on it.

4. We will comprehend the word serenity, and we will know peace.

5. No matter how far down the scale we have gone, we will see how our experience can benefit others.

6. That feeling of uselessness and self-pity will disappear.

7. We will lose interest in selfish things and gain interest in our fellows.

8. Self-seeking will slip away.

9. Our whole attitude and outlook upon life will change.

10. Fear of people and of economic insecurity will leave us.

11. We will intuitively know how to handle situations which used to baffle us.

12. We will suddenly realize that God is doing for us what we could not do for ourselves.

Are these extravagant promises? We think not. They are being fulfilled among us—sometimes quickly, sometimes slowly. They will always materialize if we work for them.

Source: The Promises is reprinted from Alcoholics Anonymous, pages 83–84, with permission from Alcoholics Anonymous World Services (A.A.W.S.); see Notes for full citation.

First Quarter

The first thirteen SFR meetings are defined by the slogan "Progress not perfection." We are learning how to do recovery, keeping it simple, and making a shift to thinking about recovery as something we do together. It begins as a way to help free the addict from the subjugation of addiction but culminates in bringing people together in ways we never expected.

At this beginning point in recovery, we don't know where this journey will take us, so we need to step out on faith. It's not enough for the addict to stop using or to work a recovery program on her own. For lasting sobriety, we need cooperation from the people who love each other most. Putting this disease into remission is not the same thing as healing a family. To heal is to make whole. Addiction pulled us apart; family recovery brings us together again.

Topic: Why Al-Anon?

Opening

Choose a round-robin order for reading and sharing. Use it to read the SFR Opening Statement.

Daily Reading

We begin our SFR journey with Step One from *How Al-Anon Works,* pages 45–47, read by the SFR counselor or chairperson. Each team member shares thoughts and insights.

Report, Discuss, Plan
Orientation by SFR counselor or chairperson followed by Q&A

1. What went well in my recovery this past week? How am I progressing on my Personal Recovery Checklist? What could be improved? Do I need someone's insight?

2. Share insights I gained from last week's SFR assignment.

3. For the upcoming week, what is my recovery goal? I will contact my accountability partner _____ times this week.

Family Recovery Discussion

For each of the three sections, a team member is selected to read and share. Team members also share thoughts and insights after each reading.

Learn Something New

It's well understood that, as human beings, we do not like to give up things even when they no longer serve the original purpose. We suffer from loss aversion. We struggle to let go of anything we perceive as ours. This can be extended to behaviors that no longer work. We can be so invested in unproductive behaviors that we believe they are still serving our needs. Admitting that these behaviors don't work triggers an innate sense of loss and a desire to hold on to them. In Al-Anon, we can admit we need help in recognizing and letting go of behaviors that felt like they work, when they don't. We can open ourselves up to what really works.

Step One

We admitted we were powerless over alcohol—
that our lives had become unmanageable.

Step One is about acceptance. We recognize that our many past attempts at controlling addiction didn't bring us the results we wanted. Paradoxically, this frees us to move out of the problem and into the solution. By admitting that we can't control outcomes, especially involving other people, we can concentrate on what we do have power over: our own choices. We can transform our own actions—acting rather than reacting. By engaging in the Twelve Steps, we begin changing our behaviors, modeling positive recovery within the family.

Working a Recovery Program

Family members are often surprised to learn that they need to play an active role in recovery because addiction doesn't feel like their problem. Calling it a family disease might seem somewhat contrived. *How is it our disease?* But addiction is pervasive, significantly affecting those who have close emotional bonds with the addict. Family members, much like the addict, often cannot see how it has changed them. Al-Anon helps lift the blinders so we can see what aspects of our lives need repair—emotional, spiritual, and physical—and then shows us how to heal. This is similar to what AA and NA do for the addict, who has also been blinded by the disease.

Assignment

Like addicted loved ones, families sometimes resist attending Twelve Step meetings, usually due to an inability to see why it's necessary. We can't know the benefits until we go. Turn to chapter 28, "My Recovery Plan." Complete the Recovery Launch Plan for Family Emotional Sobriety. Now we simply follow our plan. Share during Report, Discuss, Plan next week.

Closing

Read the SFR Closing Statement using the round-robin order.

Topic: Anger and Resentment

Opening

Choose a round-robin order for reading and sharing. Use it to read the SFR Opening Statement.

Daily Reading

For this week's topic, a team member reads his selection from a Twelve Step daily reader and shares thoughts on the reading. The other team members then share their thoughts.

Report, Discuss, Plan

Each team member takes a turn answering all questions.

1. What went well in my recovery this past week? How am I progressing on my Structured Family Recovery? What could be improved? Do I need someone's insight?

2. Share insights I gained from last week's SFR assignment.

3. For the upcoming week, what is my recovery goal? I will contact my accountability partner _____ times this week.

Family Recovery Discussion

For each of the three sections, a team member is selected to read and share. Team members also share thoughts and insights after each reading.

Learn Something New

Anger is an emotion usually tied to social interactions. We get angry when we feel trespassed against or violated in some manner. Addiction certainly does both. We hold certain expectations of people closest to us, and addiction pays no heed to these expectations. Our anger grows in proportion to the progression of the disease. Resentment is anger recycled over and over again. Resentments left unresolved can develop into difficulty trusting people, stunted emotional growth, and pessimism—all barriers to healthy relationships. Resentment stems from an inability or refusal to forgive. As Sathya Sai Baba taught, "The moment you start to resent a person, you become his slave. He controls your dreams, absorbs your digestion, robs you of your peace of mind and goodwill. . . . You cannot take a vacation without his going along. He destroys your freedom of mind and hounds you wherever you go. There is no way to escape the person you resent. . . . So if you want to be a slave, harbor your resentments!"

Step One
We admitted we were powerless over alcohol—
that our lives had become unmanageable.

When coping with addiction in the family, justifiable anger is common. Whenever we are disturbed by anger, resentments, or other negative emotions, it is almost always a Step One issue. We have expectations of others that are not being met. Resentments are an addictive state of mind. Living with resentments confuses the present with the past. Step One teaches us that we are powerless to change the past. We regain personal power by staying in the moment, understanding that we can't change yesterday and cannot predict tomorrow.

Working a Recovery Program
We often don't see our own anger. It may reside below the surface, unknowingly fueling our behaviors. Other times it's explosive, triggered by every slight. Chronic anger damages relationships, health, and overall quality of life. Working the Twelve Steps in Al-Anon gives us a way to resolve anger and resentments of the past and handle new situations. Anger keeps us stuck in the problem. Once we understand that we can only change ourselves, we are less likely to create resentments. Working a Twelve Step program moves us from anger to positive action.

Assignment
Read page 167 and 178 in the daily reader *Courage to Change*. Underline meaningful passages or write your insights in a journal. Ask yourself, *What triggers my anger and resentments? How would I prefer to live?* Share insights in a Twelve Step meeting. Ask others to share their experiences of overcoming anger and resentment. Journal insights.

Closing
Read the SFR Closing Statement using the round-robin order.

Topic: Acceptance

Opening

Choose a round-robin order for reading and sharing. Use it to read the SFR Opening Statement.

Daily Reading

For this week's topic, a team member reads her selection from a Twelve Step daily reader and shares thoughts on the reading. The other team members then share their thoughts.

Report, Discuss, Plan

1. What went well in my recovery this past week? How am I progressing on my Personal Recovery Checklist? What could be improved? Do I need someone's insight?

2. Share insights I gained from last week's SFR assignment.

3. For the upcoming week, what is my recovery goal? I will contact my accountability partner _____ times this week.

Family Recovery Discussion

For each of the three sections, a team member is selected to read and share. Team members also share thoughts and insights after each reading.

Learn Something New

Acceptance is surrendering to the reality of a situation. It is said *we surrender to win*. This is one of the key components of Twelve Step recovery. As addicts or family members trying to control active addiction, we are mired in managing the problem. We eventually lose this fight. When we surrender, we find freedom in the support of others. We see that we have choices. Recovery is now possible. Through acceptance, we can let go of our grip on the problem. As we do, we grab on to the solution. Engaging with others in recovery, we feel enough safety to let go and accept. This is how we create space for happiness in our lives.

Step One
We admitted we were powerless over alcohol—
that our lives had become unmanageable.

We do not mince words: our way has failed. Our best thinking has gotten us here. But what seems like an admission of failure is actually our gateway to freedom. We must have the humility to admit defeat so we can start over. Asking for help is an admission of our powerlessness, driven by the unmanageability in our lives. Without completing a solid Step One with our sponsor, the remaining Steps cannot work. It's through the admission of powerlessness and unmanageability that we begin our recovery journey in Al-Anon, AA, or other Twelve Step programs. "I can't, but we can." We don't recover alone.

Working a Recovery Program

The Serenity Prayer is used in Twelve Step meetings to remind us how we create manageability in our lives. "God, grant me the serenity to accept the things I cannot change, courage to change the things I can, and wisdom to know the difference." This is a prayer (or meditation) on powerlessness, acceptance, and the need of a power greater than ourselves. G-O-D can be the God of our religious beliefs, it can be Good Orderly Direction, Group of Drunks, Gifts Offered Daily, Guide of Destiny, Great Omnipotent Designer, or Giver of Deliverance. This is a program that asks us to identify something bigger than ourselves, however we understand that power. This is another form of acceptance in our recovery program.

Assignment

Read page 83 in *Courage to Change* or page 90 in *Daily Reflections*. Choose an accountability partner from the SFR team and make a call to share insights on your reading. Ask for that person's thoughts. Share insights in a Twelve Step meeting. Ask others to share their experiences with acceptance. Journal insights.

Closing

Read the SFR Closing Statement using the round-robin order.

Topic: Forgiveness

Opening

Choose a round-robin order for reading and sharing. Use it to read the SFR Opening Statement.

Daily Reading

For this week's topic, a team member reads his selection from a Twelve Step daily reader and shares thoughts on the reading. The other team members then share their thoughts.

Report, Discuss, Plan

1. What went well in my recovery this past week? How am I progressing on my Personal Recovery Checklist? What could be improved? Do I need someone's insight?

2. Share insights I gained from last week's SFR assignment.

3. For the upcoming week, what is my recovery goal? I will contact my accountability partner _____ times this week.

Family Recovery Discussion

For each of the three sections, a team member is selected to read and share. Team members also share thoughts and insights after each reading.

Learn Something New

Forgiveness may benefit those who forgive even more than the forgiven. Research shows that forgiveness is linked to our physical, mental, and spiritual health. Forgiving families are healthier families. The International Forgiveness Institute has developed a forgiveness intervention to increase forgiveness, which reduces anger, anxiety, and grief. Heart patients who complete forgiveness therapy are shown to have better blood flow to the heart. We may wonder why we should forgive so many hurts. Without forgiveness, it is we who are more depressed, less happy, and trapped in the past. Learning to forgive is an investment in ourselves.

Step One
*We admitted we were powerless over alcohol—that our lives
had become unmanageable.*

When we understand that addiction is a genetically based disease, we recognize that the addict was powerless over alcohol or other drugs. We begin to see that we've all been sharing the same problem—the symptoms of a voracious disease. Much like Alzheimer disease changes the behavior of the person suffering from it, so does addiction. Separating the disease from the person helps us forgive. It also helps the addict to forgive himself and his family.

Working a Recovery Program
Forgiveness is the key to healing resentments caused by addiction. Resentment keeps everyone in the family disconnected; forgiveness brings us back together. Working the Twelve Steps converts us into people capable of forgiving. In homes ravaged by addiction, we all need to be forgiven for something, and we all need to forgive. This is how we create new beginnings in our families.

Sometimes we have experienced wrongs that are grave and unrelated to addiction. Forgiveness seems out of reach. We may want to be free, but we can't find our way out. These are likely traumas that require the help of a specialist and therapies such as Eye Movement Desensitization and Reprocessing (EMDR).

Assignment
Forgiveness doesn't absolve the wrongs but rather cleans up our reaction to them. Discuss struggles with forgiveness, or ways you've embraced forgiveness, in a Twelve Step meeting. Journal your insights on the idea of forgiveness as medicine.

For next week, print and review the Recovery Plan Checklist found in chapter 26, "Structured Family Recovery Checklists."

Closing
Read the SFR Closing Statement using the round-robin order.

Topic: SFR Recovery Plan

Opening

Choose a round-robin order for reading and sharing. Use it to read the SFR Opening Statement.

Daily Reading

A team member reads chapter 27, "Everyone Creates a Recovery Plan." Team members share thoughts. The SFR counselor offers guidance, if the team is working with one.

Report, Discuss, Plan

1. What went well in my recovery this past week? How am I progressing on my Personal Recovery Checklist? What could be improved? Do I need someone's insight?

2. Share insights I gained from last week's SFR assignment.

3. For the upcoming week, what is my recovery goal? I will contact my accountability partner _____ times this week.

Family Recovery Discussion

For each of the three sections this week, the team will begin working on their Recovery Plans. A working meeting helps everyone move forward together.

Learn Something New

This week we're going to *do something different*: work on our SFR Recovery Plans. Check off what you complete on your Recovery Plan Checklist. For family members who haven't completed their Recovery Launch Plan or need to expand on it, do so now. The recovering person turns to and completes the Recovery Launch Plan for Sobriety and Treatment Aftercare Plan. While they are working, everyone else reads page 351 in *Courage to Change* and shares.

Step Two

Came to believe that a Power greater than ourselves could restore us to sanity.

Turn to chapter 31, "The Twelve Step Sponsor Relationship." Read the chapter using the round-robin order, paragraph by paragraph. This information is important because all team members find a sponsor to bring their Recovery Launch Plan to completion. Share insights.

Working a Recovery Program

We reinforce our recovery in two ways:

1. By celebrating. Read aloud about the "Three-Second Celebration" in chapter 22, "Put the Basics into Place."

2. By creating a plan for quickly reconnecting to our recovery in case of relapse.

As a team, take time now to complete two Recovery Plan sections: Three-Second Celebration and the Recovery Reconnection Agreement (choosing the appropriate agreement for addict or family).

Assignment

Turn to the section A Letter to My Future Self in chapter 28, "My Recovery Plan." Read the examples. Write a short letter to your future self. Bring your letter to next week's SFR meeting.

Closing

Read the SFR Closing Statement using the round-robin order.

Topic: Relapse Warning Signs

Opening

Choose a round-robin order for reading and sharing. Use it to read the SFR Opening Statement.

Daily Reading

For this week's topic, a team member reads her selection from a Twelve Step daily reader and shares thoughts on the reading. The other team members then share their thoughts.

Report, Discuss, Plan

1. What went well in my recovery this past week? How am I progressing on my Personal Recovery Checklist? What could be improved? Do I need someone's insight?

2. What insights did I gain from last week's SFR assignment? Share my Letter to My Future Self with the team.

3. For the upcoming week, what is my recovery goal? I will contact my accountability partner _____ times this week.

Family Recovery Discussion

For each of the three sections, a team member is selected to read and share. Team members also share thoughts and insights after each reading.

Learn Something New

Terence T. Gorski, noted relapse specialist and author, writes, "[Family members'] attitudes and behaviors can become such complicating factors in the addict's recovery that they can contribute to the process of relapse and even 'set-up' the addict's next episode of use. On the other hand family members can be powerful allies in helping the addict prevent fully engaging in the relapse process." Relapse always begins in our thinking process. For the addict, it leads to the next drink or drug or other addictive behavior. For the family, it leads to the loss of emotional sobriety. Turn to chapter 28,

"My Recovery Plan," and check off your top Relapse Warning Signs for family emotional sobriety or sobriety from addiction.

Step Two

Came to believe that a Power greater than ourselves could restore us to sanity.

Step Two is about looking for help outside ourselves. Our insanity comes from thinking we have all the answers. We experience a return to sanity by having the faith that answers will come from sources outside ourselves: recovering people, Twelve Step meetings, sponsors, our SFR team, and a power greater than ourselves. People find this greater power in several places: in the larger recovery community and its literature, universal love, good orderly direction, or in the God of our understanding. The help of others is what safeguards us from relapse.

Working a Recovery Program

Take time now to share your top two relapse warning signs with the rest of the team. Don't explain, just read them. Relapse prevention requires that we know our relapse warning signs. When we identify symptoms early, we can make behavior changes quickly to avoid slipping backward. When we stop taking care of ourselves, we risk relapse. We can take the H.A.L.T. quiz: *Am I Hungry, Angry, Lonely, or Tired?* If we answer yes to any of these, we need to take actions to restore balance to our lives. Working a strong program of recovery with our sponsor is one of the best ways to prevent relapse.

Assignment

Turn to chapter 28, "My Recovery Plan." In the section "Statement to My Family," read the example, then write your own statement. Bring it to next week's SFR meeting. Next, choose your Recovery Ambassadors and complete the checklist on how you want them to approach you with concerns. Then decide who you will invite to give you feedback on your Recovery Plan as well as who receives copies. You have now completed your SFR Recovery Plan—so celebrate!

Closing

Read the SFR Closing Statement using the round-robin order.

WEEK 7

Topic: Check Up

Opening

Choose a round-robin order for reading and sharing. Use it to read the SFR Opening Statement.

Daily Reading

For this week's topic, a team member reads his selection from a Twelve Step daily reader and shares thoughts on the reading. The other team members then share their thoughts.

Report, Discuss, Plan

1. What went well in my recovery this past week? How am I progressing on my Personal Recovery Checklist? What could be improved? Do I need someone's insight?

2. Share insights I gained from last week's SFR assignment. Share Recovery Plan work.

3. For the upcoming week, what is my recovery goal? I will contact my accountability partner _____ times this week.

Family Recovery Discussion

For each of the three sections, a team member is selected to read and share. Team members also share thoughts and insights after each reading.

Learn Something New

Our brains create patterns, a normal way of doing things. These patterns are so ingrained that they are easy to perform without much thought or effort. Asking our brains to change an established pattern, according to neuroscientists, is comparable to telling them something is wrong. This activates the emotional center of our brains, which then sends out a signal that there's an error or hazard. This is why change can feel threatening and why we respond with reluctance. When we tell ourselves that change is good, and it will make our lives better, we help our brains to become accepting.

Step Two

Came to believe that a Power greater than ourselves could restore us to sanity.

Change isn't as daunting when we ask for help. A positive spirituality means we leave isolation behind and reach out to others. It's in accepting help that sanity returns. Being overly self-reliant hasn't solved our problems in the past. How have we been reluctant to reach out for help from others in the program? How can we override our brain's resistance to change?

Working a Recovery Program

Where am I in my recovery today? Do I have a sponsor, a home group, a service position? Am I using my recovery checklist? Do I use an accountability partner? Have we, as a team, completed our Recovery Plans? What actions do I need to take this week to make positive changes?

Assignment

Use your recovery checklist to complete any actions left undone. Talk to your accountability partner or sponsor for support or a celebration.

Closing

Read the SFR Closing Statement using the round-robin order.

WEEK 8

Topic: Humility

Opening

Choose a round-robin order for reading and sharing. Use it to read the SFR Opening Statement.

Daily Reading

For this week's topic, a team member reads her selection from a Twelve Step daily reader and shares thoughts on the reading. The other team members then share their thoughts.

Report, Discuss, Plan

1. What went well in my recovery this past week? How am I progressing on my Personal Recovery Checklist? What could be improved? Do I need someone's insight?

2. Share insights I gained from last week's SFR assignment.

3. For the upcoming week, what is my recovery goal? I will contact my accountability partner _____ times this week.

Family Recovery Discussion

For each of the three sections, a team member is selected to read and share. Team members also share thoughts and insights after each reading.

Learn Something New

John Jay McCloy, former president of the World Bank, said, "Humility leads to strength and not to weakness. It is the highest form of self-respect to admit mistakes and to make amends for them." Humility is a relaxed form of self-assurance. It means accepting the truth about ourselves, both strengths and weaknesses. With humility, we are able to welcome positive criticism and feedback from others. When we succeed, we give credit to those who helped us. We are quick to recognize the strengths of others. Humility brings balance to our sense of self.

Step Two

Came to believe that a Power greater than ourselves could restore us to sanity.

Admitting we need help from others requires humility. We experience more spiritual growth by learning to accept help than by giving it. In Twelve Step groups, when we allow others to help us, we give them an opportunity to practice their program of recovery. It's a two-way gift.

Working a Recovery Program

Recovery from addiction is not a self-help program. It is a mutual-help program. It requires we each are willing to accept help and give help. Whichever we do, we are doing both, because every time we accept help, we give help— and vice versa. Recovery is a spiritual two-way street. It's defined by the ability to extend ourselves to others.

Assignment

This week, find a place of humility through gratitude for others who are willing to help you and the connection you make when you accept help. Journal one example each night of accepting help from someone.

Closing

Read the SFR Closing Statement using the round-robin order.

Topic: Honesty

Opening

Choose a round-robin order for reading and sharing. Use it to read the SFR Opening Statement.

Daily Reading

For this week's topic, a team member reads his selection from a Twelve Step daily reader and shares thoughts on the reading. The other team members then share their thoughts.

Report, Discuss, Plan

1. What went well in my recovery this past week? How am I progressing on my Personal Recovery Checklist? What could be improved? Do I need someone's insight?

2. Share insights I gained from last week's SFR assignment.

3. For the upcoming week, what is my recovery goal? I will contact my accountability partner _____ times this week.

Family Recovery Discussion

For each of the three sections, a team member is selected to read and share. Team members also share thoughts and insights after each reading.

Learn Something New

We become honest not by fear of punishment, but by learning the value of honesty. Researchers have found that when people are told stories about liars being punished, lying behaviors stay the same or get worse. But when they are told stories emphasizing the rewards of honesty, honesty increases. This demonstrates the power of social norms. Twelve Step recovery groups abound with stories about the rewards of honesty.

Step Two

Came to believe that a Power greater than ourselves could restore us to sanity.

When addiction takes hold of a family, an illusion of control develops. The addict uses dishonesty and the family uses enabling (which employs dishonesty) to maintain the illusion. This is a form of insanity. A power greater than ourselves restores us to sanity by returning us to honesty. As a member of Al-Anon said, "The disease of addiction had profoundly affected me, but I couldn't see the insanity in my life. I needed a place where people understood alcoholism to help me open my eyes."

Working a Recovery Program

Working a program of recovery is the beginning of change. The negative chatter in our heads doesn't matter—as long as we move our feet in the right direction. *Behavior changes attitude.* When we are honest about our feelings of reluctance but take action nonetheless, we create positive social norms and behavioral expectations. Both set an example that helps the entire family move forward in recovery.

Assignment

Focus on the spiritual practice of being honest. How is honesty linked to simplicity, trustworthiness, and peace of mind? Discuss this at a Twelve Step meeting. Journal insights.

Closing

Read the SFR Closing Statement using the round-robin order.

Topic: Twelve Step Slogans

Opening

Choose a round-robin order for reading and sharing. Use it to read the SFR Opening Statement.

Daily Reading

For this week's topic, a team member reads her selection from a Twelve Step daily reader and shares thoughts on the reading. The other team members then share their thoughts.

Report, Discuss, Plan

1. What went well in my recovery this past week? How am I progressing on my Personal Recovery Checklist? What could be improved? Do I need someone's insight?

2. Share insights I gained from last week's SFR assignment.

3. For the upcoming week, what is my recovery goal? I will contact my accountability partner _____ times this week.

Family Recovery Discussion

For each of the three sections, a team member is selected to read and share. Team members also share thoughts and insights after each reading.

Learn Something New

As a recovering alcoholic wrote in her blog *The Wild Life,* "The thing about the corny slogans is they're actually little parables that express a deeper truth." No one knows the origins of the slogans, but it's assumed the earliest ones—"Easy does it," "Live and let live," and "First things first"—originated with Bill Wilson and the first AA members. The others were passed down orally from one recovering person to the next. As an Al-Anon group describes them, "Slogans serve as gentle, calming reminders that our circumstances might not be as impossible or as desperate as they first appear. . . . A simple slogan can put the entire situation in perspective."

Step Three

Made a decision to turn our will and our lives over
to the care of God as we understood Him.

This is a decision Step: "I am willing to open myself up to guidance." Some find the word *God* troublesome, but remember, individuals choose their own Higher Power. By working this Step, we abandon "Self-will run riot" and allow ourselves to let go of controlling behaviors. The slogan "Turn it over" reminds us to relinquish the things we have no control over to our Higher Power. We always have control over choices we make for ourselves, but we can ask for guidance to help us make better choices.

Working a Recovery Program

Slogans and other recovery sayings are packets of wisdom easy to access and digest. In a flash, they can right our attitude or put our actions back on track. Slogans are the epitome of simplicity. "Easy does it . . . but do it" reminds us that when we're overwhelmed, we don't have to do everything at once; by calming down we are better able to meet our obligations. "Let go and let God" reminds us that we once expected happiness to originate from things outside ourselves, and, as a result, we tried to control what we had no control over. It was a recipe for anger, blame, and resentment. We can find a slogan to fit just about any situation we might face in recovery.

Assignment

Reference a list of slogans from Twelve Step meetings or an online source. Select two or three top choices. What slogans were common among all SFR team member picks? Choose one as the SFR team slogan; take a vote during the next SFR meeting. (The SFR secretary can coordinate tallying the top slogan choices before the next meeting.)

Closing

Read the SFR Closing Statement using the round-robin order.

Topic: Higher Power

Opening

Choose a round-robin order for reading and sharing. Use it to read the SFR Opening Statement.

Daily Reading

For this week's topic, a team member reads his selection from a Twelve Step daily reader and shares thoughts on the reading. The other team members then share their thoughts.

Report, Discuss, Plan

1. What went well in my recovery this past week? How am I progressing on my Personal Recovery Checklist? What could be improved? Do I need someone's insight?

2. Share insights I gained from last week's SFR assignment.

3. For the upcoming week, what is my recovery goal? I will contact my accountability partner _____ times this week.

Family Recovery Discussion

For each of the three sections, a team member is selected to read and share. Team members also share thoughts and insights after each reading.

Learn Something New

The term *Higher Power* was used by AA as early as the 1930s. We also hear people say "a power greater than ourselves." As some newcomers in AA say, "I'm not sure yet who my Higher Power is, but I'm pretty sure it's not me." According to a 2010 Gallup Poll, 80 percent of Americans, when asked, say they believe in God; 12 percent believe in a universal spirit; and 6 percent don't believe in either. One percent believe in something described as "other," and another 1 percent have no opinion. Among AA members, there are representatives from across the spectrum of belief.

Step Three

*Made a decision to turn our will and our lives over
to the care of God* as we understood Him.

They key to Step Three is making a decision, in everything regarding addiction and recovery, to accept guidance from a power greater than ourselves. Most of us already know or have an idea of who our Higher Power is. For those who don't, members of the recovery community give us a starting point. The "we" of the program is more powerful than the "I" of going it alone. As a recovering addict said, "I didn't know what God's will was for my life, but I was quite sure what God's will for me was not."

Working a Recovery Program

Twelve Step meetings give us a perfect opportunity to find guidance from outside of ourselves. Leaning on the experience, strength, and hope of other recovering people is a way of practicing Step Three. This helps us in our daily lives. When we find ourselves falling back into old ways of thinking or behaving, Step Three allows us to turn ourselves over to the care of a Higher Power. We can take a variety of action steps, such as to call our sponsor or a member of the SFR team, use a slogan, or say a prayer: "Your will be done, not mine."

Assignment

In your journal, write down the definition of your Higher Power. How has your belief in a power greater than yourself been helpful to you in the past? With your sponsor or in a Twelve Step meeting, ask others to share about their experience with Step Three. Journal insights.

Closing

Read the SFR Closing Statement using the round-robin order.

WEEK 12

Topic: Trusting the Process

Opening

Choose a round-robin order for reading and sharing. Use it to read the SFR Opening Statement.

Daily Reading

For this week's topic, a team member reads her selection from a Twelve Step daily reader and shares thoughts on the reading. The other team members then share their thoughts.

Report, Discuss, Plan

1. What went well in my recovery this past week? How am I progressing on my Personal Recovery Checklist? What could be improved? Do I need someone's insight?

2. Share insights I gained from last week's SFR assignment.

3. For the upcoming week, what is my recovery goal? I will contact my accountability partner _____ times this week.

Family Recovery Discussion

For each of the three sections, a team member is selected to read and share. Team members also share thoughts and insights after each reading.

Learn Something New

A man spent more than an hour watching a butterfly struggle to free itself from its cocoon without success. It had made a small hole, but its body was much too large to squeeze through. Finally, the butterfly stopped struggling and lay inside the cocoon motionless. The man became concerned and decided to cut open the cocoon. The butterfly crawled out, but its body was shriveled and its wings crumpled. The man watched, hoping the butterfly would eventually spread its wings and fly. But it never did. What the man didn't realize was that nature intended the butterfly to squeeze through that small hole. Doing so would strengthen its wings. By not trusting the process, the man took away the butterfly's necessary struggle and its chance to fly.

Step Three
Made a decision to turn our will and our lives over
to the care of God as we understood Him.

Trusting the process means we need to have faith and patience. We didn't get here overnight, and the solutions are going to take time. When we see our loved ones struggle—especially the addict—we may want to step in and begin working her program. But we have to stop to remember that our loved ones must go through their own struggles so they can mature and grow. When we are tempted to "help," that is when we need to think of Step Three and say, "My loved ones have their own Higher Power, and it is not me."

Working a Recovery Program
In Twelve Step circles, a popular slogan is "Time takes time." We get into recovery, and in short order we want everything fixed. But recovery is a process of growth, and growth takes time. We need to work our programs "One day at a time" to collect the experiences that eventually bring us long-term results. As we continue, we learn to trust the process and worry less.

Assignment
This week think of your recovery as planting a garden. Once the seed goes into the ground, you have to wait for the roots to take hold before the plant grows, the leaves sprout, and the flowers bloom. Along the way, you must do your part, watering the plant, weeding the garden, and fertilizing the soil. Most important, you must have patience. Journal your thoughts and insights about doing your part to grow your recovery program.

Closing
Read the SFR Closing Statement using the round-robin order.

WEEK 13

Topic: Choices

Opening

Choose a round-robin order for reading and sharing. Use it to read the SFR Opening Statement.

Daily Reading

For this week's topic, a team member reads his selection from a Twelve Step daily reader and shares thoughts on the reading. The other team members then share their thoughts.

Report, Discuss, Plan

1. What went well in my recovery this past week? How am I progressing on my Personal Recovery Checklist? What could be improved? Do I need someone's insight?

2. Share insights I gained from last week's SFR assignment.

3. For the upcoming week, what is my recovery goal? I will contact my accountability partner _____ times this week.

Family Recovery Discussion

For each of the three sections, a team member is selected to read and share. Team members also share thoughts and insights after each reading.

Learn Something New

Daily, we make hundreds of choices. How do we find the guidance to make the best choices in the most important areas of our lives? When we are living in the crisis or aftermath of addiction, stress creates tunnel vision. We're less able to absorb all the information available to us. Worry, anxiety, and fear distort choices, and our brains suffer from decision fatigue. Structured Family Recovery avoids these pitfalls by completing Recovery Plans, making choices prior to crisis, using checklists, identifying triggers to spark behaviors—all ways to simplify recovery.

Step Three
Made a decision to turn our will and our lives over
to the care of God as we understood Him.

In AA's *Twelve Steps and Twelve Traditions,* it is said, "Practicing Step Three is like opening a door which to all appearances is still closed. All we need is a key, and the decision to swing the door open." The key, of course, is willingness. Once we are willing, making the choice to open the door is easy. This Step is asking us to make a *decision* to turn our lives and will over to the *care* of a power greater than ourselves, however defined. Our will is our thinking, and our life is our actions. By making this choice, we prepare ourselves for the Steps to come.

Working a Recovery Program
Once the disease has found its way into our family, the way out is working a program of recovery. It can seem hard to make a lasting commitment to recovery—for both family and addict. But when we think about recovery in the same way we think about our jobs, it's easier. We don't always consciously make a daily choice about whether we're going to work. Work is a commitment—we know we are going and when we need to be there. We go to work for the positive rewards, to provide for ourselves and our family, and to avoid negative consequences, such as dismissal. The same is true of recovery. It's a commitment. We don't have to make a new decision every day; we just do it.

Assignment
Are you still making daily choices about your involvement in recovery or have you made a commitment? How does commitment simplify recovery? Talk to your Twelve Step sponsor about commitment. Journal insights.

Closing
Read the SFR Closing Statement using the round-robin order.

Second Quarter

The next twelve weeks focus on issues common to this stage of recovery. By this time, members of the recovery team are working a Twelve Step program of recovery and understand that recovery is more than keeping the addict abstinent. By following the directions, we are beginning to see some results by now. Even though we are still in the earliest stage of recovery, working a program of recovery has given us a constructive role to play.

We expect that team members have chosen a home group, have found a sponsor, and have begun working the Twelve Steps. We move ahead based on what we need to help us through the next phase of recovery. We will begin working the action Steps: Steps Four and Five. For the addict, these are the first Steps toward physical and emotional sobriety. For the families, these Steps are about achieving emotional sobriety. Actively work with your Twelve Step sponsor on these Steps while following the guidance of your SFR meetings. This ushers in a period of recovery that increases comfort and willingness.

WEEK 14

Topic: Open and Willing

Opening

Choose a round-robin order for reading and sharing. Use it to read the SFR Opening Statement.

Daily Reading

For this week's topic, a team member reads her selection from a Twelve Step daily reader and shares thoughts on the reading. The other team members then share their thoughts.

Report, Discuss, Plan

1. What went well in my recovery this past week? How am I progressing on my Personal Recovery Checklist? What could be improved? Do I need someone's insight?

2. Share insights I gained from last week's SFR assignment.

3. For the upcoming week, what is my recovery goal? I will contact my accountability partner _____ times this week.

Family Recovery Discussion

For each of the three sections, a team member is selected to read and share. Team members also share thoughts and insights after each reading.

Learn Something New

Gaylord Nelson, former U.S. senator and governor of Wisconsin, said, "The ultimate test of man's conscience may be his willingness to sacrifice something today for future generations whose words of thanks will not be heard." Working the Twelve Steps requires that we do some rigorous inside work. When a family does this work together, it's transformative on a larger scale, changing the very legacy of a family. The recovery work we do today is an inheritance for the generations to come. Instead of handing down the behaviors molded by addiction, a kind of spiritual illness, we pass on an emotional stability that provides the ability to regulate behaviors. In the words of Bill Wilson, this results in "easy, happy, and good living."

Steps Four and Five

Made a searching and fearless moral inventory of ourselves.

*Admitted to God, to ourselves, and to another human being
the exact nature of our wrongs.*

Steps Four and Five are simply about taking an inventory of ourselves. For most of us, the addiction has been our primary focus; these Steps help us put the focus back where it belongs, on us. It requires using the HOW of the program: being Honest, Open, and Willing. We can experience reluctance to the idea of taking a personal inventory. By using the wisdom and insights of Steps One, Two, and Three, we find the courage to take a fearless look at ourselves.

Working a Recovery Program

The founders of AA stated that failure to do a thoroughly honest Fourth and Fifth Step is one of the primary causes of relapse. This is as true for families as for alcoholics. With the guidance of our sponsor, we write our Fourth Step inventory on paper. Being honest about ourselves is as liberating as it is frightening. We do a Fifth Step by reading our inventory to our Twelve Step sponsor or someone experienced at hearing Fifth Steps, such as a pastor or an addictions counselor. As it says in the Big Book, "We pocket our pride and go to it, illuminating every twist of character, every dark cranny of the past. Once we have taken this step, withholding nothing, we are delighted. We can look the world in the eye. We can be alone at perfect peace and ease."

Assignment

Read about Steps Four and Five in *Twelve Steps and Twelve Traditions, How Al-Anon Works,* or *Twelve Steps for Adult Children* (good for all family members). Highlight passages, write notes in the margins, and share these with your sponsor.

Closing

Read the SFR Closing Statement using the round-robin order.

Topic: Secrets

Opening

Choose a round-robin order for reading and sharing. Use it to read the SFR Opening Statement.

Daily Reading

For this week's topic, a team member reads his selection from a Twelve Step daily reader and shares thoughts on the reading. The other team members then share their thoughts.

Report, Discuss, Plan

1. What went well in my recovery this past week? How am I progressing on my Personal Recovery Checklist? What could be improved? Do I need someone's insight?

2. Share insights I gained from last week's SFR assignment.

3. For the upcoming week, what is my recovery goal? I will contact my accountability partner _____ times this week.

Family Recovery Discussion

For each of the three sections, a team member is selected to read and share. Team members also share thoughts and insights after each reading.

Learn Something New

Holding in secrets takes a lot out of us. *It's eating me up alive.* When we're hanging on to secrets and resentments, we hedge ourselves in. This takes a toll on us. Depression and anxiety often increase, as do body aches and pains. Appropriately letting go of secrets and harbored resentments is correlated with better mental and physical health. Neuroscientists tell us that secrets cause the brain to fight with itself, whereas just the act of writing secrets down on paper can release the stress.

Steps Four and Five

Made a searching and fearless moral inventory of ourselves.

Admitted to God, to ourselves, and to another human being the exact nature of our wrongs.

Steps Four and Five are often the first tools of the program that help us come to a point of feeling okay about ourselves at a deep level. All the little secrets and hidden feelings that drag us down are brought to light. As they say in Twelve Step groups, "We're only as sick as our secrets." Working these Steps with our sponsor gives us a safe and appropriate place to reclaim parts of ourselves that were buried by secrets and disturbed emotions. It's much easier to live with ourselves once we've cleaned house.

Working a Recovery Program

These two Steps bring us to a place of complete honesty. The addict—for the first time—is taking account of the havoc the disease has had on his life and the lives of others. Through this inventory process, family members are able to identify the role they played in the saga of the family disease. When everyone completes a personal Fourth and Fifth Step, the family can begin to do away with the hierarchy of relationships within it—who is better and who is worse. These two Steps are the great equalizers. By taking our own inventory, we are less likely to sit in judgment of one another. Instead, we have a common bond in recovery.

Assignment

Begin talking with your sponsor about Steps Four and Five. Ask others at Twelve Step meetings to share their experiences doing a Fourth and Fifth Step. Journal insights.

Closing

Read the SFR Closing Statement using the round-robin order.

Topic: Character Defects

Opening

Choose a round-robin order for reading and sharing. Use it to read the SFR Opening Statement.

Daily Reading

For this week's topic, a team member reads her selection from a Twelve Step daily reader and shares thoughts on the reading. The other team members then share their thoughts.

Report, Discuss, Plan

1. What went well in my recovery this past week? How am I progressing on my Personal Recovery Checklist? What could be improved? Do I need someone's insight?

2. Share insights I gained from last week's SFR assignment.

3. For the upcoming week, what is my recovery goal? I will contact my accountability partner _____ times this week.

Family Recovery Discussion

For each of the three sections, a team member is selected to read and share. Team members also share thoughts and insights after each reading.

Learn Something New

Character defects are patterns we've developed that don't work for us anymore. We developed many of these patterns of thought and behavior to cope with the ongoing crisis of addiction. They made perfect sense in the short run, but as our lives filled with crisis—or the threat of crisis—these patterns became ingrained habits. Though they sometimes developed to protect us and serve a purpose, now they block healthy relationships and spiritual growth. Usually, we're not even cognizant of doing them. The next step in our recovery is simply to identify our patterns and share them with our sponsor.

Steps Four and Five

Made a searching and fearless moral inventory of ourselves.

Admitted to God, to ourselves, and to another human being the exact nature of our wrongs.

Taking an inventory of the ways we've been coping (refraining from taking the inventory of others), we consider these common patterns and discuss them with our sponsor:

anger	impatience	aloofness	self-justification
dishonesty	people-pleasing	fear	intolerance
controlling behavior	self-pity	perfectionism	criticizing
resentment	false pride	irritability	self-condemnation

Whichever we relate to, we must remember that these began as ways to create a safe place for ourselves and others. They no longer work for us because survival skills have an expiration date after which they go bad. Used habitually, they start causing problems, signaling that we must make changes in our lives. That we've needed them for so long in the face of addiction isn't our fault.

Working a Recovery Program

Sponsors help us by sharing their personal experience working the Steps. They aren't asking us to do anything they haven't done. Sponsors tell us how they did it, what helped them, and how they would like us to do it. We are not alone in this process; we just need to follow the directions. Many a sponsor, when asked the best time to start a Fourth and Fifth Step, replies, "When you want to stop hurting."

Assignment

Take time this week to consider the defects you could relate to, and notice when they crop up in your daily life. Discuss in your Twelve Step meetings and journal insights.

Closing

Read the SFR Closing Statement using the round-robin order.

Topic: Gentleness

Opening

Choose a round-robin order for reading and sharing. Use it to read the SFR Opening Statement.

Daily Reading

For this week's topic, a team member reads his selection from a Twelve Step daily reader and shares thoughts on the reading. The other team members then share their thoughts.

Report, Discuss, Plan

1. What went well in my recovery this past week? How am I progressing on my Personal Recovery Checklist? What could be improved? Do I need someone's insight?

2. Share insights I gained from last week's SFR assignment.

3. For the upcoming week, what is my recovery goal? I will contact my accountability partner _____ times this week.

Family Recovery Discussion

For each of the three sections, a team member is selected to read and share. Team members also share thoughts and insights after each reading.

Learn Something New

"If you are gentle with yourself, you will become gentle with others."

—Lama Yeshe

Moving through Steps Four and Five, we must first be gentle with ourselves. In doing so, we temper negative feelings we have toward ourselves. When we come with gentleness, we bring patience and kindness.

Steps Four and Five

Made a searching and fearless moral inventory of ourselves.

Admitted to God, to ourselves, and to another human being the exact nature of our wrongs.

George Mann, MD, founder of The Retreat, describes Step Four as critical for the development of a good self-image. To complete a *fearless* and *searching* inventory, we aren't called to log just negative but also positive attributes. In the video *Touch Life Gently,* Dr. Mann says, "We need to look at our positives too and say, 'This is who I am!'" What made the difference for him in doing a Fourth Step was realizing he was a good person. "Goodness is an inherent quality. . . . I can make mistakes and do dumb things, and I can take wrong turns. But my basic goodness is an ongoing characteristic."

Working a Recovery Program

Some find taking an inventory of their positive characteristics more difficult than the negatives. When we attend a Twelve Step meeting, we hear others share about overcoming negative characteristics by turning them into positives. The perfectionist, for instance, becomes a person who strives for excellence but understands that this requires allowing for mistakes. Positive characteristics include the following:

honest	empathetic	courageous	optimistic	forgiving
gentle	gracious	generous	enthusiastic	sincere
fair	cheerful	passionate	creative	loyal
kind	hospitable	supportive	curious	grateful
loving	fun	inspiring	joyful	warm-hearted

Assignment

Sit with your eyes closed for one minute, asking yourself, "What are my most positive characteristics, the parts of me that shine?" Circle positives you relate to from the preceding list. Write these in your journal and share with your sponsor.

Closing

Read the SFR Closing Statement using the round-robin order.

Topic: Empathy

Opening

Choose a round-robin order for reading and sharing. Use it to read the SFR Opening Statement.

Daily Reading

For this week's topic, a team member reads her selection from a Twelve Step daily reader and shares thoughts on the reading. The other team members then share their thoughts.

Report, Discuss, Plan

1. What went well in my recovery this past week? How am I progressing on my Personal Recovery Checklist? What could be improved? Do I need someone's insight?

2. Share insights I gained from last week's SFR assignment.

3. For the upcoming week, what is my recovery goal? I will contact my accountability partner _____ times this week.

Family Recovery Discussion

For each of the three sections, a team member is selected to read and share. Team members also share thoughts and insights after each reading.

Learn Something New

Empathy is experiencing what another person is facing or going through from that person's perspective. Isn't this what we all want from others? When a family has been coping with addiction, each member—including the addict—scrambled to find ways to survive the destructive nature of the disease. We can often more easily see the harmful patterns in others' lives than in our own. Let's begin by understanding the attempt to survive from the perspective of each member of our family. How is it different from the viewpoint we've taken in the past?

Steps Four and Five

Made a searching and fearless moral inventory of ourselves.

*Admitted to God, to ourselves, and to another human being
the exact nature of our wrongs.*

Since our brains experience negatives more intensely than positives, let's challenge any unfavorable thinking toward our family. What positive qualities are true of our family and its members? Here are some examples to help us take this inventory:

We are committed to the well-being of each one of us.

We make an effort to spend time and do things together.

We communicate with positive emotions.

We express appreciation.

We engage in problem solving together.

We show flexibility and tolerance toward each other.

We treat each other kindly and delight in each other.

We are willing to work together to strengthen and improve our family.

Working a Recovery Program

By working a program of recovery, we begin to let go of fear. Finally able to raise our heads out of the foxhole, we can afford to feel empathy. Everyone is actually on the same team; it was the chaos of addiction that separated us. Attending Twelve Step meetings, we know our family is not alone. Others have experienced what we have and worse—and they gladly share what worked for them. Empathy is our way out of spiritual isolation.

Assignment

Empathy builders: challenge preconceived notions, listen carefully to others, imagine living another's life, heal past hurts, pay attention to what you have in common with others, and initiate pleasant family encounters. Select one empathy building action and incorporate it into daily life this week. Discuss with your accountability partner. Journal insights.

Closing

Read the SFR Closing Statement using the round-robin order.

Topic: Patience

Opening

Choose a round-robin order for reading and sharing. Use it to read the SFR Opening Statement.

Daily Reading

For this week's topic, a team member reads his selection from a Twelve Step daily reader and shares thoughts on the reading. The other team members then share their thoughts.

Report, Discuss, Plan

1. What went well in my recovery this past week? How am I progressing on my Personal Recovery Checklist? What could be improved? Do I need someone's insight?

2. Share insights I gained from last week's SFR assignment.

3. For the upcoming week, what is my recovery goal? I will contact my accountability partner _____ times this week.

Family Recovery Discussion

For each of the three sections, a team member is selected to read and share. Team members also share thoughts and insights after each reading.

Learn Something New

When we have patience, we are better able to endure hardship. Patience is how much we can tolerate before our negative thinking sets in. It shows itself as perseverance even when we don't know the outcome of our efforts. Cognitive neuroscience has identified patience as a decision-making process. In recovery, we choose the valuable rewards that come with steadfastness over immediate gratification. Our natural inclination, however, is to take the less valuable reward of immediate gratification. Perhaps this is why patience is one of the highest virtues in world religions.

Steps Four and Five

Made a searching and fearless moral inventory of ourselves.

*Admitted to God, to ourselves, and to another human being
the exact nature of our wrongs.*

When we begin identifying character defects—our unhelpful patterns of behavior—we want them gone instantly. But they are well practiced and have created stable pathways in our brains. We may find we're not yet ready to give some of them up. For now, we will practice patience. We are called only to identify our character defects and admit their exact nature to ourselves, our Higher Power, and another human being.

Working a Recovery Program

A Twelve Step slogan, "Live and let live," helps us remember patience. It tells us we do not need to tie ourselves into knots thinking about what others need to do. When we find ourselves becoming impatient with another person, it's usually because that person isn't doing what we want. This popular slogan reminds us that, just as we want to live free of others' controlling behaviors, we can't micromanage another's life or recovery. As we each work our own program, our rate of personal growth will vary, but with patience and right behavior, results come.

Assignment

Unrealistic expectations often trigger impatience. Make patience a goal for the week. Slow down. Take time to think about expectations. Delay gratification. Take walks. Call your sponsor when feeling impatient. Discuss patience in a Twelve Step group. Journal insights.

Closing

Read the SFR Closing Statement using the round-robin order.

Topic: Fear

Opening

Choose a round-robin order for reading and sharing. Use it to read the SFR Opening Statement.

Daily Reading

For this week's topic, a team member reads her selection from a Twelve Step daily reader and shares thoughts on the reading. The other team members then share their thoughts.

Report, Discuss, Plan

1. What went well in my recovery this past week? How am I progressing on my Personal Recovery Checklist? What could be improved? Do I need someone's insight?

2. Share insights I gained from last week's SFR assignment.

3. For the upcoming week, what is my recovery goal? I will contact my accountability partner _____ times this week.

Family Recovery Discussion

For each of the three sections, a team member is selected to read and share. Team members also share thoughts and insights after each reading.

Learn Something New

> I must say a word about fear. It is life's only true opponent. Only fear can defeat life. It is a clever, treacherous adversary, how well I know. It has no decency, respects no law or convention, shows no mercy. It goes for your weakest spot, which it finds with unnerving ease. It begins in your mind, always . . . so you must fight hard to express it. You must fight hard to shine the light of words upon it. Because if you don't, if your fear becomes a wordless darkness that you avoid, perhaps even manage to forget, you open yourself to further

attacks of fear because you never truly fought the opponent
who defeated you.

—*Yann Martel,* Life of Pi

Steps Four and Five

Made a searching and fearless moral inventory of ourselves.

*Admitted to God, to ourselves, and to another human being
the exact nature of our wrongs.*

When living with addiction, fear becomes the governing force in our lives.
Since it is ever-present, we may no longer even recognize that it's our constant companion. Fear is behind most of our character defects. If we peek
behind anger, we're likely to find fear. Look at the root of perfectionism;
you'll probably find fear. Controlling behavior is a way to keep us safe from
what we fear. Self-pity, dishonesty, negative thinking—all can have their
roots in fear. It's promised that one of the results of doing a Fifth Step is
"Our fears fall from us."

Working a Recovery Program

Fear tells us what we can't do. Fear tells us good things won't last. Fear tells
us we don't have what it takes. Fear finds faults in our loved ones. Fear pre-
dicts the worst possible future. Fear produces dread. But we can overcome
fear by staying in the moment, doing the next right thing, and getting involved with other people in the recovery community. When others share
their experience, strength, and hope, they help extinguish our fears, reminding us that everything is going to be all right. In Steps Four and Five,
we take an inventory of when fear stopped us from doing what we needed
to do. By doing so, we begin to understand the ways fear undermines us.

Assignment

Ask in a Twelve Step meeting how people use the Steps and recovery slogans
to deal with fear. Journal insights.

Closing

Read the SFR Closing Statement using the round-robin order.

WEEK 21

Topic: Self-Centeredness

Opening

Choose a round-robin order for reading and sharing. Use it to read the SFR Opening Statement.

Daily Reading

For this week's topic, a team member reads his selection from a Twelve Step daily reader and shares thoughts on the reading. The other team members then share their thoughts.

Report, Discuss, Plan

1. What went well in my recovery this past week? How am I progressing on my Personal Recovery Checklist? What could be improved? Do I need someone's insight?

2. Share insights I gained from last week's SFR assignment.

3. For the upcoming week, what is my recovery goal? I will contact my accountability partner _____ times this week.

Family Recovery Discussion

For each of the three sections, a team member is selected to read and share. Team members also share thoughts and insights after each reading.

Learn Something New

Bill Wilson wrote in the Big Book, "Selfishness—self-centeredness! That, we think, is the root of our troubles." Self-centeredness keeps us isolated from others and a power greater than ourselves. At the core of self-centeredness is fear. In recovery, we move past self-centeredness by working closely with a sponsor and other recovering people to replace self-centeredness with healthy self-reflection.

Steps Four and Five

Made a searching and fearless moral inventory of ourselves.

*Admitted to God, to ourselves, and to another human being
the exact nature of our wrongs.*

The inventory process provides a method for identifying and rooting out selfish and self-centered behaviors driven by fears we often cannot see. By taking a close look at these defects, we can come to understand the underlying fears that motivate them. Our sponsor can provide additional insight and guidance in the Fifth Step process. We must root out self-centered behaviors if we hope to maintain physical and emotional sobriety, and rebuild relationships.

Working a Recovery Program

In the past, self-centeredness has been a cocoon used for protection. In recovery, we can take the risks of creating more authentic relationships based on our common welfare. The greatest relief from self-centeredness always comes from working with others. This is the paradoxical magic of the Twelve Step program. By extending ourselves to others, we find relief from the demands of the big "I." A recovering friend, sober more than twenty years from heroin addiction, said, "I'd followed the directions for the first time and worked with my sponsor to do a thorough Fourth and Fifth Step. It was a rite of passage and a great relief. I'd never felt more a part of the fellowship of AA."

Assignment

Take time after your next Twelve Step meeting to reach out to someone who shared something that resonated with you. Take a few moments to talk and to offer thanks. Journal about this interaction.

Closing

Read the SFR Closing Statement using the round-robin order.

Topic: Self-Pity

Opening

Choose a round-robin order for reading and sharing. Use it to read the SFR Opening Statement.

Daily Reading

For this week's topic, a team member reads her selection from a Twelve Step daily reader and shares thoughts on the reading. The other team members then share their thoughts.

Report, Discuss, Plan

1. What went well in my recovery this past week? How am I progressing on my Personal Recovery Checklist? What could be improved? Do I need someone's insight?

2. Share insights I gained from last week's SFR assignment.

3. For the upcoming week, what is my recovery goal? I will contact my accountability partner _____ times this week.

Family Recovery Discussion

For each of the three sections, a team member is selected to read and share. Team members also share thoughts and insights after each reading.

Learn Something New

"Self-pity is easily the most destructive of the non-pharmaceutical narcotics; it is addictive, gives momentary pleasure and separates the victim from reality," wrote the novelist John Gardner. Self-pity is a call for others to repeatedly come to our rescue. It requires that we mire ourselves in helplessness and blame. I've heard it said that the recipe for self-pity is misery plus self-obsession. For addicts, self-pity is an especially threatening relapse symptom: "Poor me, poor me, pour me a drink." The antidote for self-pity is gratitude.

Steps Four and Five

Made a searching and fearless moral inventory of ourselves.

Admitted to God, to ourselves, and to another human being the exact nature of our wrongs.

Step Four is when we begin to see the ways self-pity or pity-seeking takes a toll on our lives and our relationships, as we look to others to validate us. What's less obvious is that this is a symptom of resentment and self-centeredness. Some call self-pity, resentment, and self-centeredness a character defect three-pack. Recovery requires us to use Step Four to squarely face self-pity and the relentless belief that life isn't working out for us. By doing so, we begin taking responsibility for ourselves.

Working a Recovery Program

The more active we are in our recovery—attending meetings, spending time with other recovering people, working the Steps with our sponsor, and doing service work—the less time we have to dwell on ourselves. The ingredients for self-pity—resentment and self-centeredness—begin to wither away as we work an enthusiastic recovery program.

Assignment

Think about times when you've felt self-pity or engaged in pity-seeking. Discuss the antidote—gratitude—with your sponsor or in a Twelve Step meeting. Journal insights.

Closing

Read the SFR Closing Statement using the round-robin order.

Topic: People-Pleasing

Opening

Choose a round-robin order for reading and sharing. Use it to read the SFR Opening Statement.

Daily Reading

For this week's topic, a team member reads his selection from a Twelve Step daily reader and shares thoughts on the reading. The other team members then share their thoughts.

Report, Discuss, Plan

1. What went well in my recovery this past week? How am I progressing on my Personal Recovery Checklist? What could be improved? Do I need someone's insight?

2. Share insights I gained from last week's SFR assignment.

3. For the upcoming week, what is my recovery goal? I will contact my accountability partner _____ times this week.

Family Recovery Discussion

For each of the three sections, a team member is selected to read and share. Team members also share thoughts and insights after each reading.

Learn Something New

Earnie Larsen, the late recovery author and lecturer, wrote in his book *Stage II Recovery,* "People-pleasers have learned that their self-esteem is based on never making anyone angry." People-pleasers have difficulty saying no because they fear displeasing their loved ones and friends. For this reason, people-pleasers aren't free to be honest about what they think or how they feel. They don't get what they need and, as a result, harbor hidden resentments. They sacrifice themselves for the approval of others and peace in the moment.

Steps Four and Five

Made a searching and fearless moral inventory of ourselves.

Admitted to God, to ourselves, and to another human being the exact nature of our wrongs.

People-pleasers cannot begin caring for themselves until they face this character defect. Steps Four and Five help us understand how people-pleasing blocks healthy relationships with ourselves and others. These Steps prepare people-pleasers to remove this defect. Once removed, they are free from always having to agree, from taking responsibility for other's feelings, from constantly having to say yes, and from sacrificing themselves to make others happy.

Working a Recovery Program

Recovering people model honesty and openness. There is no safer place for people-pleasers to begin testing these waters than Twelve Step meetings. Experiencing acceptance when expressing honest thoughts and true feelings is liberating. By completing a Fourth and Fifth Step, they learn that they can be honest about their resentments and fears without being abandoned. Rather, they are readily welcomed into the recovery community. In Al-Anon, they hear other recovering people-pleasers share how they began respecting themselves. Little by little, people-pleasers begin losing their fears, letting go of resentments, and living a more fulfilling emotional life.

Assignment

Earnie Larsen was known for asking, "Who's driving your bus?" Ask yourself, "What character defects are driving my bus?" Schedule your Fifth Step with your sponsor sometime in the upcoming two weeks, if you haven't already done so. Following the suggestions of a sponsor experienced in doing Fifth Steps, you'll find the experience exceptional. It's also a recovery milestone.

Closing

Read the SFR Closing Statement using the round-robin order.

WEEK 24

Topic: Regret

Opening

Choose a round-robin order for reading and sharing. Use it to read the SFR Opening Statement.

Daily Reading

For this week's topic, a team member reads her selection from a Twelve Step daily reader and shares thoughts on the reading. The other team members then share their thoughts.

Report, Discuss, Plan

1. What went well in my recovery this past week? How am I progressing on my Personal Recovery Checklist? What could be improved? Do I need someone's insight?

2. Share insights I gained from last week's SFR assignment.

3. For the upcoming week, what is my recovery goal? I will contact my accountability partner _____ times this week.

Family Recovery Discussion

For each of the three sections, a team member is selected to read and share. Team members also share thoughts and insights after each reading.

Learn Something New

Regret binds us to the past. Recovering people often say, "You can't move forward when you are facing backward." For addicts, the negative consequences of addiction can be devastating. Their life is often in shambles, and the heartache is unbearable. The family, too, is grieving many losses. Family members often say, "I wish we'd gotten into recovery years ago." But we are powerless to change the past. Self-forgiveness and gratitude for today can close the door on regret. Then we can turn toward the future and move on.

Steps Four and Five

Made a searching and fearless moral inventory of ourselves.

*Admitted to God, to ourselves, and to another human being
the exact nature of our wrongs.*

We write about our regrets in Step Four and share them with our sponsor in Step Five. Being thoroughly honest and specific about the nature of our regrets, we can rid ourselves of their power over us, bringing about a renewed peace of mind. The Fourth and Fifth Steps are housekeeping for the soul.

Working a Recovery Program

"The past is done and can't be returned. So if we can do a good job this day we are doing the best we possibly can." This quote comes from the pamphlet *A Guide to the Twelve Steps of Alcoholics Anonymous.* It reminds us that we have power only over today. The past has let us go; let's let it go. The wisdom that comes from working a daily recovery program will prepare us to address our defects of character.

Assignment

Display the above AA quote about the past someplace where you'll see it every day. Ask members of your Twelve Step group how they moved past their most troublesome regrets. Journal insights.

Closing

Read the SFR Closing Statement using the round-robin order.

WEEK 25

Topic: A New Freedom

Opening

Choose a round-robin order for reading and sharing. Use it to read the SFR Opening Statement.

Daily Reading

For this week's topic, a team member reads his selection from a Twelve Step daily reader and shares thoughts on the reading. The other team members then share their thoughts.

Report, Discuss, Plan

1. What went well in my recovery this past week? How am I progressing on my Personal Recovery Checklist? What could be improved? Do I need someone's insight?

2. Share insights I gained from last week's SFR assignment.

3. For the upcoming week, what is my recovery goal? I will contact my accountability partner _____ times this week.

Family Recovery Discussion

For each of the three sections, a team member is selected to read and share. Team members also share thoughts and insights after each reading.

Learn Something New

When we identify harmful behavior patterns, we are preparing the ground for new seeds. Harvest time will bring a bounty of spiritual gifts. According to a parable on integrity and honesty, "If you plant honesty, you will reap trust. If you plant goodness, you will reap friends. If you plant humility, you will reap greatness. If you plant perseverance, you will reap victory. If you plant consideration, you will reap harmony. If you plant hard work, you will reap success. If you plant forgiveness, you will reap reconciliation. If you plant openness, you will reap intimacy. If you plant patience, you will reap improvements. If you plant faith, you will reap miracles."

Steps Four and Five

Made a searching and fearless moral inventory of ourselves.

Admitted to God, to ourselves, and to another human being the exact nature of our wrongs.

We can experience a new freedom after completing Steps Four and Five, but only if we've been truly thorough in our inventory. Some people omit a particularly embarrassing incident from their Fifth Step, thinking erroneously that it will have been enough to write it in their Fourth Step. The relief we seek from these Steps will not be realized until we make an admission of powerlessness over the past and clear out all our baggage.

Working a Recovery Program

A blog written by a member of AA called *Mr. SponsorPants* presents an honest account of the changes that come from working the Twelve Steps:

> I am sharing about the storm on the surface because, if I don't, it gets worse. But rest assured, like the depths of the ocean, there is a core of peace which AA helped me to develop, and it is always there. Some would go further, saying it's a living connection with a God consciousness, and on some days I would more easily agree with them than others, but it is there regardless. . . . Find the seeds inside yourself and develop them, because from that place will come a connection to a power greater than yourself. From that place will come an ability to empathize with other people's struggles. . . . From that place will come the ability to maintain your physical sobriety . . . and then to grow into mental, emotional, and spiritual sobriety as well.

Assignment

Completing Steps Four and Five is a rite of passage in Twelve Step programs. It's the single most important thing you can do to galvanize your recovery. Many people treat themselves to something special after completing this process. Reach out to others and celebrate this milestone.

Closing

Read the SFR Closing Statement using the round-robin order.

Third Quarter

The next twelve weeks focus on issues common to the seventh, eighth, and ninth months of recovery. At this point, by following the directions, family members and addict are likely to be starting to truly enjoy this journey. New and different things are happening, trust is being rebuilt, and recovery is beginning to bear fruit.

We expect that team members have completed Steps Four and Five by this point. Now it's time to get to the heart of recovery by working Steps Six, Seven, Eight, and Nine. It's easy to overlook these Steps, but they are transformational. It's said they separate the men from the boys and the women from the girls. Actively work with your Twelve Step sponsor on these Steps while following the guidance of your SFR meetings.

Topic: Attitude

Opening

Choose a round-robin order for reading and sharing. Use it to read the SFR Opening Statement.

Daily Reading

For this week's topic, a team member reads her selection from a Twelve Step daily reader and shares thoughts on the reading. The other team members then share their thoughts.

Report, Discuss, Plan

1. What went well in my recovery this past week? How am I progressing on my Personal Recovery Checklist? What could be improved? Do I need someone's insight?

2. Share insights I gained from last week's SFR assignment.

3. For the upcoming week, what is my recovery goal? I will contact my accountability partner _____ times this week.

Family Recovery Discussion

For each of the three sections, a team member is selected to read and share. Team members also share thoughts and insights after each reading.

Learn Something New

Attitude is a way of thinking and feeling that colors how we evaluate our relationships and circumstances. The Latin root words for attitude—*apto* and *acto*—mean "to do or to act." They understood a clear connection between attitude and action. It wasn't until the mid-1800s that psychologists began using the word to mean "an internal state of preparation for action." It's behavior that leads to changes in attitude, not the other way around. The effective message for change is "It works when you work it."

Step Six

Were entirely ready to have God remove all these defects of character.

This Step is about action leading to a new attitude. We admitted our defects; now we are asked to be entirely ready to let them be removed from us. This Step isn't asking us to remove our own character defects—something none of us has been able to manage—but to trust that a power greater than ourselves can and will remove them. Our action in this Step is simply *readiness*.

Working a Recovery Program

Twelve Step programs work so well because members do exactly what social scientists say works best. First, they engage in the behaviors of recovery, which lead to changed attitudes. Second, they share how their lives are changed as a result of working a program. Newcomers witnessing the authenticity in Twelve Step groups are likely to choose these behaviors for themselves. This is how attitudes change.

Assignment

What recovery behaviors are you exhibiting on a daily basis? Are you walking the walk? How have your attitudes changed as a result? Talk about this with your sponsor and in a Twelve Step meeting. Journal insights.

Closing

Read the SFR Closing Statement using the round-robin order.

Topic: Readiness

Opening

Choose a round-robin order for reading and sharing. Use it to read the SFR Opening Statement.

Daily Reading

For this week's topic, a team member reads his selection from a Twelve Step daily reader and shares thoughts on the reading. The other team members then share their thoughts.

Report, Discuss, Plan

1. What went well in my recovery this past week? How am I progressing on my Personal Recovery Checklist? What could be improved? Do I need someone's insight?

2. Share insights I gained from last week's SFR assignment.

3. For the upcoming week, what is my recovery goal? I will contact my accountability partner _____ times this week.

Family Recovery Discussion

For each of the three sections, a team member is selected to read and share. Team members also share thoughts and insights after each reading.

Learn Something New

Poet and author C. JoyBell C. writes, "We can't be afraid of change. You may feel very secure in the pond that you are in, but if you never venture out of it, you will never know that there is such a thing as an ocean, a sea." Becoming ready to change is a process of decision-making. The brain starts scanning for evidence for why a change will benefit us. But if we rely only on the information at hand and never throw ourselves into the sea, we're likely to decide staying in the pond is just fine. We don't make great strides sitting around waiting to feel ready. We need to stand up and move our feet. Having completed Steps Four and Five, we have taken the action steps necessary to get us ready for Step Six.

Step Six

Were entirely ready to have God remove all these defects of character.

Our readiness is usually a result of wanting to stop the pain. If our harmful patterns of behavior aren't causing us enough pain, when the pain is diminished, or when we don't identify patterns as the source of our pain, we might remain ambivalent. This is when we have to go back to our fearless and searching inventory. What kind of life are we willing to settle for? Is the pond still okay? Or have we had enough?

Working a Recovery Program

"When we tried to clean ourselves up with our own power and 'discipline,' we kept ourselves agitated, confused, in denial, and worn out, and we were in almost constant emotional pain," writes J. Keith Miller in his book *A Hunger for Healing*. We think we can do Step Six easily ourselves, that naming our character defects means we can just let them go. It's a form of denial about our true relationship with these behaviors. We've used them for a long while, we trust them, they're comfortable, they work for us in the short run (remember our propensity for immediate gratification in the near term), and they feel good when we use them. It's going to take a power greater than ourselves to remove them. Our part is in the readiness.

Assignment

Discuss with your sponsor the character defect you will have the most difficulty letting go, and the one that will be easiest. Journal insights.

Closing

Read the SFR Closing Statement using the round-robin order.

Topic: Letting Go

Opening

Choose a round-robin order for reading and sharing. Use it to read the SFR Opening Statement.

Daily Reading

For this week's topic, a team member reads her selection from a Twelve Step daily reader and shares thoughts on the reading. The other team members then share their thoughts.

Report, Discuss, Plan

1. What went well in my recovery this past week? How am I progressing on my Personal Recovery Checklist? What could be improved? Do I need someone's insight?

2. Share insights I gained from last week's SFR assignment.

3. For the upcoming week, what is my recovery goal? I will contact my accountability partner _____ times this week.

Family Recovery Discussion

For each of the three sections, a team member is selected to read and share. Team members also share thoughts and insights after each reading.

Learn Something New

Michelangelo, Italian sculptor and painter of the High Renaissance, upon finishing one of the most remarkable pieces of sculpture ever created, was asked how he did it. It is said that he replied, "I saw David in this block of marble, and I then chipped away everything that wasn't David." That block of marble represents us encased in the character defects caused by coping with the disease of addiction. In Step Six, we're ready to have our Higher Power chip away everything that isn't our best self, ready to live our best life in recovery.

Step Six

Were entirely ready to have God remove all these defects of character.

What is our reluctance? What is it about a particular pattern of behaviors that is so comforting to us, even when it blocks our relationships with others? Do we believe we can continue relying on defects without hurting those we love and ourselves? Since we don't always feel entirely ready, we must ask ourselves which behaviors will lead to the best results over time. Look away from the moment to see the big picture.

Working a Recovery Program

We are often afraid of letting go of well-used character defects because we don't know what will replace them. They have protected us and helped us cope. It's in working a recovery program that we are given the skills to replace old behaviors. We don't need to be afraid of letting go anymore. We are constantly developing new patterns that bring us a better way of living. Working a recovery program creates solutions, making readiness a natural part of the process.

Assignment

Take fifteen minutes to journal your vision of new ways of interacting with others and yourself after leaving behind old patterns of behavior for new recovery behaviors. What are the benefits?

Closing

Read the SFR Closing Statement using the round-robin order.

WEEK 29

Topic: Self-Acceptance

Opening

Choose a round-robin order for reading and sharing. Use it to read the SFR Opening Statement.

Daily Reading

For this week's topic, a team member reads his selection from a Twelve Step daily reader and shares thoughts on the reading. The other team members then share their thoughts.

Report, Discuss, Plan

1. What went well in my recovery this past week? How am I progressing on my Personal Recovery Checklist? What could be improved? Do I need someone's insight?

2. Share insights I gained from last week's SFR assignment.

3. For the upcoming week, what is my recovery goal? I will contact my accountability partner _____ times this week.

Family Recovery Discussion

For each of the three sections, a team member is selected to read and share. Team members also share thoughts and insights after each reading.

Learn Something New

Moving through the Steps, from Four to Seven, is a quest to realize our best selves. In the past, we put more faith into our trusted, but eventually ineffective, ways of responding to crisis. Now we must take a good look at what is worth saving and ask our Higher Power to help us chip away the rest. Removing these defects is no easy task, but opportunities present themselves daily. We reach for the help of our Twelve Step program, other recovering people, and our SFR team. All serve as conduits for our Higher Power.

Step Seven

Humbly asked Him to remove our shortcomings.

Approaching Step Seven humbly means we are accepting ourselves as we are, in this moment. We are not perfect, and we do not have all the answers. Humility means accepting reality. By asking to have our shortcomings removed, we are trusting that our Higher Power will help us on the next stage of our spiritual growth.

Working a Recovery Program

A recovering friend said to me, "These two Steps, Six and Seven, gave me inner peace and a sense of beauty about myself. I was finally comfortable in my own skin." Step Seven tells us we can leave all the good stuff—meaning our true best selves—in place, while our Higher Power helps us remove everything that distracts from the good. God *as we understand Him* doesn't just come along and lop it all off with a single stroke. Defects of character are chipped away one day at a time. Our Higher Power comes to our assistance in many different forms through our program of recovery.

Assignment

Every morning for the next week, spend thirty seconds with your eyes closed asking your Higher Power to remove a specific defect of character for today. Spend another thirty seconds with your eyes closed identifying one characteristic of your better self you will implement today.

Closing

Read the SFR Closing Statement using the round-robin order.

WEEK 30

Topic: Service

Opening

Choose a round-robin order for reading and sharing. Use it to read the SFR Opening Statement.

Daily Reading

For this week's topic, a team member reads her selection from a Twelve Step daily reader and shares thoughts on the reading. The other team members then share their thoughts.

Report, Discuss, Plan

1. What went well in my recovery this past week? How am I progressing on my Personal Recovery Checklist? What could be improved? Do I need someone's insight?

2. Share insights I gained from last week's SFR assignment.

3. For the upcoming week, what is my recovery goal? I will contact my accountability partner _____ times this week.

Family Recovery Discussion

For each of the three sections, a team member is selected to read and share. Team members also share thoughts and insights after each reading.

Learn Something New

In the words of Rabindranath Tagore, Nobel Laureate in Literature, "I slept and dreamt that life was joy. I awoke and saw that life was service. I acted and behold, service was joy." Service brings out the best in us. It's an external act of considering others before self. It is how we show gratitude for our recovery by giving back. In Twelve Step service, we gain a sense of belonging and feel the warmth of other people. Much of our positive spirituality comes through the outward journey of service.

Step Seven

Humbly asked Him to remove our shortcomings.

Our shortcomings separate us from others. When we humbly ask our Higher Power to remove these defects, we are also asking for this separation to be removed. By asking for help, we stop excluding others from the solution and give our Higher Power something to work with. An anonymous recovering academic wrote, "Asking for help is the turning point. After that, the story changes tone, from anxiety to hope, from tragedy to laughter. That story is called recovery. And that is where it gets good."

Working a Recovery Program

In the Hazelden pamphlet *Step 6 & 7: Ready, Willing, and Able,* it's suggested we have a conversation with our Higher Power: "I am willing to let down the barriers between me and the rest of the world. Please remove all my defects and help me to become my best self. I am ready to go out and do the work that calls me without the swords and shields I thought I needed." Or we can use the Seventh Step Prayer from the Big Book of Alcoholics Anonymous: "My Creator, I am now willing that you should have all of me, good and bad. I pray that you now remove from me every single defect of character which stands in the way of my usefulness to you and my fellows." We work Step Seven when on the verge of putting a character defect into action.

Assignment

Discuss with your sponsor how you will use the Seventh Step daily in a meaningful way.

Closing

Read the SFR Closing Statement using the round-robin order.

Topic: Change

Opening

Choose a round-robin order for reading and sharing. Use it to read the SFR Opening Statement.

Daily Reading

For this week's topic, a team member reads his selection from a Twelve Step daily reader and shares thoughts on the reading. The other team members then share their thoughts.

Report, Discuss, Plan

1. What went well in my recovery this past week? How am I progressing on my Personal Recovery Checklist? What could be improved? Do I need someone's insight?

2. Share insights I gained from last week's SFR assignment.

3. For the upcoming week, what is my recovery goal? I will contact my accountability partner _____ times this week.

Family Recovery Discussion

For each of the three sections, a team member is selected to read and share. Team members also share thoughts and insights after each reading.

Learn Something New

Everywhere, people resist change. Change occurs continually in the business world because of competition, yet many business leaders are always dealing with employees' resistance to change. It's one of the greatest contributors to loss of productivity and lowered quality of service. Change requires moving in the direction of the unknown, and most of us prefer to stay in the known—even when it's no longer relevant or effective in dealing with our current situation. Fear of change is common on a social level too. We connect with people using our established patterns of behavior. It's how we're used to relating to each other. Anything that falls outside of our comfort zone feels unnatural. For this reason, recovery asks us to take change in small steps.

Step Eight

*Made a list of all persons we had harmed,
and became willing to make amends to them all.*

This is the first Step that directly touches on our personal relationships. We take a look around to see who we've harmed. We do this for two good reasons: (1) to consider how we can develop the best possible relationship with the people in our lives, and (2) to end emotional isolation and begin ridding ourselves of the weight we carry. This is a preparation Step.

Working a Recovery Program

In AA and NA, members cannot deny that their disease has caused others harm. In Al-Anon, it's harder to imagine the necessity of this Step. We say, "I haven't hurt anyone! I was the responsible one. I was the one who took the brunt of all the problems." But when we are defending ourselves from addiction in the family, we develop survival skills that, over time, hurt us and others. Working with our sponsor and listening to others in Twelve Step meetings, we open our eyes and begin to see. In Steps Four through Seven, we cleaned up past selves; now we are preparing to clean up our relationships. This is an act of integrity.

Assignment

Discuss Step Eight with your sponsor this week. Ask others in your Twelve Step meetings about their experiences with Step Eight. Journal insights.

Closing

Read the SFR Closing Statement using the round-robin order.

Topic: Progress

Opening

Choose a round-robin order for reading and sharing. Use it to read the SFR Opening Statement.

Daily Reading

For this week's topic, a team member reads her selection from a Twelve Step daily reader and shares thoughts on the reading. The other team members then share their thoughts.

Report, Discuss, Plan

1. What went well in my recovery this past week? How am I progressing on my Personal Recovery Checklist? What could be improved? Do I need someone's insight?

2. Share insights I gained from last week's SFR assignment.

3. For the upcoming week, what is my recovery goal? I will contact my accountability partner _____ times this week.

Family Recovery Discussion

For each of the three sections, a team member is selected to read and share. Team members also share thoughts and insights after each reading.

Learn Something New

In the words of Ernest Hemingway, "There is nothing noble in being superior to your fellow man; true nobility is being superior to your former self." By now, in working our Twelve Step program and meeting weekly with our SFR team, we most assuredly are "superior to our former selves." How do we know? By the quality of our relationships. Take a look at your inventory and notice the things you are not doing anymore—and acknowledge how you're doing things differently now. Let's take a moment to smell the roses.

Step Eight
Made a list of all persons we had harmed,
and became willing to make amends to them all.

If everything we've done in recovery thus far has brought us to this point, Steps Eight and Nine represent a quantum leap forward in our relationships with others and ourselves. Taking these Steps, we become aware that we're people of worth. It's paradoxical. By becoming willing to make amends to all whom we've harmed—acknowledging our wrongs—we clear away the debris that prevents us from seeing what's right in our life. We live in the present with no regrets or fears about the past. It is a marvelous feeling.

Working a Recovery Program

We work Steps Eight and Nine with our Twelve Step sponsor. We need guidance on taking these Steps so we don't use them in a way that further injures others or ourselves. We also need help avoiding reluctance to "make amends to them all." Self-interest is a natural reaction to these Steps, which fuels avoidance. But with power we've gained from working the previous Steps, we are now working from our better selves. We have already brought our best qualities to the world: willingness, thoroughness, courage, honesty, and acceptance. These qualities are all we need to make our list.

Assignment

Talk with your sponsor about the ways working a Twelve Step program has changed your relationships. This is the positive part of your relationship inventory, revealing the fruits of your efforts. It also helps you see the value of taking this next Step. Journal your insights.

Closing

Read the SFR Closing Statement using the round-robin order.

Topic: Self-Awareness

Opening

Choose a round-robin order for reading and sharing. Use it to read the SFR Opening Statement.

Daily Reading

For this week's topic, a team member reads his selection from a Twelve Step daily reader and shares thoughts on the reading. The other team members then share their thoughts.

Report, Discuss, Plan

1. What went well in my recovery this past week? How am I progressing on my Personal Recovery Checklist? What could be improved?

2. Share insights I gained from last week's SFR assignment.

3. For the upcoming week, what is my recovery goal? I will contact my accountability partner _____ times this week.

Family Recovery Discussion

For each of the three sections, a team member is selected to read and share. Team members also share thoughts and insights after each reading.

Learn Something New

Self-awareness is being conscious of the true condition of our existence. When we're living with addiction, we are so vigilant about what the alcoholic or addict is doing, we are no longer fully aware of ourselves. We even lose our grasp on just how bad things have become. Without sufficient self-awareness, we cannot clearly see our strengths or our limitations. Working the Twelve Steps wakes us up. We go through a series of Steps that help us look at ourselves and become aware of others in a new way. We may be bruised and battered—both alcoholic and family—but these Steps heal and strengthen us.

Step Eight

Made a list of all persons we had harmed,
and became willing to make amends to them all.

This Step gives us clear directions: make a list. But our lack of self-awareness can blind us to how we've harmed others. How do we begin to get ready if we can't see our part in a harm that has occurred? Here are some questions to ask: *How has my contempt for the addict hurt others? Have I turned people against each other by what I've said? Whom have I taken my frustrations out on? How have my character defects harmed others, directly or indirectly? Have I withdrawn from others? In what ways have I neglected others, especially children? Where have I placed blame?* Living with addiction twists all of our behaviors; it's the nature of the disease.

Working a Recovery Program

Working a Twelve Step program is a gift because it provides a place where everyone understands what it's like to live with the disease of addiction; where everyone is open and honest about personal shortcomings and wrongdoings; where everyone takes action to thoroughly clean house; where everyone clears out blame, anger, and resentment and knows how to accept the past. Working a Twelve Step program brings about real change.

Assignment

Look back to your Fourth Step inventory to help you write your list for Step Eight. Do this with your sponsor's guidance.

Closing

Read the SFR Closing Statement using the round-robin order.

Topic: Easy Does It

Opening

Choose a round-robin order for reading and sharing. Use it to read the SFR Opening Statement.

Daily Reading

For this week's topic, a team member reads her selection from a Twelve Step daily reader and shares thoughts on the reading. The other team members then share their thoughts.

Report, Discuss, Plan

1. What went well in my recovery this past week? How am I progressing on my Personal Recovery Checklist? What could be improved? Do I need someone's insight?

2. Share insights I gained from last week's SFR assignment.

3. For the upcoming week, what is my recovery goal? I will contact my accountability partner _____ times this week.

Family Recovery Discussion

For each of the three sections, a team member is selected to read and share. Team members also share thoughts and insights after each reading.

Learn Something New

"Easy does it" is one of the most useful Twelve Step slogans. Many people may treat it scornfully as simplistic, but they overlook the power behind the words. The slogan means relax. First relax your muscles, then the expression on your face. Allow the corners of your mouth to lift up to make a touch of a smile. Breathe in and out of your nose slowly. Notice the little space between your inhale and exhale. Some call it the "God space." Observe how your mind is following the example of your body as it begins to relax too. This one slogan has saved many people from themselves—especially when working the Steps for the first time.

Step Eight
Made a list of all persons we had harmed,
and became willing to make amends to them all.

There are four common reasons people postpone taking this Step: fear, pride, procrastination, and the belief that we haven't harmed others. Whichever one we might be experiencing, our sponsor can help us examine our motives. Do we want to look good to others? Are we afraid our amends will be received poorly? Do we only see the ways we've been caught up in another's bad behaviors, without seeing our own role? When we are justifying or rationalizing, putting it off, or projecting into the future what might happen when we make amends, it's an indication we may just need to relax and remind ourselves, "Easy does it."

Working a Recovery Program

Most of us came to Step Four with trepidation but found it easier than we imagined. Now we are making another list that proves not to be as difficult as we think. We will follow our sponsor's lead. We can even take this Step with a bit of excitement, thinking how good it will feel to finally have a thoroughly clean house.

Assignment

Talk with your sponsor about any trepidation you have about working this Step. Ask how she benefitted by completing Steps Eight and Nine. Then schedule a time to write your list.

Closing

Read the SFR Closing Statement using the round-robin order.

Topic: Repairing the Past

Opening

Choose a round-robin order for reading and sharing. Use it to read the SFR Opening Statement.

Daily Reading

For this week's topic, a team member reads his selection from a Twelve Step daily reader and shares thoughts on the reading. The other team members then share their thoughts.

Report, Discuss, Plan

1. What went well in my recovery this past week? How am I progressing on my Personal Recovery Checklist? What could be improved? Do I need someone's insight?

2. Share insights I gained from last week's SFR assignment.

3. For the upcoming week, what is my recovery goal? I will contact my accountability partner _____ times this week.

Family Recovery Discussion

For each of the three sections, a team member is selected to read and share. Team members also share thoughts and insights after each reading.

Learn Something New

Members of Al-Anon describe their experiences with Step Nine:

> "My sponsor insisted I make amends to myself before approaching others."
>
> "My sponsor guided me on how to make amends to each person on my list."
>
> "It was very humbling. I hadn't realized that I'd played a part in the alcoholism."
>
> "I couldn't make amends to someone on my list. My sponsor had me make 'living amends' by changing my behavior."
>
> "I was scared, but making amends made a huge difference in my life."
>
> "Amends were about me getting my affairs in order, not an attempt to seek forgiveness."

Step Nine
Made direct amends to such people wherever possible,
except when to do so would injure them or others.

Making amends is easier when we bring a love to the process that asks for nothing in return. The only expectation we have is for ourselves. Complete this Step under the guidance of a sponsor, move forward courageously, do no harm to anyone, be thorough, make amends to yourself, and keep it simple.

Working a Recovery Program

Working the previous eight Steps makes it possible to do Step Nine. We couldn't have done it any sooner because we wouldn't have known what this Step required. Making amends isn't the same as saying empty words of apology. As is true of the rest of the program, Step Nine requires a change in behavior. We are cleaning up our side of the street and don't want to sully it in the months and years to come. Once we've completed this Step, we move into *living amends*: treating others the way we want to be treated.

Assignment

Sit down with your sponsor, go over your list, and decide the best way to proceed for each person you've listed. Ask yourself, "Am I leaving anyone off this list?"

Closing

Read the SFR Closing Statement using the round-robin order.

Topic: Forgiveness

Opening

Choose a round-robin order for reading and sharing. Use it to read the SFR Opening Statement.

Daily Reading

For this week's topic, a team member reads her selection from a Twelve Step daily reader and shares thoughts on the reading. The other team members then share their thoughts.

Report, Discuss, Plan

1. What went well in my recovery this past week? How am I progressing on my Personal Recovery Checklist? What could be improved? Do I need someone's insight?

2. Share insights I gained from last week's SFR assignment.

3. For the upcoming week, what is my recovery goal? I will contact my accountability partner _____ times this week.

Family Recovery Discussion

For each of the three sections, a team member is selected to read and share. Team members also share thoughts and insights after each reading.

Learn Something New

It's important to recognize if we are still harboring anger, blame, or resentment toward anyone on our list. We need to work through these feelings before we make our amends. We are back to the topic of forgiveness. It's an important skill in all areas of life. In an article in *Forbes,* Amanda Neville writes about forgiveness: "Forgiveness is a process. It takes time and effort. Start by reflecting on what happened and try to see the other point of view. If you have a hard time seeing their side, try putting yourself in their shoes and write a letter to yourself outlining what happened. Think about how your choices and actions contributed to the situation. Evaluate the cost of holding on to your negative emotions versus letting go of them in the name of forgiveness. The key is to reconnect with your empathy, with a more centered sense of reality."

Step Nine
*Made direct amends to such people wherever possible,
except when to do so would injure them or others.*

We are asked to make amends unless it will hurt that person or someone else. Determine with your sponsor if there is someone on your list you could harm. In these cases, we make creative amends, which provide other ways to clean up our part of the problem. Be sure your motives in avoiding direct amends are honest and not a case of avoidance, because amends relieve us of much of our shame, guilt, and regrets. It's emotional accountability that cleans up the last vestiges of the wreckage of the past. It lifts the weight off our shoulders.

Working a Recovery Program
If we struggle to forgive someone on our list, we must use the program to help us. Anger, blame, and resentments are treacherous for recovering people. Such emotions cause alcoholics to drink and addicts to use. These feelings can cause families to lose emotional sobriety. With your sponsor, discuss the danger of hanging on to these negative emotions. It is in our best interest to take necessary measures to overcome these lingering feelings. We do this by surrendering to Step Nine. It is then that we transcend ourselves and discover that the beauty of making amends includes forgiving ourselves.

Assignment
Go back to Steps One, Two, and Three to ready yourself for making amends. Ask your sponsor and members of your Twelve Step group how they've dealt with the difficulties of letting go of blaming others and focusing on our part instead. Journal insights.

Closing
Read the SFR Closing Statement using the round-robin order.

Topic: The Promises

Opening

Choose a round-robin order for reading and sharing. Use it to read the SFR Opening Statement.

Daily Reading

For this week's topic, a team member reads his selection from a Twelve Step daily reader and shares thoughts on the reading. The other team members then share their thoughts.

Report, Discuss, Plan

1. What went well in my recovery this past week? How am I progressing on my Personal Recovery Checklist? What could be improved? Do I need someone's insight?

2. Share insights I gained from last week's SFR assignment.

3. For the upcoming week, what is my recovery goal? I will contact my accountability partner _____ times this week.

Family Recovery Discussion

For each of the three sections, a team member is selected to read and share. Team members also share thoughts and insights after each reading.

Learn Something New

We close each SFR meeting with "The Promises." They are rightly titled "The Ninth Step Promises," because it is after making amends—clearing out the rest of the debris—that all of the promises can materialize. Sitting in AA, NA, or Al-Anon meetings, you'll hear people who've *painstakingly* completed Steps One through Nine say these promises have come true for them—usually adding that they never believed it would happen and were quite amazed when it did.

Step Nine

*Made direct amends to such people wherever possible,
except when to do so would injure them or others.*

When we make amends, we need to keep our expectations in check. If we move forward expecting certain things from the people to whom we are making amends, we set ourselves up for disappointment. Their responses aren't our business. Our only job is to be honest about what we have done. We may hope to restore relationships, but we cannot control results. If someone remains angry, we know we did our best. These Steps have helped us grow along spiritual lines, but we must remember, not everyone has made spiritual progress to the point of being able to forgive some things, and they may have reasons why they can't at this time in their lives.

Working a Recovery Program

We didn't know what to expect when we attended our first Al-Anon, AA, or NA meeting, and may not have known why we needed to go. Now, after a relatively brief amount of time in the grand scheme of things, we are likely to have made significant spiritual progress together as a family. We have become better at keeping our commitments to one another and demonstrating trustworthiness. We are completing (or have completed) the last of the action Steps. It's a good time to take one minute to close our eyes in silent gratitude.

Assignment

Once you've completed your Ninth Step, turn to "The Promises" in this book or the Big Book and read them slowly to yourself or with your sponsor. This is the legacy you've earned.

Closing

Read the SFR Closing Statement using the round-robin order.

Fourth Quarter

The next thirteen weeks focus on issues common to the tenth, eleventh, and twelfth months of recovery. As bad memories of active addiction begin to dim, this is a period when addict and family can begin to experience some complacency. Everyone on the team is in danger of becoming overconfident that the disease has been licked. It's more important than ever to continue following directions and work your recovery program.

This is also a time to begin planning again. The newly recovering person has been advised in treatment and by his sponsor not to make big changes in the first year of sobriety. Now, approaching the one-year anniversary of sobriety, he may initiate discussions about going back to school, career advancement, and any needed work on relationships.

We expect that team members have completed Steps Six, Seven, Eight, and Nine with their sponsors. By now, as a result of doing these Steps, we realize a positive spirituality is working in our lives. The team now comes to Steps Ten, Eleven, and Twelve. Step Ten involves continuing to take a personal inventory on a daily basis. Step Eleven compresses the whole program into one sentence, where we make our reliance on our Higher Power a daily practice. Step Twelve is the practice of helping others. Actively work with your Twelve Step sponsor on these Steps while following the guidance of your SFR meetings.

Topic: Trustworthiness

Opening

Choose a round-robin order for reading and sharing. Use it to read the SFR Opening Statement.

Daily Reading

For this week's topic, a team member reads her selection from a Twelve Step daily reader and shares thoughts on the reading. The other team members then share their thoughts.

Report, Discuss, Plan

1. What went well in my recovery this past week? How am I progressing on my Personal Recovery Checklist? What could be improved? Do I need someone's insight?

2. Share insights I gained from last week's SFR assignment.

3. For the upcoming week, what is my recovery goal? I will contact my accountability partner _____ times this week.

Family Recovery Discussion

For each of the three sections, a team member is selected to read and share. Team members also share thoughts and insights after each reading.

Learn Something New

We are genetically wired to trust; it's tied to our survival and the need to co-operate with one another. Those we are most likely to trust are the people who share our DNA. Studies at the University of London show that we humans have a tendency to trust people who look more like us than those who don't. In the online magazine *Evolution,* Dan Jones writes, "In the case of humans, it's possible that when people cooperate with us, treat us kindly or show us altruism, we tend to see them as more like family, and this influences the way we perceive their physical features." This demonstrates the important role trust plays in our sense of who belongs to us. Is it any wonder it's often the first thing addicts are concerned about in treatment: *How do I get my family to trust me again?* In other words, *How do I belong to my family again?*

Step Ten
Continued to take personal inventory and when we were wrong promptly admitted it.

Step Ten is the trustworthiness Step. It is a daily inventory of our trustworthiness. *How did I do today? Did I trespass against someone or something? What amends do I need to make? How soon can I get it done?* If we do this every day, we are living as a trustworthy person. We don't have to be perfect; we just need to promptly admit when we were wrong and then change that particular behavior—starting now. *Humbly asked Him to remove our shortcomings.*

Working a Recovery Program
We learn about what it means to be trustworthy from listening to others share their experience, strength, and hope. Not just the obvious stuff, either, but the subtle little ways we're untrustworthy. These are easy to ignore or overlook. It's the stuff in the corners and under the bed. By taking a good Tenth Step on a daily basis, the house stays well scrubbed. We have peace of mind and clean relationships.

Assignment
Commit to faithfully working a Tenth Step. Identify your daily recovery trigger for your Tenth Step. Discuss with your sponsor and during a Twelve Step meeting. Journal insights.

Closing
Read the SFR Closing Statement using the round-robin order.

Topic: Inventory

Opening

Choose a round-robin order for reading and sharing. Use it to read the SFR Opening Statement.

Daily Reading

For this week's topic, a team member reads his selection from a Twelve Step daily reader and shares thoughts on the reading. The other team members then share their thoughts.

Report, Discuss, Plan

1. What went well in my recovery this past week? How am I progressing on my Personal Recovery Checklist? What could be improved? Do I need someone's insight?

2. Share insights I gained from last week's SFR assignment.

3. For the upcoming week, what is my recovery goal? I will contact my accountability partner _____ times this week.

Family Recovery Discussion

For each of the three sections, a team member is selected to read and share. Team members also share thoughts and insights after each reading.

Learn Something New

Taking a personal inventory—or self-assessment—is an important personal activity that allows us to monitor our strengths and shortcomings daily. If we identify a shortcoming in our Fourth Step but don't take action, we can damage our sense of self-worth. Remember, taking an inventory is only the first step; the next step asks, "What do I need to do with this information?" As we learned in Steps Four through Nine, inventories are meant to give rise to positive actions and self-betterment. The same holds true for Step Ten.

Step Ten
Continued to take personal inventory and when we were wrong
promptly admitted it.

Using Step Ten to promptly admit we were wrong not only gives us an immediate opportunity to put things right, but also gives the people we hurt, angered, or disappointed an opportunity to forgive us, cleaning up their reaction toward our transgression. Doing a Tenth Step opens doors for us both. As the American poet Emily Dickinson wrote, "Not knowing when the dawn will come, I open every door."

Working a Recovery Program
We depend on inventories because, with addiction in the family, we've been preoccupied with trying to manage and second-guess the disease. As it says in AA's *Twelve Steps and Twelve Traditions,* "A great many of us have never really acquired the habit of accurate self-appraisal." Working our recovery program with a daily Tenth Step changes the quality of how we live each day. We learn to depend on this Step to keep us looking forward.

Assignment
Ask your sponsor and other members of your Twelve Step group to share how using Step Ten has changed their relationship with themselves and others. Journal insights.

Closing
Read the SFR Closing Statement using the round-robin order.

Topic: Self-Righteousness

Opening

Choose a round-robin order for reading and sharing. Use it to read the SFR Opening Statement.

Daily Reading

For this week's topic, a team member reads her selection from a Twelve Step daily reader and shares thoughts on the reading. The other team members then share their thoughts.

Report, Discuss, Plan

1. What went well in my recovery this past week? How am I progressing on my Personal Recovery Checklist? What could be improved? Do I need someone's insight?

2. Share insights I gained from last week's SFR assignment.

3. For the upcoming week, what is my recovery goal? I will contact my accountability partner _____ times this week.

Family Recovery Discussion

For each of the three sections, a team member is selected to read and share. Team members also share thoughts and insights after each reading.

Learn Something New

The power of spiritual inventories (what some call "soul inventories") is understood throughout world religions. For instance, Yom Kippur, the holiest day of the year among Jewish people, is a time for taking inventory of the previous year. Rabbi Ben A. Romer, writing for the *Richmond Times-Dispatch*, says, "We can all too regularly be sure we are holding the higher moral ground. Too often we build our walls of assured righteousness, refusing to see the complicated lives of others." Only after this soul checking, he says, is it possible for us to move forward humanly and spiritually. Self-righteousness blocks compassion and trusting relationships.

Step Ten

Continued to take personal inventory and when we were wrong promptly admitted it.

We can use our Tenth Step inventory to monitor our tendencies to insist on being right. Messages that implicitly or explicitly say, "I know better; I'm right, you're not; you need to do it my way," are often symptoms of our controlling behaviors, our inability to trust other people, feelings of perfectionism, or fear of mistakes. Sometimes our insistence on being right can wrong others.

Working a Recovery Program

Recovering people often ask, "Would I rather be right or be happy?" The way we answer this question tells us much about ourselves and our relationships. "A light sprinkle of self-righteousness," as author Stephen King says, "'spread over all your scruples' can keep one from becoming milquetoast, but an overdose makes us insufferable." Working a program helps us create a balance. By taking even the most admirable characteristics too far in one direction or the other, we produce defects. We rely on the experiences and wisdom of other recovering people to help enlighten our thinking about balance. With this ever-increasing self-knowledge, our Tenth Step becomes a richer experience.

Assignment

In your Tenth Step, ask yourself if you are being true to the structure you built to support your recovery. By maintaining the structure, you will keep your balance during times that are rough or unpredictable. Use your Personal Recovery Checklist to remind yourself of the components of your recovery structure. Is something being neglected? Talk about it with your sponsor.

Closing

Read the SFR Closing Statement using the round-robin order.

Topic: Meditation

Opening

Choose a round-robin order for reading and sharing. Use it to read the SFR Opening Statement.

Daily Reading

For this week's topic, a team member reads his selection from a Twelve Step daily reader and shares thoughts on the reading. The other team members then share their thoughts.

Report, Discuss, Plan

1. What went well in my recovery this past week? How am I progressing on my Personal Recovery Checklist? What could be improved? Do I need someone's insight?

2. Share insights I gained from last week's SFR assignment.

3. For the upcoming week, what is my recovery goal? I will contact my accountability partner _____ times this week.

Family Recovery Discussion

For each of the three sections, a team member is selected to read and share. Team members also share thoughts and insights after each reading.

Learn Something New

If you constantly stir a glass of muddy water, the sediment continues to swirl, keeping the water cloudy and opaque, but by letting the water settle for a while, soon it clears. We can't stop our thoughts during meditation, but we find quiet between thoughts. Begin by sitting up comfortably. Repeat a positive statement, such as "Happiness is with me in this moment." With closed eyes, we breathe in and out slowly for a few moments between our positive statement, noticing that each inhale goes uphill, and exhales go down the other side. This is a simple but effective meditation. We end the meditation by asking our Higher Power to guide our thoughts and behaviors using Step Three.

Step Eleven

Sought through prayer and meditation to improve our conscious contact with God as we understood Him, praying only for knowledge of His will for us and the power to carry that out.

Whereas Step Ten asks us to review our day, Step Eleven asks us to begin each day by considering what we will make of it. This is our time to consider the day ahead. Through meditation or prayer, we ask our Higher Power to guide our thinking so we don't fall into destructive patterns. We're assured in the Big Book that if we do this daily, "Our thought-life will be placed on a much higher plane when our thinking is cleared of wrong motives." We'll also have much less to be concerned with when doing our Tenth Step later.

Working a Recovery Program

Step Eleven harkens us back to Steps Two and Three, working in partnership with a power greater than ourselves. This Step encourages the good in us, helping us flower and grow. We maintain a positive spirituality by turning ourselves over to the care of our Higher Power every morning. As for prayer and what to pray for, the Greek philosopher Pythagoras wrote, "Do not pray for yourself: You do not know what will help you."

Assignment

Begin meditating or praying for one or two minutes when you rise each morning. Identify a recovery trigger for this. Discuss practicing Step Eleven with your sponsor. For your next SFR meeting, go to lovefirst.net/sfr-resources/. Click on SFR Assignment Readings, and read Saint Teresa of Avila's poem "Clarity Is Freedom." Print a copy for your use in SFR week 42.

Closing

Read the SFR Closing Statement using the round-robin order.

WEEK 42

Topic: Guidance

Opening

Choose a round-robin order for reading and sharing. Use it to read the SFR Opening Statement.

Daily Reading

For this week's topic, a team member reads her selection from a Twelve Step daily reader and shares thoughts on the reading. The other team members then share their thoughts.

Report, Discuss, Plan

1. What went well in my recovery this past week? How am I progressing on my Personal Recovery Checklist? What could be improved? Do I need someone's insight?

2. Share insights I gained from last week's SFR assignment.

3. For the upcoming week, what is my recovery goal? I will contact my accountability partner _____ times this week.

Family Recovery Discussion

For each of the three sections, a team member is selected to read and share. Team members also share thoughts and insights after each reading.

Learn Something New

From last week's assignment, read aloud Saint Teresa of Avila's poem "Clarity Is Freedom," which speaks to the need for guidance. Steps Three and Eleven both ask us to turn to a power greater than ourselves for guidance. The guidance we are seeking aligns us with what is good. We must first know if something is good to know it is right to desire it. What would Love have me do? What would Patience have me do? What would Kindness have me do? What would Courage have me do? These self-directed questions contribute to the maintenance of our spiritual condition.

Step Eleven

Sought through prayer and meditation to improve our conscious contact with God as we understood Him, praying only for knowledge of His will for us and the power to carry that out.

One definition of guidance is the act of setting and holding a course. After coming this far in the Twelve Step program, we are working the final three Steps that help us stay the course. They are called the maintenance Steps. We may be tempted to think, at this point, that we've arrived. But much like physical exercise, once you are in an optimal place, you need to maintain it. In recovery, this means receiving ongoing guidance from those in the program and from our Higher Power.

Working a Recovery Program

The purpose of this Step is to make contact with our Higher Power and embrace a higher purpose for our lives. Again, we are called to access a power greater than ourselves to achieve what we could not achieve on our own. We have witnessed a power at work in our Twelve Step groups. Those of us who've worked these Steps with rigorous honesty find ourselves in a place we couldn't imagine just months ago. These are changes that go far beyond the addict's sobriety, but every single one is necessary for the continuation of sobriety, both physical and emotional.

Assignment

With your sponsor, discuss what guidance you need in this stage of your recovery. How does Step Eleven bring you back to Steps Two and Three? For your next SFR meeting, go to lovefirst.net/sfr-resources/. Click on SFR Assignment Readings and read Hafiz's poem, "Just Sit There Right Now." Print a copy for your use during SFR Week 43.

Closing

Read the SFR Closing Statement using the round-robin order.

WEEK 43

Topic: Conscious Contact

Opening

Choose a round-robin order for reading and sharing. Use it to read the SFR Opening Statement.

Daily Reading

For this week's topic, a team member reads his selection from a Twelve Step daily reader and shares thoughts on the reading. The other team members then share their thoughts.

Report, Discuss, Plan

1. What went well in my recovery this past week? How am I progressing on my Personal Recovery Checklist? What could be improved? Do I need someone's insight?

2. Share insights I gained from last week's SFR assignment.

3. For the upcoming week, what is my recovery goal? I will contact my accountability partner _____ times this week.

Family Recovery Discussion

For each of the three sections, a team member is selected to read and share. Team members also share thoughts and insights after each reading.

Learn Something New

From last week's assignment, read aloud Hafiz's poem, which speaks to the need for conscious contact. When we didn't know where to turn or how to move forward, a program of recovery offered a cushion for our heads. As our recovery evolves, we may come up against plateaus in our personal growth. Again, our fellow travelers in recovery are there for us—lighting the way to conscious contact—and soothing us: "Be gentle, be kind with yourself."

Poet Mary Oliver writes in her book *Felicity*, "God, or the gods, are invisible . . . but holiness is visible entirely." Perhaps it's what is holy in this world—things too great to express in words—that we can contact consciously.

Discuss with your sponsor how "improving conscious contact" has helped in all areas of your life. For your next SFR meeting, go to lovefirst .net/sfr-resources/. Click on SFR Assignment Readings and read Rumi's poem "The Silk Worm." Print a copy for your use during SFR Week 44.

Step Eleven
Sought through prayer and meditation to improve our conscious contact with God as we understood Him, praying only for knowledge of His will for us and the power to carry that out.

Recovering people often say that prayer is talking to God; meditation is listening. Making conscious contact with our Higher Power moves us beyond our wants to higher aspirations and a willingness to help others. This Step tells us to pray for the knowledge of what our Higher Power would have us do in these next twenty-four hours and ask for the power to carry it out. It's a replacement for self-centeredness and an ultimate recipe for emotional sobriety. As Søren Kierkegaard wrote, "The function of prayer is not to influence God, but rather to change the nature of the one who prays."

Working a Recovery Program
Step Eleven isn't used in isolation from the rest of the program. We need recovering people to "bring us trays of food and cushion our head" as we search for this conscious contact. Step Eleven is about living our way into this higher place. Staying close to others in recovery who have the wisdom to see what we cannot see helps us from veering off in an unanticipated direction. Some people get on their knees—not necessarily in a religious fashion—to keep themselves humble enough to make a connection.

Assignment
Discuss the accomplishment of "improving conscious contact" in all areas of your life as a result of practicing these Steps. Write a gratitude list. Share in next week's Report, Discuss, and Plan.

Closing
Read the SFR Closing Statement using the round-robin order.

WEEK 44

Topic: Spiritual Awakening

Opening

Choose a round-robin order for reading and sharing. Use it to read the SFR Opening Statement.

Daily Reading

For this week's topic, a team member reads her selection from a Twelve Step daily reader and shares thoughts on the reading. The other team members then share their thoughts.

Report, Discuss, Plan

1. What went well in my recovery this past week? How am I progressing on my Personal Recovery Checklist? What could be improved? Do I need someone's insight?

2. Share insights I gained from last week's SFR assignment.

3. For the upcoming week, what is my recovery goal? I will contact my accountability partner _____ times this week.

Family Recovery Discussion

For each of the three sections, a team member is selected to read and share. Team members also share thoughts and insights after each reading.

Learn Something New

From last week's assignment, read aloud Rumi's poem "The Silk Worm," which speaks to spiritual awakening. It speaks to the limitless nature of our spirit—its capacity for awakening. Unlike a physical awakening—an event of becoming awake at the end of a night's sleep—a spiritual awakening can continue without end. In Rumi's poem, it is his heart that tells him what is possible. This leads to a moment of choice. Will we begin? Will we not cease?

Step Eleven

Sought through prayer and meditation to improve our conscious contact with God as we understood Him, *praying only for knowledge of His will for us and the power to carry that out.*

A spiritual experience is often believed to be something ethereal, brought on by mystical powers. Nothing could be further from what happens in Twelve Step groups. The spiritual awakening we are talking about is earned. We create a space for grace. These Twelve Steps move us toward our awakening. It's very real and practical in nature. What might be thought of as mystical, or soul filling, comes as we work on these Steps with a sponsor, practicing honesty, forgiveness, and service. Thus, our lives are different today. We started in such a dark, hopeless place, but we aren't there any longer. Life is not meant to be perfect, but we have a serenity we didn't have before.

Working a Recovery Program

The blog *AA Redux* posts: "A typical 'view of the world' as seen by an alcoholic in the depths of his disease focused mainly on only its most immediate, close by features. Being crazily 'self-absorbed' as a result of the spiritual malady, the most obvious part of the world seemed to center on the most recent threat. From that point of view, successful living seemed to have everything to do with surviving the latest 'attack' and very little to do with a more reasoned idea about living successfully on a planet with another six or seven billion people, the majority of whom had no interest in 'attacking' us at all." We family members can also relate to this malady. This is what working a program of the Twelve Steps has helped us leave behind. Our awakening is clear by comparison.

Assignment

Sit with your sponsor and look over the road you have traveled. Now, at Step Eleven, what are your fruits? How have you changed as a family member? As a friend? How has your SFR team, as a whole, changed you and your life together as family? Journal insights.

Closing

Read the SFR Closing Statement using the round-robin order.

Topic: Serenity

Opening

Choose a round-robin order for reading and sharing. Use it to read the SFR Opening Statement.

Daily Reading

For this week's topic, a team member reads his selection from a Twelve Step daily reader and shares thoughts on the reading. The other team members then share their thoughts.

Report, Discuss, Plan

1. What went well in my recovery this past week? How am I progressing on my Personal Recovery Checklist? What could be improved? Do I need someone's insight?

2. Share insights I gained from last week's SFR assignment.

3. For the upcoming week, what is my recovery goal? I will contact my accountability partner _____ times this week.

Family Recovery Discussion

For each of the three sections, a team member is selected to read and share. Team members also share thoughts and insights after each reading.

Learn Something New

The Serenity Prayer tells us we must have serenity, courage, and wisdom. The Ninth Step Promises also speak of serenity, courage, and wisdom. Both family and addict may offer a litany of reasons why they want lasting sobriety, but in the end, whether we understand it or not, the goal of recovery is to achieve serenity. Once we've reached this inner peace, we have handled most everything we had the power to change. It's our serenity that allows us to accept the things we cannot change. Finally reaching this place of inner peace required courage and wisdom; we needed both to help us take the necessary steps to get here.

Step Twelve

Having had a spiritual awakening as a result of these steps, we tried to carry this message to others, and to practice these principles in all our affairs.

Step Twelve tells us serenity is already within us as a result of the spiritual awakening we've had working the Steps. Suddenly, it seemed to material-ize. As a recovering friend of mine said, "It's as if I took a long deep breath, and there it was." Serenity is necessary for lasting sobriety. We desire inner peace, and if we don't find it, we will search for something to fill the void or slow the agitation. For the addict, it's another drink or drug.

Working a Recovery Program

After working a program of recovery for a couple of years or more, having largely put our lives back together, new outside issues begin to arise. A girl-friend leaves. There is friction with the boss. A beloved grandparent dies. Improved circumstances and relationships come with losses and difficulties too. It's the internal benefits of recovery—the deep well of serenity—and our ability to reach out for help that carry us through. Spiritual maintenance is required so we don't relapse over life.

Assignment

How do Steps Ten, Eleven, and Twelve work together to maintain your spiritual condition on a daily basis? Discuss with your sponsor. Journal insights.

Closing

Read the SFR Closing Statement using the round-robin order.

Topic: Service

Opening

Choose a round-robin order for reading and sharing. Use it to read the SFR Opening Statement.

Daily Reading

For this week's topic, a team member reads her selection from a Twelve Step daily reader and shares thoughts on the reading. The other team members then share their thoughts.

Report, Discuss, Plan

1. What went well in my recovery this past week? How am I progressing on my Personal Recovery Checklist? What could be improved? Do I need someone's insight?

2. Share insights I gained from last week's SFR assignment.

3. For the upcoming week, what is my recovery goal? I will contact my accountability partner _____ times this week.

Family Recovery Discussion

For each of the three sections, a team member is selected to read and share. Team members also share thoughts and insights after each reading.

Learn Something New

Service work in Twelve Step groups is a form of gratitude, a kind of giving that asks for no reward. We experience the program in an entirely new way when we begin to sponsor others. It also requires that we maintain our own recovery program. In this way, service also becomes accountability. But sweetest of all are the dear friendships that come from offering service to the newly recovering alcoholic, addict, or family member. These mutual bonds of sponsorship provide remarkable friendships, some lasting a lifetime.

Step Twelve

Having had a spiritual awakening as a result of these steps, we tried to carry this message to others, and to practice these principles in all our affairs.

Every word in Al-Anon's Twelve Steps is the same as in AA's Twelve Steps except one. In this last Step, *alcoholics* became *others*. We recognize that when we come to Step Twelve, we have already had a spiritual awakening. It is at this time that we are ready to offer service to new members through Twelve Step sponsorship. But first we must have that awakening, as we define it. When we are asked to carry the message, we must have a message to carry.

Working a Recovery Program

Being asked to carry the message can be a startling notion at first. *AA Redux* explains, "The fact is that *sobriety reveals an immense and unexpected decency in us!* What greater—or more complicated—reason is needed to explain why we would be so determined to help others facing the same malady we once suffered ourselves!" Going from addiction (including the family's role) to being a person qualified to help others is a testament to the transformative effects of this program. As the song "Amazing Grace" says, we were blind, but now we see.

Assignment

Discuss with your sponsor your readiness to offer your services in sponsorship to a newcomer.

Closing

Read the SFR Closing Statement using the round-robin order.

Topic: In All Our Affairs

Opening

Choose a round-robin order for reading and sharing. Use it to read the SFR Opening Statement.

Daily Reading

For this week's topic, a team member reads his selection from a Twelve Step daily reader and shares thoughts on the reading. The other team members then share their thoughts.

Report, Discuss, Plan

1. What went well in my recovery this past week? How am I progressing on my Personal Recovery Checklist? What could be improved? Do I need someone's insight?

2. Share insights I gained from last week's SFR assignment.

3. For the upcoming week, what is my recovery goal? I will contact my accountability partner _____ times this week.

Family Recovery Discussion

For each of the three sections, a team member is selected to read and share. Team members also share thoughts and insights after each reading.

Learn Something New

According to author and AA historian Bill Pittman, "The principles of Twelve Step recovery are the opposite of our character defects." As we work the Twelve Step program, it turns shortcomings into principles. Pittman offers examples: "We work to change fear into faith, hate into love, egoism into humility, anxiety and worry into serenity, complacency into action, denial into acceptance, jealousy into trust, fantasizing into reality, selfishness into service, resentment into forgiveness, judgmentalism into tolerance, despair into hope, self-hate into self-respect, and loneliness into fellowship." We live the Twelve Step principles as we are working our program.

Step Twelve

Having had a spiritual awakening as a result of these steps, we tried to carry this message to others, and to practice these principles in all our affairs.

In Twelve Step programs, we won't find a list of principles to somehow apply to our lives. We come to know these principles through our actions. They are infused within us because we worked to achieve them. They become us. Once this happens, practicing them in all our affairs is as automatic as a heartbeat.

Working a Recovery Program

By exhibiting great interest and sincerity toward the newcomer, we practice these principles. By following the Golden Rule (doing unto others as we would have them do unto us) in our communities, we practice these principles. By creating a loving and serene home life, we practice these principles. By demonstrating self-care, we practice these principles. By treating those in the workplace with dignity and respect, we practice these principles. Practicing these principles in all our affairs is our outward show of gratitude.

Assignment

Ask yourself, *How do I practice these principles in my home, work, social life, and community?* Discuss with your sponsor. Journal insights.

Closing

Read the SFR Closing Statement using the round-robin order.

Topic: Happy, Joyous, and Free

Opening

Choose a round-robin order for reading and sharing. Use it to read the SFR Opening Statement.

Daily Reading

For this week's topic, a team member reads her selection from a Twelve Step daily reader and shares thoughts on the reading. The other team members then share their thoughts.

Report, Discuss, Plan

1. What went well in my recovery this past week? How am I progressing on my Personal Recovery Checklist? What could be improved? Do I need someone's insight?

2. Share insights I gained from last week's SFR assignment.

3. For the upcoming week, what is my recovery goal? I will contact my accountability partner _____ times this week.

Family Recovery Discussion

For each of the three sections, a team member is selected to read and share. Team members also share thoughts and insights after each reading.

Learn Something New

At dinner with a group of AA members, there was more raucous laughter and fun at our table than anywhere in the place. In recovery, as a friend of mine said, if we're not happy, joyous, and free, what's the point? Elizabeth Berg wrote in *The Art of Mending*, "There are random moments—tossing a salad, coming up the driveway to the house, ironing the seams flat on a quilt square, standing at the kitchen window and looking out at the delphiniums, hearing a burst of laughter from one of my children's rooms—when I feel a wavelike rush of joy. This is my true religion: arbitrary moments of nearly painful happiness for a life I feel privileged to lead." Having come to this place in recovery, most of us can find happiness almost anywhere.

The Twelve Steps

Working these marvelous Steps, painstakingly and with rigorous honesty, we come to know the gift. We understand those who have said that the Twelve Steps are among the greatest treasures the United States has given the world. But we cannot hang on to this treasure by having done the Steps. This is a living program. The Steps change and expand as we change and expand. We haven't reached a destination; the best is yet to come as we help another work the Steps. Alice Munro, winner of the 2013 Nobel Prize in Literature, writes, "Few people, very few, have a treasure, and if you do you must hang onto it. You must not let yourself be waylaid, and have it taken from you."

Working a Recovery Program

People in recovery are some of the best people in the world. How could they not be? Our gift comes out of our desperation. After trying everything else, desperation brought us to this place. As Sister Molly Monahan writes in *Seeds of Grace,* "Thanks be to God for Alcoholics Anonymous." And we send thanks, too, for the Twelve Step program that serves those who love the alcoholics and addicts.

Assignment

Pay attention to the "arbitrary moments of nearly painful happiness" in your life and, when you experience these moments, take a moment—right then—to give thanks.

Closing

Read the SFR Closing Statement using the round-robin order.

Topic: Family

Opening

Choose a round-robin order for reading and sharing. Use it to read the SFR Opening Statement.

Daily Reading

For this week's topic, a team member reads his selection from a Twelve Step daily reader and shares thoughts on the reading. The other team members then share their thoughts.

Report, Discuss, Plan

1. What went well in my recovery this past week? How am I progressing on my Personal Recovery Checklist? What could be improved? Do I need someone's insight?

2. Share insights I gained from last week's SFR assignment.

3. For the upcoming week, what is my recovery goal? I will contact my accountability partner _____ times this week.

Family Recovery Discussion

For each of the three sections, a team member is selected to read and share. Team members also share thoughts and insights after each reading.

Learn Something New

Resilience was once thought to be a personality trait, but we now understand that it is a result of taking specific actions. *Family resilience* is a term we use when the entire family develops traits that lead to successful change. In Structured Family Recovery, we have done that. We've stayed active in Twelve Step recovery, shared our experiences with one another, grown closer, communicate differently, and learned to express love. How we live this change is in our daily relationships with ourselves and our family. We live it with our recovery community. We live it with our co-workers, our neighbors, our friends, and the clerk at the grocery store.

The Twelve Steps

Lovely and inspiring writing about self-improvement and spiritual growth abounds. But in the end, does just reading about these ideals create lasting change? Our brain is so easily fooled into believing that reading something today will change our tomorrows. It doesn't. The Twelve Steps require action. They only change us when we've taken action each step of the way—rising to the challenge of doing the next right thing, knowing we grow by sticking with it, having patience to let things unfold as they are meant to, and trusting the process. But, at Step Twelve, we are not done. The disease is never cured. It's the love of recovery that ensures we hold on to the treasure we have found. We keep it close. It brings good things into our lives.

Working a Recovery Program

Where are we going now as a family? We've taken this journey through early recovery and can celebrate the commitment we've kept and the new places we've found in ourselves and each other. But we may be remembering that the addicted doctors—those recovery winners—didn't stop here. They keep going—meeting, talking, staying accountable to each other. Most of all, they keep recovery at the top of their list. The rest of their lives depend upon it. So do ours. In the words of Abraham Lincoln, "I am a slow walker, but I never walk back."

Assignment

As a family, we decide not only how to keep recovery growing and expanding, but also how we keep this unique connection with each other. Will we take the time to keep our family recovery team united and walking forward together? Will we continue our SFR journey? We decide this together.

Closing

Read the SFR Closing Statement using the round-robin order.

WEEK 50

Topic: Where Do We Go Now?

Opening

Choose a round-robin order for reading and sharing.

Daily Reading

A team member reads page 366 from *Courage to Change* and shares her thoughts. The other team members then share their thoughts.

Group Decision

As we take the time to reflect upon the collective accomplishment of our family over this past year, we are also faced with making a collective decision: *Do we stop here, or do we continue?* Many families choose to continue; others do not. As one team member wrote, "SFR has introduced us to the healing presence that now gathers our commitment and we still want to see where we can go with it. . . . We now trust each other in ways that would have been hard to imagine at the beginning." Perhaps we take some days or weeks to decide. Maybe we know now. Take some time to allow the team members to share their thoughts.

What Are Our Choices?

If we want to continue with our SFR meetings, what are our choices? What have other families done? Can we create our own path forward? After completing a year of SFR, there are a number of ways to move forward. You may think of some of your own. The SFR team can also reconsider the frequency of meetings. Do you want to meet every week, every other week, once a month? Some team members may stay on the team; others may end their involvement. Perhaps you invite somebody new. You have put together a recovery foundation after a year of SFR. You can now consider possibilities for building on it. Take some time to allow team members to share their thoughts.

SFR Meeting Ideas for Year Two and Beyond

Listed below are some ideas for continuing SFR meetings. Review and make a decision with the consensus of the group. Despite having different perspectives, all team members should feel they can accept the final choice.

- Start again from the beginning of the book and repeat the year. Many families choose this option, finding their perspectives on topics are very different now.
- Have each team member list favorite topics from the year. Combine the lists and repeat those weeks.
- For each meeting, a team member chooses a topic and reading from any variety of Twelve Step daily readers or meditation books. Take turns sharing on the topic.
- Focus exclusively on the Steps, choosing readings from the books *Twelve Steps and Twelve Traditions, How Al-Anon Works,* the Big Book, *Twelve Steps for Adult Children,* daily readers, and other Twelve Step literature.
- Use meetings to do a Big Book study and *How Al-Anon Works* study. Read passages from chapters in each book. Discuss.
- Combine recovery and self-care topics. Discuss.
- As a team, be creative. Imagine other possibilities.

Set up a time frame for making a decision. If you have already decided that your team will move forward, determine the date and time of your next SFR meeting.

Closing

Read the Twelve Steps of Al-Anon (page 367 from *Courage to Change*) and then the SFR Closing Statement using the round-robin order.

Twelve Step Resources

Alcoholics Anonymous World Services
aa.org
Use this site to find AA meetings around the world and much more.

Narcotics Anonymous World Services
na.org
Use this site to find NA meetings around the world and much more.

Al-Anon Family Groups
al-anon.alateen.org
Use this site to find Al-Anon meetings around the world, meetings for teens, and much more.

Families Anonymous Recovery Fellowship
familiesanonymous.org
Use this site to find FA in the United States and twelve other countries, and much more.

Nar-Anon Family Groups
nar-anon.org
Use this site to find Nar-Anon meetings around the world, meetings for teens, and much more.

The Twelve Steps of Al-Anon

These Twelve Steps, adapted nearly word for word from the Twelve Steps of Alcoholics Anonymous, have been a tool for spiritual growth for millions of Al-Anon/Alateen members. At meetings, Al-Anon/Alateen members share with each other the personal lessons they have learned from practicing from these Steps.

1. We admitted we were powerless over alcohol—that our lives had become unmanageable.

2. Came to believe that a Power greater than ourselves could restore us to sanity.

3. Made a decision to turn our will and our lives over to the care of God *as we understood Him.*

4. Made a searching and fearless moral inventory of ourselves.

5. Admitted to God, to ourselves, and to another human being the exact nature of our wrongs.

6. Were entirely ready to have God remove all these defects of character.

7. Humbly asked Him to remove our shortcomings.

8. Made a list of all persons we had harmed, and became willing to make amends to them all.

9. Made direct amends to such people wherever possible, except when to do so would injure them or others.

10. Continued to take personal inventory and when we were wrong promptly admitted it.

11. Sought through prayer and meditation to improve our conscious contact with God *as we understood Him,* praying only for knowledge of His will for us and the power to carry that out.

12. Having had a spiritual awakening as the result of these steps, we tried to carry this message to others, and to practice these principles in all our affairs.

Source: The Twelve Steps of Al-Anon, copyright 1996, is reprinted with permission from Al-Anon Family Group Headquarters; see Notes for full citation.

The Twelve Traditions
of Alcoholics Anonymous

1. Our common welfare should come first; personal recovery depends upon A.A. unity.

2. For our group purpose there is but one ultimate authority—a loving God as He may express Himself in our group conscience. Our leaders are but trusted servants; they do not govern.

3. The only requirement for A.A. membership is a desire to stop drinking.

4. Each group should be autonomous except in matters affecting other groups or A.A. as a whole.

5. Each group has but one primary purpose—to carry its message to the alcoholic who still suffers.

6. An A.A. group ought never endorse, finance, or lend the A.A. name to any related facility or outside enterprise, lest problems of money, property, and prestige divert us from our primary purpose.

7. Every A.A. group ought to be fully self-supporting, declining outside contributions.

8. Alcoholics Anonymous should remain forever nonprofessional, but our service centers may employ special workers.

9. A.A., as such, ought never be organized; but we may create service boards or committees directly responsible to those they serve.

10. Alcoholics Anonymous has no opinion on outside issues; hence the A.A. name ought never be drawn into public controversy.

11. Our public relations policy is based on attraction rather than promotion; we need always maintain personal anonymity at the level of press, radio, and films.

12. Anonymity is the spiritual foundation of all our traditions, ever reminding us to place principles before personalities.

Source: The Twelve Traditions of Alcoholics Anonymous is reprinted with permission from Alcoholics Anonymous World Services (A.A.W.S.); see Notes for full citation.

Notes

The number that begins each note indicates the page in this book where the cited material appears.

Introduction

3 *"We were a strange little band of characters"*: Erma Bombeck, "Erma Bombeck Quotes," GoodReads, www.goodreads.com/quotes/209784-the -family-we-were-a-strange-little-band-of-characters (accessed December 7, 2020).

Part 1

5 *"You never change things by fighting the existing reality"*: found in: L. Steven Sieden, *A Fuller View—Buckminster Fuller's Vision of Hope and Abundance for All* (Divine Arts Media, 2011), 358.

Chapter 1

7 *Fifty to 90 percent of alcoholics and addicts relapse:* Since research on outcomes for the general population post-treatment are few and validity varies, a statistical range of 50 to 90 percent is commonly used. No one statistic can claim accuracy in reporting relapse rates. To complicate matters, levels of support and time in treatment vary widely, as do the environments addicted persons return to after treatment. If you would like to research this further, here are some beginning points: R. L. Hubbard, M. E. Marsden, E. Cavanaugh, and J. V. Rachal, "Drug Use After Drug Treatment," background paper prepared for the IOM/NAS Committee on a National Strategy for HIV/AIDS, April 1986; Rudolf H. Moos, John W. Finney, and Ruth C. Cronkite, *Alcoholism Treatment: Context, Process, and Outcome* (New York: Oxford University Press, 1990); J. W. Finney and R. H. Moos, "The Long-Term Course of Treated Alcoholism: I. Mortality, Remission, and Relapse Rates and Comparisons with

Community Controls," *Journal of Studies on Alcohol* 52 (1991): 44–54; J. Humphrey, R. H. Moos, and C. Cohen, "Social and Community Resources and Long-Term Recovery from Treated and Untreated Alcoholism," *Journal of Studies on Alcohol* 58, no. 3 (1997): 231–38; D. C. Walsh, R. W. Hingson, D. M. Merrigan, S. M. Levenson, et al., "A Randomized Trial of Treatment Options for Alcohol-Abusing Workers," *New England Journal of Medicine* 325 (1991): 775–82. Another helpful article: Omar Manejwala, "How Often Do Long-Term Sober Alcoholics and Addicts Relapse?" *Psychology Today,* February 14, 2014.

9   *Integrating the Twelve Steps into the treatment plan:* Nowinski, Joseph, *If You Work It, It Works* (Center City, MN: Hazelden, 2015), 60–69.

10   *"Consumers, unfortunately, are typically getting data":* Eric Topol, *The Creative Destruction of Medicine: How the Digital Revolution Will Create Better Health Care* (New York: Basic Books, 2013), 30.

11   *What if I told you there was a group:* Robert L. DuPont, A. T. McLellan, W. L. White, et al., "Setting the Standard for Recovery: Physicians' Health Programs," *Journal of Substance Abuse Treatment* 36, no. 2 (March 2009): 159–71.

11   *"Managing good sobriety without much help":* Stephen King, "Stephen King on James Frey's *Million Little Pieces,*" *Entertainment Weekly,* February 1, 2007.

12   *Research shows that among patients:* Marie T. Brown and Jennifer K. Bussell, "Medical Adherence: WHO Cares?" *Mayo Clinic Proceedings* 86, no. 4 (April 2011): 304–14.

Chapter 2

15   *Let's put a doctor's risk for relapse into perspective:* Douglas R. Scott II, "The Direct Medical Costs of Healthcare-Associated Infections in U.S. Hospitals and the Benefits of Prevention," Division of Healthcare Quality Promotion; National Center for Preparedness, Detection, and Control of Infectious Diseases; Coordinating Center for Infectious Diseases; Centers for Disease Control and Prevention, March 2009, www.cdc.gov/hai/pdfs/hai/scott_costpaper.pdf (accessed December 7, 2020).

16   *A drug court in Hawaii found that the future threat:* National Institute of Justice, "'Swift and Certain' Sanctions in Probation Are Highly Effective: Evaluation of the HOPE Program," National Institute of Justice, February 2, 2012, www.nij.gov/topics/corrections/community/drug-offenders/Pages/hawaii-hope.aspx (accessed December 7, 2020).

17   *In 2007, researchers conducted the largest study to date:* Robert L. DuPont, A. T. McLellan, W. L. White, et al., "Setting the Standard for Recovery: Physicians' Health Programs," *Journal of Substance Abuse Treatment* 36, no. 2 (March 2009): 159–71.

17   *Based on evidence and reasoning:* DuPont et al., "Setting the Standard for Recovery," 159–71.

19   *When doctors relapse, the PHP process re-intervenes:* G. E. Skipper and R. L. DuPont, "The Physician Health Program: A Replicable Model of Sustained Recovery Management," in *Addiction Recovery Management,* Current Clinical Psychiatry series, ed. J. F. Kelly and W. L. White (Totowa, NJ: Humana Press), https://doi.org/10.1007/978-1-60327-960-4_15.

Chapter 3

21   *William Duncan Silkworth, MD:* Dr. Silkworth and his ideas are so well known that there is a book about him with this phrase as a subtitle: Dale Mitchel, *Silkworth: The Little Doctor Who Loved Drunks* (Center City, MN: Hazelden, 2002).

22   *"I once heard a Jesuit assert":* Molly Monahan, *Seeds of Grace: A Nun's Reflection on the Spirituality of Alcoholics Anonymous* (New York: Riverhead Books, 2001).

22   *"There is room for all shades of belief and nonbelief":* This originated with Bill Wilson. It was used in *A Newcomer Asks* (New York: Alcoholics Anonymous World Services, 1980).

25   *"If any feel that as psychiatrists":* William Duncan Silkworth, MD, "The Doctor's Opinion," in *Alcoholics Anonymous,* 4th ed. (New York: Alcoholics Anonymous World Services, 2000), xvii.

25   *"I used to think my life":* William G. Borchert, *The Lois Wilson Story: When Love Is Not Enough* (Center City, MN: Hazelden, 2005), x.

25   *"I am sorry for families who have not taken refuge":* Al-Anon Faces Alcoholism, 2nd ed., (New York: Al-Anon Family Group Headquarters, 1984), 98.

Chapter 5

35   *Nearly two thousand years ago:* Lucius Annaeus Seneca, *Letters from a Stoic,* trans. Robin Campbell (London: Penguin Books, 1969).

35   *"The man who drinks for pleasure":* "Inebriety as a Disease," *Scientific American,* January 27, 1877.

36   *An 1885 issue of the same journal:* T. L. Wright, "The Property of Alcohol Which Allures the Neurotic to Drink," *Scientific American Supplement* 474 (January 31, 1885).

36 *By the mid-nineteenth century:* American Association for the Study and
Cure of Inebriety, "The Disease of Inebriety: From Alcohol, Opium and
Other Narcotic Drugs, Its Etiology, Pathology, Treatment and Medivo-Legal
Relations" (New York: E. B. Treat, 1893).

36 *"Much misapprehension exists":* Isaiah De Zouche, "On Inebriety and the
Duty of the State with Regard to Inebriates" (Dunedin, New Zealand:
Joseph Brajthwaite, 1885).

36 *These same advocates would surely be shocked:* Silkworth, "The Doctor's
Opinion," *Alcoholics Anonymous,* xvii.

37 *Some people metabolize intoxicants differently:* Mitchel, *Silkworth.*

37 *"Your genetics load the gun":* Gretchen Voss, "Disease and Diet: Outsmart
Your DNA Destiny," *Women's Health,* January 19, 2012.

37 *The concept of alcoholism as an inherited disease:* Since researchers cannot
decisively determine exactly the ratio between the genetics of addiction
and environmental factors (such as the drinking culture one inhabits), a
statistical range of 50 to 65 percent is commonly used. If you would like
to research the genetics of addiction further, including twin and adoption
studies and animal studies, here are some beginning points: Matt McGue,
Behavioral Genetics Models of Alcoholism and Drinking (New York: Guild-
ford Press, 1999); A. C. Heath, K. K. Bucholz, P. A. Madden, S. H. Din-
widdie, et al., "Genetic and Environmental Contributions to Alcohol
Dependence Risk in a National Twin Sample: Consistency of Findings
in Women and Men," National Institute on Alcohol Abuse and Alcoholism, 1997; Danielle M. Dick and Arpana Agrawal, "The Genetics of
Alcohol and Other Drug Dependence," National Institute on Alcohol Abuse
and Alcoholism, 2008; R. L. Bell, Z. A. Rodd, L. Lumeng, J. M. Murphy,
and W. J. McBride, "The Alcohol-Preferring P Rat and Animal Models of
Excessive Alcohol Drinking," National Institute on Alcohol Abuse and
Alcoholism, 2006; and T. K. Li, L. Lumeng, W. J. McBride, and J. M. Murphy, "An Experimental Approach to Understanding the Genetic and Neu-
robiological Basis of Alcoholism," *Transactions of the American Clinical
and Climatological Association* 104 (1993): 61–73. Additionally, refer to
Howard J. Edenberg, "The Collaborative Study on the Genetics of Alco-
holism," *Alcohol Health and Research World,* 1995; and "Genetics: The
Blueprint of Health and Disease," *Topics in Brief: Genetics of Addiction,*
(National Institute on Drug Abuse, 2008). For twins research in the United
States, see C. A. Prescott and K. S. Kendler, "Genetic and Environmental

Contributions to Alcohol Abuse and Dependence in a Population-Based Sample of Male Twins," *American Journal of Psychiatry* 156 (1999): 34–40. The statement that alcoholism is one of the most complex genetic diseases to study came from a 1999 conversation the author had with Robert W. Karp, director of the Genetics Program, National Institute on Alcohol Abuse and Alcoholism, National Institutes of Health from 1991 to 2001.

40 *"Our human compassion binds us the one to another":* Nelson Mandela, untitled speech (Healing and Reconciliation Service, Johannesburg, South Africa, December 6, 2000).

42 *"I remember the day Nancy Reagan suggested":* Harry Haroutunian, *Being Sober: A Step-by-Step Plan to Getting to, Getting through, and Living in Recovery* (New York: Rodale Books, 2013).

45 *Exerting self-control may consume self-control strength:* Mark Muraven and Roy F. Baumeister, "Self-Regulation and Depletion of Limited Resources: Does Self-Control Resemble Muscle?" *Psychological Bulletin* 126, no. 2 (2000), 247–59.

46 *The researchers at Case Western Reserve University:* Muraven and Baumeister, "Self-Regulation and Depletion of Limited Resources" *Psychological Bulletin.*

47 *When I had been in A.A. only a short while:* Alcoholics Anonymous, 553.

Chapter 6

49 *We know the weight loss and diet control market:* Weight loss and diet control numbers come from "The U.S. Weight Loss & Diet Control Market," Research and Markets, report 4753379, Feburary 2019, researchandmarkets .com/research/qm2gts/the_72_billion?w=4 (accessed December 7, 2020). Health and fitness club numbers come from Melissa Rodriguez, "Latest IHRSA Data: Over 6B Visits to 39,570 Gyms in 2018," March 28, 2019, ihrsa.org/about/media-center/press-releases/latest-ihrsa-data-over-6b -visits-to-39-570-gyms-in-2018/ (accessed December 7, 2020). Overweight and obesity percentages were reported by the Centers for Disease Control, National Center for Health Statistics: Obesity and Overweight, cdc.gov /nchs/fastats/obesity-overweight.htm (accessed December 7, 2020).

50 *Danish researchers reviewed 900 scientific articles:* C. Ayyad and T. Andersen, "Long-Term Efficacy of Dietary Treatment of Obesity: A Systematic Review of Studies Published between 1931 and 1999," *Obesity Reviews* 1 (2000): 113–19.

50 *Jeni Cross, PhD, . . . says that our greatest obstacle to change:* Jeni Cross, "Three Myths of Behavior Change: What You Think You Know That You Don't," TEDxCSU, 2013, youtube.com/watch?v=l5d8G W6GdR0 (accessed June 22, 2014).

52 *Research has shown that when we are exposed to positive social behaviors:* Jessica M. Nolan, P. Wesley Shultz, and Robert B. Scaldini, et al., "Normative Social Influence Is Underdetected," *Personality and Social Psychology Bulletin* 34 (July 2008): 913–23.

55 *"There is a principle which is a bar against all information":* Herbert Spencer in *Alcoholics Anonymous,* 568.

Chapter 7

64 *"To goodness and wisdom":* *A Day at a Time: Daily Reflections for Recovering People* (Center City, MN: Hazelden, 1987), September 13 meditation.

64 *People who abuse alcohol or other drugs:* These statistics have been commonly used since Dr. Silkworth achieved a success rate of about 2 percent while working with alcoholics prior to the formation of Alcoholics Anonymous. Since research in this area is limited and varies in validity, and findings may have limitations, it is difficult to know exact numbers. Research sometimes combines alcoholics with alcohol abusers (substance use disorder) and often doesn't report switched addictions (switching to another type of intoxicant). If you would like to research this further, here is a beginning point: Rudolf H. Moos and Bernice S. Moos, "Rates and Predictors of Relapse after Natural and Treated Remission from Alcohol Use Disorder," *Addiction* 101, no. 2 (February 2006): 212–22.

66 *"We began to get the feeling that we could be forgiven":* Alcoholics Anonymous, *Twelve Steps and Twelve Traditions* (New York: Alcoholics Anonymous World Services, 2002), 58.

68 *"Someone will say something profound":* Elizabeth Landau, "Alcoholics Anonymous as a Spiritual Experience," *The Chart,* CNN Health, December 14, 2010, thechart.blogs.cnn.com/2010/12/14/alcoholics-anonymous -as-a-spiritual-experience (accessed December 7, 2020).

72 *Recovering alcoholics who receive criticism from their spouses:* Buddy T., "Spouse's Attitude Can Affect Alcoholic's Relapse," About.com, alcoholism .about.com/library/weekly/aa020101a.htm (accessed June 22, 2014); Buddy T., "Spousal Support Can Improve an Alcoholic or Addict's Recovery," VerywellMind, updated July 17, 2019, verywellmind.com/spouses-attitude -can-affect-alcoholics-relapse-3952335 (accessed December 7, 2020).

Chapter 8

73   *""Every solution to every problem is simple.":* Derek Landy, *Skullduggery Pleasant,* (London: HarperCollins, 2007).

73   *Dr. Fogg describes a model he created:* Based on the author's personal experience at a professional workshop with Dr. Fogg, 2013, and B. J. Fogg, "Fogg Method: Three Steps to Changing Behavior," www.foggmethod.com (accessed December 7, 2020).

74   *"Relying primarily on motivation":* B. J. Fogg, "Forget Big Change, Start with a Tiny Habit," TEDxFremont, www.youtube.com/watch?v=AdKUJxjn-R8 (accessed December 7, 2020).

76   *Every day, approximately 350 alcoholics and addicts . . . die:* National Institute on Drug Abuse, "Shatter the Myths: General Questions About Drug Abuse," National Institute on Drug Abuse, drugfactsweek.drugabuse.gov/chat/chat faqs_topics/general_questions.php (accessed June 22, 2014).

77   *Many of us exclaimed, "What an order!":* Alcoholics Anonymous, 60.

78   *Al-Anon reminds me to "Keep it simple":* Al-Anon, *Courage to Change: One Day at a Time in AlAnon II* (New York: Al-Anon Family Group Headquarters, 1992).

79   *"There are two or three things that flashed into my mind":* Robert Smith, "Dr. Bob's Farewell Talk," Alcoholics Anonymous, www.aa.org/pages/en_US/dr -bobs-farewell-talk (accessed December 7, 2020).

82   *But, since social science research repeatedly shows:* Jeni Cross, "Three Myths of Behavior Change: What You Think You Know That You Don't," TEDxCSU, 2013, www.youtube.com/watch?v=l5d8GW 6GdR0 (accessed June 22, 2014).

83   *"We are going to know a new freedom and a new happiness":* This excerpt from *Alcoholics Anonymous,* pages 83–84, is reprinted with permission of Alcoholics Anonymous World Services, Inc. ("A.A.W.S."). Permission to use this excerpt does not mean that A.A.W.S. has reviewed or approved the contents of this publication, or that A.A.W.S. necessarily agrees with the views expressed therein. A.A. is a program of recovery from alcoholism only—use of this material in connection with programs and activities which are patterned after A.A., but which address other problems or concerns, or in any other non-A.A. context, does not imply otherwise.

83   *"You are learning lessons of life":* Joseph Martin, "The Promises of AA," www .youtube.com/watch?v=vvDmSV8yktM (accessed December 7, 2020).

Chapter 9

87 *"An old belief is like an old shoe"*: Robert Brault, *Round Up the Usual Subjects: Thoughts on Just About Everything* (self-published, CreateSpace Independent Publishing Platform, 2014).

90 *"It's helpless . . . it's absence of control"*: Toni Morrison, interview by Bob Swaim, Wired for Books, September 15, 1987, www.wiredforbooks.org /tonimorrison (accessed June 22, 2014).

95 *"Too often we underestimate the power of a touch"*: Leo Buscaglia, *Love* (Greenwich, CT: Fawcett, 1972).

Chapter 10

97 *"Stress can wreak havoc with your metabolism,:* Robert M. Sapolsky, *Why Zebras Don't Get Ulcers,* 3rd ed. (New York: Holt Paperbacks, 2004).

98 *Stress hormones can do some truly nasty things:* John J. Medina, *Brain Rules: 12 Principles for Surviving and Thriving at Work, Home, and School* (Seattle: Pear Press, 2014).

99 *Stress is changing our neural anatomy.:* Jonah Lehrer, "The Reinvention of the Self," *SEED,* February/March 2006, 58–67.

99 *Researchers at Yale have found that the prefrontal cortex:* Amy Arnesten, "Creative Minds: Making Sense of Stress and the Brain," *NIH Director's Blog,* National Institutes of Health, March 18, 2014, http://directorsblog.nih .gov/2014/03/18/creative-minds-making-sense-of-stress-and-the-brain (accessed December 7, 2020).

100 *According to the National Sleep Foundation:* National Sleep Foundation, www.sleepfoundation.org.

100 *Chronic insomnia disrupts the brain's ability:* Jeffrey Iliff, "How Our Brains Wash Away the Gunk during Sleep," Brain Institute, Oregon Health and Science University, 2002, www.ohsu.edu/blogs/brain/2013/10/30 /how-our-brains-wash-away-the-gunk-during-sleep (accessed December 7, 2020).

100 *Another stress-related phenomenon:* Christopher Peterson, Steven F. Maier, and Martin E. P. Seligman, *Learned Helplessness: A Theory for the Age of Personal Control* (New York: Oxford University Press, 1995).

101 *Another scientist, Donald Hiroto:* Douglas A. Bernstein, *Essentials of Psychology* (Stamford, CT: Cengage Learning, 2013).

Chapter 11

107 *"In the face of clear evidence that children"*: Sis Wenger, "The Challenge: Drawn by Anger . . . Motivated By Hope," National Association for Children of Alcoholics, Summer 2008, http://www.nacoa.net/pdfs/Summer _08_comment.pdf (accessed January 25, 2021).

109 *Imagine the lives of those babies*: Molly Monahan, *Seeds of Grace: A Nun's Reflection on the Spirituality of Alcoholics Anonymous* (New York: Riverhead Books, 2001).

110 *"It takes much courage and strength"*: Jerry Moe, written specifically for inclusion in *It Takes a Family*, 2014.

Chapter 12

113 *Dr. Kevin McCauley points out that when people say they are "craving"*: Kevin McCauley, *Pleasure Unwoven: A Personal Journey about Addiction* (DVD), The Institute for Addiction Study, 2010.

114 *"The problem drinker gets pulled over and arrested"*: "The Alcoholic vs. the Problem Drinker," Mr. SponsorPants: An AA Sponsor Blog, January 21, 2016, https://mrsponsorpants.typepad.com/mr_sponsorpants/page/7/ (accessed December 7, 2020).

114 *Also writing . . . a physician shared about his life as an alcoholic and addict*: "Acceptance Was the Answer," *Alcoholics Anonymous*, 409.

Part 2

Chapter 14

129 *"Nothing in the world could make human life happier"*: David R. Mace, "Family Strengths," Encyclopedia.com., www.encyclopedia.com/doc/1G2-3406900165 .html (accessed December 7, 2020).

131 *Doctors are neither easy to treat nor compliant*: Robert L. DuPont, A. T. McLellan, W. L. White, et al., "Setting the standard for recovery: Physicians' Health Programs," *Journal of Substance Abuse Treatment* 36, no. 2 (March 2009): 159–71.

Chapter 15

134 *"Nuclear families in this era"*: "The Nuclear Family Was a Mistake," David Brooks, *The Atlantic*, March 2020, https://www.theatlantic.com/magazine /archive/2020/03/the-nuclear-family-was-a-mistake/605536/ (accessed De- December 7, 2020).

134 *"High-performing teams are high in cohesiveness,"* "The Science behind Expert Teams: Insights from Sport Psychology," *AASP Blog,* Association for Applied Sport Psychology, https://appliedsportpsych.org/blog/2017/01/the-science-behind-expert-teams-insights-from-sport-psychology/, January 31, 2017 (accessed December 7, 2020).

141 *"Want to have a happier family?":* Bruce Feiler, *The Secrets of Happy Families: Improve Your Mornings, Rethink Family Dinner, Fight Smarter, Go Out and Play, and Much More* (New York: William Morrow, 2013).

Chapter 18

173 *"It's a design flaw—not a personal flaw.":* B. J. Fogg, *Tiny Habits: The Small Changes That Change Everything,* (Boston: HMH Books, 2019), 130.

184 *Second, team members will also need a daily reader:* Al-Anon Family Groups, *Courage to Change: One Day at a Time in Al-Anon* (Virginia Beach, VA: Al-Anon); A.A. Members, *Daily Reflections: A Book of Reflections by A.A. Members for A.A. Members* (New York: Alcoholics Anonymous World Services, 2017).

185 *"Unless commitment is made, there are only promises and hopes":* Peter F. Drucker, *Management* (Abingdon, UK: Routledge, 2012), 123; www.azquotes.com/quote/81884.

187 *In* Tiny Habits, *B. J. Fogg, PhD, points out:* Fogg, *Tiny Habits.*

188 *"[T]he quick dispersal of exuberant or triumphant emotion":* Kay R. Jamison, *Exuberance: The Passion for Life* (New York: Vintage Books, 2005), 138.

Chapter 25

207 *In an essay on human fallibility:* Randy Mayeux, "Two Great Dilemmas: Ignorance and Ineptitude—Insights from Atul Gawande's The Checklist Manifesto," First Friday Book Synopsis, February 23, 2010, http://ffbsccn.wordpress.com/2010/02/23/two-great-dilemmas-ignorance-and-ineptitude-insight-from-atul-gawandes-the-checklist-manifesto/ (accessed December 7, 2020).

207 *"Checklists seem to provide protection against such failures:* Atul Gawande, *The Checklist Manifesto: How to Get Things Right* (New York: Picador, 2011).

208 *Dr. Gawande found that physicians, on average:* Atul Gawande, *The Checklist Manifesto: How to Get Things Right* (New York: Henry Holt and Company, 2010), 183.

208 *"Discipline is hard—harder than trustworthiness":* Gawande, *The Checklist Manifesto.*

Chapter 28

228 *Relapse Warning Signs Threatening Family Emotional Sobriety:* This checklist is adapted and expanded from the work of Terence T. Gorski; used with permission of Terence T. Gorski.

231 *"When you celebrate effectively, you tap into the reward circuitry":* Fogg, *Tiny Habits.*

Chapter 29

246 *The latest Cochrane Review's findings show:* Austin Frakt and Aaron Carroll, "Alcoholics Anonymous vs. Other Approaches: The Evidence Is Now In," *New York Times,* March 11, 2020, https://www.nytimes.com/2020/03/11/upshot/alcoholics-anonymous-new-evidence.html (accessed December 7, 2020).

Chapter 31

259 *"I was sitting there . . . with someone who knew who I was":* Carol W., "My Sponsor's Unconditional Love Was the Turning Point," *The Forum,* December 2012, www.al-anon.org/forum-magazines-stories/item/539-my-sponsor's-unconditional-love-was-the-turning-point (accessed June 22, 2014).

260 *"Whether you are a newcomer who is hesitant":* Questions and Answers on *Sponsorship* (New York: Alcoholics Anonymous World Services, 1983).

Chapter 32

264 *"The manners and mores of a community":* David Brooks, "Other People's Views," *New York Times,* February 6, 2014, www.nytimes.com/2014/02/07/opinion/brooks-other-peoples-views.html?partner=rssnyt&emc=rss&_r=1 (accessed December 7, 2020).

264 *"Before you know what kindness really is":* Naomi Shihab Nye, "Kindness," in *Words Under the Words: Selected Poems* (Portland, OR: Eighth Mountain Press, 1994). Used with permission.

265 *"Yesterday I was clever":* Mamta Sehgal, *Rooh-e-Rumi: Seeking God Is Seeking Love* (Chennai, India: Notion Press, 2019), 18.

266 *"Negative emotions generally involve more thinking":* Alina Tugend, "Praise Is Fleeting, but Brickbats We Recall," *New York Times,* March 23, 2012, www.nytimes.com/2012/03/24/your-money/why-people-remember-negative-events-more-than-positive-ones.html?pagewanted=1&.tsrc=sun&partner=yahoofinance (accessed December 7, 2020).

266 *"Negative emotions are often crucial for survival—but only in time present.:* George Vaillant, *Spiritual Evolution: A Scientific Defense of Faith* (New York: Harmony, 2009).

268 *"An acquaintance merely enjoys your company":* E. A. Bucchianeri, *Brushstrokes of a Gadfly* (Fatima, Portugal: Batalha Publishers, May 21, 2011).

Chapter 33

272 *It's estimated that it takes five good experiences to overcome one bad:* Mark Muraven and Roy F. Baumeister, "Self-Regulation and Depletion of Limited Resources: Does Self-Control Resemble Muscle?" *Psychological Bulletin* 126, no. 2 (2000): 247–59.

272 *"If you want to belong, you need to engage in social play":* The National Institute for Play, www.nifplay.org (accessed December 7. 2020).

273 *Play refreshes our relationship:* Stuart Brown, "Play Is More Than Fun" March 12, 2009, TED video, 26:42. https://www.youtube.com/watch?v =HHwXlcHcTHc.

Chapter 34

275 *"The last ten years have been the best of my life":* Eric Clapton, *Clapton: The Autobiography* (New York: Three Rivers Press, 2008).

Epilogue

277 *"A hero ventures forth from the world of common day":* Joseph Campbell, *The Hero with a Thousand Faces,* 3rd ed., (Novato, CA: New World Library, 2008).

Part 3, SFR Closing

282 *The Promises: Alcoholics Anonymous,* 4th ed. (New York: Alcoholics Anonymous World Services, 2000), 83–84; see full citation for page 83.

Part 3, First Quarter

284 *Week 1, Daily Reading reference to How Al-Anon Works:* Al-Anon, *Courage to Change,* 45–47.

286 *Week 2, "The moment you start to resent a person":* Sathya Sai Baba, *Sathya Sai Speaks: Discourses of Bhagavan Sri Sathya Sai Baba Delivered During 1970* (Sri Sathya Sai Books and Publications Trust, 1999).

294 *Week 6, "[Family members'] attitudes and behaviors:* Terence T. Gorski and Merlene Miller, *Staying Sober: A Guide for Relapse Prevention,* 1st ed. (Independence, MO: Independence Press, 1986).

298 *Week 8, "Humility leads to strength"*: John J. McCloy, "Thoughts on the Business of Life," *Forbes,* http://thoughts.forbes.com/thoughts/john-j-mccloy (accessed June 23, 2014).

302 *Week 10, "The thing about the corny slogans"*: Bridgette Boudreau, "What I Learned from 12-Step Slogans," *The Wild Life Blog,* March 5, 2009, bridgetteboudreau.com/2009/03/05/what-i-learned-from-aa-slogans (accessed June 22, 2014).

304 *Week 11, Learn Something New*: Audrey Barrick, "Most Americans Still Believe in God; Nonbelief Rises," *The Christian Post,* June 3, 2011, www.christianpost.com/news/most-americans-still-believe-in-god-nonbelief-rises-50791 (accessed December 7, 2020).

309 *Week 13, Step Three*: Alcoholics Anonymous, *Twelve Steps and Twelve Traditions,* 34.

Part 3, Second Quarter

313 *Week 14, "We pocket our pride"*: Alcoholics Anonymous, 75.

318 *Week 17, "If you are gentle with yourself"*: Lama Yeshe, *The Enlightened Experience: Collected Teachings, Volumes 1–3* (Lincoln, MA: Lama Yeshe Wisdom Archive, September 20, 2020), https://www.lamayeshe.com/article/e-letter-no-207-september-2020.

319 *Week 17, "We need to look at our positives too"*: George Mann and Dick Rice, *Touch Life Gently—Step Four,* The Retreat, Wayzata, MN, 1987, www.youtube.com/watch?v=zR3W8N_H5O4 (accessed December 7, 2020).

324 *Week 20, "I must say a word about fear"*: Yann Martel, *Life of Pi* (Toronto: Alfred A. Knopf Canada, 2001), 161.

326 *Week 21, "Selfishness—self-centeredness"*: Alcoholics Anonymous, 62.

330 *Week 23, "People-pleasers have learned"*: Earnie Larsen, *Stage II Recovery: Life Beyond Addiction,* (San Francisco, CA: Harper & Row, 1988).

333 *Week 24, "The past is done and can't be returned"*: "A Guide to the Twelve Steps of Alcoholics Anonymous" (Akron, OH: Akron Area Intergroup Council of Alcoholics Anonymous, 1941/2007).

334 *Week 25, "If you plant honesty, you will reap trust"*: Author Unknown, "Planting and Reaping," HumanityAndLove.com, humanityandlove.com/amazing_facts/Planting_and_Reaping.htm (accessed December 8, 2020).

335 *Week 25, "I am sharing about the storm on the surface"*: "Questions via Email: If You Are Sober a Long Time and Still Have a Hard Time, What's the Point?" *Mr. SponsorPants: An AA Sponsor Blog,* October 19, 2010, mrsponsorpants.typepad.com/mr_sponsorpants/2010/10/questions-via-email-if-you

-are-sober-a-long-time-and-still-have-a-hard-time-whats-the-point.html (accessed December 8, 2020).

Part 3, Third Quarter

340 *Week 27, "We can't be afraid of change"*: C. JoyBell C., *Vade Mecum: (n) a needed thing carried around everywhere; a useful handbook or guidebook always kept on one's person; lit. "go with me"* (self-published, CreateSpace Independent Publishing Platform, 2013).

341 *Week 27, "When we tried to clean ourselves up"*: J. Keith Miller, *A Hunger for Healing: The Twelve Steps as a Classic Model for Christian Spiritual Growth* (San Francisco, CA: HarperSanFrancisco, 1992).

347 *Week 30, "I am willing to let down the barriers"*: *Step 6 & 7: Ready, Willing, and Able* (Center City, MN: Hazelden, 1992).

347 *Week 30, "My Creator, I am now willing"*: "Seventh Step Prayer," *Alcoholics Anonymous*, 76.

358 *Week 36, "Forgiveness is a process"*: Amanda Neville, "How Forgiveness Can Save Your Business," *Forbes*, June 21, 2013, forbes.com/sites/amanda neville/2013/06/21/how-forgiveness-can-save-your-business (accessed December 8, 2020).

Part 3, Fourth Quarter

364 *Week 38, Studies at the University of London show*: University of Royal Holloway London, "Study Shows Trustworthy People Perceived to Look Similar to Ourselves," *Science Daily*, November 7, 2013, sciencedaily.com /releases/2013/11/131107094406.htm (accessed December 8, 2020).

364 *Week 38, "In the case of humans, it's possible"*: Dan Jones, "Trustworthy People Are Seen as More Similar to Ourselves," *Evolution: This View of Life*, January 11, 2014, thisviewoflife.com/index.php/magazine/articles /trustworthy-people-are-seen-as-more-similar-to-ourselves (accessed June 23, 2014).

367 *Week 39, "Not knowing when the dawn will come"*: "Part Two: Nature, LXXXIX," Emily Dickinson, *The Complete Poems of Emily Dickinson*, (Boston: Little, Brown, 1924; Bartleby.com, 2000).

367 *Week 39, "A great many of us have never really acquired the habit"*: *Twelve Steps and Twelve Traditions*, 192.

368 *Week 40, "We can all too regularly be sure"*: Ben Romer, "Yom Kippur" The Time of Year for Soul Inventory," *Richmond Times-Dispatch*, September 27, 2009, updated September 19, 2019, https://richmond.com/news

/yom-kippur-the-time-of-year-for-soul-inventory/article_cfa6554f-bc32
-5c31-8bda-c86702af6045.html.

371 *Week 41, "Our thought-life will be placed on a much higher plane"*: Alcoholics Anonymous, 86.

374 *Week 43, "God, or the gods, are invisible"*: Mary Oliver, "Leaves and Blossoms Along the Way," *Felicity: poems,* (New York: Penguin Books, 2015), 17.

377 *Week 44, "A typical 'view of the world"*: Anonymous, "Sponsorship in the 21st Century," *AA Redux,* https://www.aareduxgroup.com/ (accessed December 8, 2020).

381 *Week 46, "The fact is that sobriety reveals an immense and unexpected decency in us!"*: "Sponsorship in the 21st Century," AA Redux.

382 *Week 47, "The principles of Twelve Step recovery are the opposite"*: Bill Pittman, *Practice These Principles and What Is the Oxford Group?* (Center City, MN: Hazelden, 1997), xi.

384 *Week 48, "There are random moments—tossing a salad"*: Elizabeth Berg, *The Art of Mending* (New York: Random House, 2004), chapter 16.

385 *Week 48, "Few people, very few, have a treasure"*: Alice Munro, *Runaway* (New York: Knopf, 2004).

385 *Week 48, "Thanks be to God for Alcoholics Anonymous"*: Molly Monahan, *Seeds of Grace: A Nun's Reflection on the Spirituality of Alcoholics Anonymous* (New York: Riverhead Books, 2001).

391 *Twelve Steps of Al-Anon:* From Al-Anon's Twelve Steps, Al-Anon Family Group Headquarters, Inc., 1996. Reprinted by permission of Al-Anon Family Group Headquarters, Inc. Permission to reprint these excerpts does not mean that Al-Anon Family Group Headquarters, Inc. has reviewed or approved the contents of this publication, or that Al-Anon Family Group Headquarters, Inc. necessarily agrees with the views expressed herein. Al-Anon is a program of recovery for families and friends of alcoholics— use of these excerpts in any non Al-Anon context does not imply endorsement or affiliation by Al-Anon. The Twelve Steps as adapted by Al-Anon with permission of Alcoholics Anonymous Services World, Inc. ("A.A.W.S.") are reprinted with permission of Al-Anon. Permission to reprint Al-Anon's Steps does not mean that A.A.W.S. has reviewed or approved the contents of this publication, or that A.A.W.S. necessarily agrees with the views expressed therein. A.A. is a program of recovery from alcoholism *only*—use or permissible adaptation of A.A.'s Twelve Steps in connection with programs and activities which are patterned after A.A.,

but which address other problems, or in any other non-A.A. context, does not imply otherwise.

392 *Twelve Traditions of AA:* The Twelve Traditions are reprinted with permission of Alcoholics Anonymous World Services, Inc. ("A.A.W.S."). Permission to reprint the Twelve Traditions does not mean that A.A.W.S. has reviewed or approved the contents of this publication, or that A.A. necessarily agrees with the views expressed herein. A.A. is a program of recovery from alcoholism *only*—use of the Twelve Traditions in connection with programs and activities which are patterned after A.A., but which address other problems, or in any other non-A.A. context, does not imply otherwise.

Index

About the Author

 Debra Jay is the coauthor with Jeff Jay of Hazelden's best-selling *Love First*. She is cofounder of Love First Family Recovery, a private practice providing national-level services for clinical intervention, SFR, and other counseling services for families and addicted loved ones. She is also the author of *No More Letting Go* (Bantam, 2006), coauthor of *Aging and Addiction* (Hazelden 2002), and numerous journal and magazine articles on addiction. She appeared on *The Oprah Winfrey Show* as an addiction expert for three seasons and on *The Dr. Oz Show,* among other TV shows, and is an in-demand keynote speaker at behavioral health conferences and treatment centers nationally. She designs and cofacilitates professional trainings for clinical interventionists and SFR counselors internationally. She launched *The Best Minds Podcast* and has also co-designed two informative websites for families: lovefirst.net and GetHelpGiveHelp.info.

Debra lives in Michigan with her husband and their Yorkshire Terrier, Wilhelmina.

About Hazelden Publishing

As part of the Hazelden Betty Ford Foundation, Hazelden Publishing offers both cutting-edge educational resources and inspirational books. Our print and digital works help guide individuals in treatment and recovery, and their loved ones. Professionals who work to prevent and treat addiction also turn to Hazelden Publishing for evidence-based curricula, digital content solutions, and videos for use in schools, treatment programs, correctional programs, and electronic health records systems. We also offer training for implementation of our curricula.

Through published and digital works, Hazelden Publishing extends the reach of healing and hope to individuals, families, and communities affected by addiction and related issues.

For more information about Hazelden publications,
please call **800-328-9000**
or visit us online at **hazelden.org/bookstore**.